The Police in a Free Society

Safeguarding Rights While Enforcing the Law

Todd Douglas

PRAEGER ™

An Imprint of ABC-CLIO, LLC

Santa Barbara, California • Denver, Colorado

Library of Congress Cataloging-in-Publication Data

Names: Douglas, Todd.
Title: The police in a free society : safeguarding rights while enforcing the law / Todd Douglas.
Description: Santa Barbara, California : ABC-CLIO, 2017. | Includes bibliographical references and index.
Identifiers: LCCN 2017023446 (print) | LCCN 2017023720 (ebook) | ISBN 9781440852916 (ebook) | ISBN 9781440852909 (alk.paper : alk. paper)
Subjects: LCSH: Police—United States. | Police power—United States. | Law enforcement—United States. | Police misconduct—United States.
Classification: LCC KF5399 (ebook) | LCC KF5399 .D68 2017 (print) | DDC 363.20973—dc23
LC record available at https://lccn.loc.gov/2017023446

ISBN: 978-1-4408-5290-9
EISBN: 978-1-4408-5291-6

21 20 19 18 17   1 2 3 4 5

This book is also available as an eBook.

Praeger
An Imprint of ABC-CLIO, LLC

ABC-CLIO, LLC
130 Cremona Drive, P.O. Box 1911
Santa Barbara, California 93116-1911
www.abc-clio.com

This book is printed on acid-free paper ∞

Manufactured in the United States of America

For my parents, Doug and Sylvia

Contents

Preface

Just before noon on August 9, 2014, a robbery took place at the Ferguson Market and Liquor Store in the small St. Louis suburb of Ferguson, Missouri. Michael Brown, a 6-foot-5-inch-tall man, weighing 289 pounds, stole several packs of Cigarillos and physically overpowered an employee who attempted to block his exit from the store. Employees of the store called the police, who sent a radio broadcast alerting their patrols of the crime, along with a description of Brown and his companion.

Several minutes later, as he was on his way to lunch with his fiancée, Officer Darren Wilson observed two young men walking single file directly down the center of Canfield Drive. Officer Wilson slowed, approaching the men, and said, "What's wrong with the sidewalk?" Brown responded, "F*** what you have to say!" As he passed Brown, he observed Cigarillo packs in his hand and immediately suspected he had been involved in the robbery, as the physical description of the perpetrator also matched Brown's appearance.

Wilson radioed his dispatch for backup, advising he was stopping two individuals on Canfield Drive, and then positioned his patrol car in front of the two men to impede their path up the street. Officer Wilson then opened his door, calling to Brown as he did so, saying, "Hey, come here." Before Wilson could get his leg out of the car, Brown said, "What the f[***] you gonna do?" and slammed the car door shut, throwing Officer Wilson back into his seat. He attempted to open the door again, telling Brown "Get back" and was again blocked by Brown. Officer Wilson tried and failed a third time, telling Brown, "Get the f[***] back."

Brown then lunged into the interior of the patrol vehicle and viscously attacked Officer Wilson, punching him repeatedly in the jaw and side of the face and grabbing wildly at his shirt, arms, and hands. Officer Wilson, fearing he would lose consciousness as a result of the assault, had

three options available: mace on his left hip, which would likely incapaci-
tate him if he used it within the car; an expandable baton, unreachable on
the back of his duty belt and without the space needed to expand it; and
his sidearm on his right side, away from his attacker.

Officer Wilson drew his weapon and pointed it at Brown, ordering him
to stop or he would shoot, to which Brown responded "You're too much of
a pussy to shoot!" and grabbed the officer's hand, forcing the gun down
toward Wilson's right hip. Realizing that Brown's massive size, coupled
with his advantage over a seated opponent, made him "completely vulnerable," Wilson mustered a herculean effort to twist his body and lift the
gun toward Brown. He then pulled the trigger twice to no effect, as
Brown's hand was interfering with the weapon's function. On the third
pull, the weapon fired with a deafening explosion inside the car.

Brown appeared momentarily startled and backed away slightly;
investigation would reveal that Brown had been shot through the fleshy
part of his right hand below the thumb. He then became "enraged"
and flung his torso back into the cruiser and resumed his beating of Officer Wilson. While he tried to shield his face and head from Brown's
punches, Wilson attempted to fire his weapon with his right hand, but it
jammed. Wilson then lifted the gun in front of him and, using both
hands while still trying to shield his head, manually cleared the weapon.
He then fired a second shot but believed he missed. At that point, Brown
began running away. Officer Wilson radioed for assistance, indicating
that shots had been fired, and gave chase on foot, keeping his weapon
pointed downward in the *low-ready* position.

Ignoring Officer Wilson's repeated commands to stop, Brown continued running down the street, until he suddenly stopped abruptly when
Wilson was approximately 20–30 feet away. He then made a guttural
grunting sound and charged Officer Wilson at a dead run. Fearing for his
life—he would later testify that he knew if Brown got a hold of him, he
"would be done"—Wilson backed away from the charging Brown. In his
first few strides, Brown reached under his shirt toward his waistband,
possibly reaching for a weapon, whereupon Wilson fired multiple shots.
At that point, Brown paused briefly, and Officer Wilson again yelled for
him to stop and get on the ground. Brown then charged the policeman
again, with his hand still in his waistband; again, Officer Wilson backed
away and fired a second volley of shots; again, there was a brief pause, followed by Brown charging at the officer. Confused as to how and why
Brown was continuing his attack, Officer Wilson backed up further.
When he was approximately 10 feet away, Brown lowered his head preparing to tackle the officer. Officer Wilson fired one last time, with a

bullet entering the top of Brown's head and finally stopping the assault. About 2 minutes had passed since the incident began.[1]

This incident, in a tiny city of 21,000 on the outskirts of St. Louis,[2] would touch off a firestorm of racial protests and violence and unleash a wave of criticism and violence against police that continues to this day. Michael Brown was black and Officer Wilson was white. Local, state, and federal investigations found no wrongdoing whatsoever on the part of Officer Wilson and no credibility to witnesses who changed their initial statements to later claim that Brown had held his hands up before he was shot. Nonetheless, the day after the shooting, the fury of the black community over their treatment under the laws of the city exploded in nine days of rioting involving looting, arson, and attacks on police and citizens. Eventually, the state police and National Guard would be required to restore order.

On the same day that the Justice Department released their report on the shooting that cleared Officer Wilson, they published a separate investigation, conducted by its Civil Rights Division, into the Ferguson Police Department. That report was harshly critical of both the police department and the city government, accusing the city of using its municipal lawmaking authority to fleece the mainly low-income residents of the majority African American population. The Justice Department would also accuse the police department of a pattern of tactics that disproportionally impacted the black community, making frequent unlawful stops, searches, and arrests and engaging in pervasive racial profiling.[3] In retrospect, it is apparent that the anger unleashed in August 2014 was more a result of long-simmering tensions over city policies and police misconduct and imperious, improper behavior rather than the shooting death of Michael Brown, which served as the trigger for the violence.

The result has been a sporadic and mostly incoherent discussion of police tactics generally, with some tangential analysis of the larger criminal justice system as a whole. Following the Michael Brown shooting, protestors everywhere, from the streets to the NBA and NFL, repeated the chant of "Hands up, don't shoot," perpetuating the lie that Brown was an innocent, unarmed teenager standing with his hands in the air when he was gunned down just for being black. The attacks on the integrity of police officers in general have been continuous and withering. Violent and peaceful protests have been held nationwide with chants of "What do we want? Dead cops! When do we want it? Now!"[4] and "Pigs in a blanket, fry 'em like bacon."[5] Norfolk, Virginia, City councilwoman Angelia Williams Graves proclaimed at a meeting of the NAACP that

"Modern racists have taken off their white hats and white-sheeted robes and put on police uniforms."[6]

The ongoing controversy has spawned the creation of a group calling themselves Black Lives Matter, whose informal leaders and followers have called for everything from police reform, to the abolition of police and prisons, to the targeted assassination of police officers.[7] The issues regarding alleged mistreatment of African Americans by members of the police have logically led to a larger discussion about race in America and the tensions and problems that remain some five decades on from the civil rights movement of the 1960s. Race relations have declined dramatically since Barack Obama took office as president in 2009, going from +44 percent viewing relations as generally good to –4 percent.[8]

A number of deaths of unarmed black suspects have poured additional fuel on the fire that began on that tragic August day in Ferguson. The names of the dead have become household terms, especially for those who believe that America's police are out of control: Eric Garner, Michael Brown, Eric Harris, Walter Scott, Freddie Gray, Philando Castile, and others. Some of these shootings have been criminal acts and some have been entirely justified. With each new incident—whether later ruled justifiable or not—claims of widespread police racism, calls for reform, and angry protests have followed.

While many of the questions about race relations and the general feeling of the African American community are much larger than simply matters involving the police, it is nonetheless incumbent upon police leaders and administrators to address the eroding respect for officers of the law. Regardless of whether any given police shooting of a citizen is reasonable and necessary, the police must educate the public about the concerns and considerations of the police and the applicable laws.

The following chapters discuss the challenges facing the police in the coming decades. I will trace the history of policing, from the shire reeve of old England to the genesis of the modern, uniformed officer, to the transformation from appointed political flunkie to professional police officer.

America's police have come a long way since the racial riots of the 1960s put a spotlight on improper police tactics and began a push toward improved training and professionalization. Yet, as the police have moved from sub-professionals to better-paid quasi-professionals, the war on crime, war on drugs, and war on terror have transformed the professional police officer into the *law enforcement officer* of today. Where the policeman of the 1950s and 1960s concerned himself with maintaining the peace, today's law enforcement officer too often sees himself or herself as a soldier engaged in an epic struggle of good and evil, too often is busy enforcing too many laws too aggressively, and lacks an understanding of his or her proper role as a keeper of the peace and defender of the peoples' liberty.

To ensure that the police are able to carry out their function, steps must be taken to restore the legitimacy of the law and of the police in general. Police leaders can improve training and begin to properly indoctrinate their officers, but the larger issues of the law, the courts, and the corrections system require the participation of the citizenry and action from our elected officials. America's police officers are generally dedicated and earnest individuals drawn to the work out of a desire to do good. It is up to their leaders and the government they support to ensure that they understand their proper role and that the integrity and legitimacy of our system of laws is maintained.

CHAPTER ONE

The Paradox of Policing a Free Society

Order without liberty and liberty without order are equally destructive.

—Theodore Roosevelt

The concept of liberty is so ingrained in the American consciousness that, for many, unexpected restrictions on their movement or other activity generates immediate, reflexive hostility. Americans instinctively regard personal liberty—personal privacy and freedom of movement, speech, assembly, religion, and the like—as their birthright.

In the free and open societies of the Western world and the United States in particular, the commitment to freedom in our governing documents and the tradition of unfettered personal liberties make the existence of police officers somewhat paradoxical and present those officers with unique challenges. On the one hand, we live in a free and open society where, generally speaking, citizens should be free from the hand of government in the conduct of their business and personal affairs. On the other hand, we employ individuals endowed with the power of the state to enforce laws and, under certain conditions, to restrict movements and limit or disperse public assemblies. Moreover, these officers carry the exclusive power of the state to use violence to enforce compliance. In a free society such as America's, every enforcement action taken by a police officer may be immediately suspect and is often subjected to rigorous scrutiny. While this is as it should be, it can create extreme difficulties for those charged with carrying out the police function of the state.

Nonetheless, policing remains vital to a free society. In order for citizens to exercise their natural rights to life, liberty, and the pursuit of happiness, as laid out in our founding documents, we must operate under a uniform set of laws that prevent one citizen from infringing upon the rights of another. As Thomas Jefferson said, "Rightful liberty is unobstructed action according to our will within limits drawn around us by the equal rights of others."[1] As others have phrased it, "your rights end where mine begin." Though he was not speaking about the police, Jefferson encapsulated the central paradox that applies to the police; the people are free insofar as their actions do not infringe upon the rights of others. The police are the frontline interpreters and guardians of those limits.

The Bill of Rights guarantees all Americans the right to freedom of speech, assembly, and religion and freedom from self-incrimination and unreasonable searches and seizures. Yet, it is the American police officer who is charged with enforcing the defined limits of those rights, who tries to coax the guilty into confession and argues for the right to search for evidence and to seize the guilty.

Americans have always cherished their near-absolute right to freedom of speech and to peaceful protest. However broad those rights are, there are limits, and it is the police who must enforce them. It falls to the police to ensure the safety of protesters from others who disagree with their viewpoints and also to ensure protesters refrain from infringing upon the rights of others by obstructing their freedom of movement. In these situations, the police find themselves pressed not only on one side by their responsibility to enforce the laws of the state and on the other by their duty to protect the rights of protesters but also from a third direction, requiring that they attempt to balance the freedoms of different groups of citizens.

An American's home is sacrosanct; citizens can rightfully defend their homes with deadly force, with no duty to retreat even if possible. The state is barred from entering, searching, or listening to what citizens do inside their residence. This right to be free from government intrusion into our personal affairs is enshrined in the Fourth Amendment and taken for granted by nearly everyone. Still, the police are responsible for ferreting out criminal activity and solving crimes reported to them by victims, and this often requires searches of the homes, the vehicles, or the person of citizens suspected of being guilty. So it is the police officer who makes the case to a judge for government intrusion into someone's houses, papers, and effects or does so without a judicial warrant under legal exceptions and must make his or her case for legality after the fact.

Police in a free and open society face another dilemma as well; they must treat citizens with the utmost respect, while at the same time obliging even the most defiant and violent to comply with the law and their lawful commands. A free society does not want its police officers to be feared, yet those officers are at times duty bound to force people to obey the law. Unfortunately, there are vicious and remorseless people who live among us, and they must be controlled to protect the rights of the innocent. The dilemma is how to make the lawbreaker fear the police enough to submit, without unduly intimidating the guiltless. The naked truth is that a certain segment of society does not respect the rights of others and would violently resist the police at every encounter except for the fact that they fear the consequences of such resistance. This ugly truth is often unknown to those outside of policing and is one of the most important reasons the police and their critics find themselves talking past one another.

It is often claimed that George Orwell said, "We sleep safe in our beds because rough men stand ready in the night to visit violence on those who would do us harm."[2] In our world, this remains an unfortunate truth; there are indeed dangerous predators who live among us, and it is only the laws and the men and women who enforce them that keep the wolves away from the doors of the weak and innocent. That being said, our continued freedom relies upon those rough men (and women) using their power to inflict violence with the utmost restraint and care. The nobility of their duty, however, cannot be used as an excuse to place themselves above reproach, criticism, or especially the law itself.

Americans have a fascination with the police. There has never been a time in the past half century when there was not a television drama or motion picture playing about the world of the police. Police work's appeal lies not only in the danger and autonomy of the officer's duties but in the intense morality struggle that attends so many of the officer's decisions. The police officer is also perceived to be the person who *knows* things. Police officers are privy to all sorts of intimate details of people's lives: they know what a murder scene looks like, what human blood and human decomposition smell like, what it's like to watch someone die, what the couple upstairs was fighting about, why there were four cop cars at the building on the corner, and what happened in the park beyond where the crime scene tape was strung up. In the 1973 film *Serpico*, taken from Peter Maas's novel of the same name, Officer Frank Serpico describes why he wanted to become a cop:

> All my life I wanted to be a cop, you know? It's like I can remember nothing else. I remember this one time . . . there was—Something happened. A domestic argument or something; somebody stabbed somebody. And there was this crowd around this tenement. I must have been nine, ten years

old . . . I went over to see what was going on. I noticed the red light goin'
around and around . . . all these people, and I couldn't see. I kept saying,
"Do you know what's goin' on? Do you know?" Nobody knew. It was like a
big mystery behind that—that crowd there. All of a sudden . . . the crowd
just parted . . . like the Red Sea, you see? And there were these guys in
blue, and I said . . . "They know." What do they know? What do they
know? It's amazing. It's incredible.[3]

As with all people of interest in our land, Americans are fascinated with
watching them fall from grace. Stories of police crime and corruption
capture the popular imagination and make for national front-page news.
This makes life tough for police and police agencies; when a local dentist
is caught fondling his anesthetized patients in Chicago, it doesn't appear
on the front page of the local paper in Atlanta.

Americans also have some peculiar attitudes toward the law. While not
a unique mind-set, Americans especially have a tendency to view laws as
a good idea when they are applied to others but not when they are applied
to them personally. Many people are quick to declare "there ought to be a
law!" but when called to account for their own infractions believe the law
is being unjustly applied or that their particular case calls for an
exception.

In a very real sense, the police occupy the physical space where the
laws made by their government impact upon the citizenry. This is a difficult position to find oneself in. In 21st-century America, citizens in general are utterly detached from government. They have precious little
information about the representatives that make their state's laws and
generally neither know nor care who they are. As such, they are certainly
not involved in any debate about the merits of the laws they find themselves living under. This results in the creation of statutes that large
swaths of the population may disagree with, or at least are ambivalent
toward. Combine this with the all-too-common human tendency to think
that a given law is a good idea but only for everyone else to obey, and
policing becomes a difficult endeavor at best. Aspiring police officers and
civilians alike vastly underestimate the extent to which police activity is
driven by lawmakers.

Until the latter part of the 20th century, there were very few standards
for police training.[4] Qualifications in many states were minimal to nonexistent, with decisions about hiring and firing of officers left to the whim of
the chief, sheriff, or local politicians. Low-level corruption was rampant
and oversight rare and inadequate. The notion of the police officer as a
true professional is a concept that has begun to evolve only in the past

half century, with many still arguing that policing does not meet the criteria for a genuine profession.[5]

The notion that some experts do not consider policing to be a true profession often comes as a shock to police officers and administrators who consider themselves to be professionals and who take great pride in their work. While the argument is to some extent a matter of semantics, since anyone who performs any function requiring specialized training for pay is by definition a professional, it nonetheless is an important discussion. A profession is generally thought of as having certain characteristics that separate it from mere physical labor and occupations that require little knowledge or specialized training. The level of professionalization varies widely from one agency to another; however, a *profession* has some characteristics that the police as a group have not fully attained. While there is no clear consensus about all the specific characteristics that mark a true profession, some of the more common elements of a profession in the extant literature include the following.

- Specialized knowledge and training: Members are required to hold a college-level degree in their field or have extensive specialized training, as well as ongoing education in new research and techniques. While police to have specialized training, in many agencies it is sorely lacking in both depth and breadth, and few police take part in active research or efforts at innovation.

- Certification: Members of a profession are expected to be certified as competent and qualified by a licensing or accrediting body that independently verifies the member's credentials to practice in the field. Some states issue official certification for officers who successfully complete an approved local police academy while others do not.

- Significant responsibility: A profession's members are often thought to be in positions of importance and responsibility to those they serve. The professional is charged with taking care that a client is protected from harm and given proper and fair treatment and deals in areas of importance such as health, safety, law, and financial or psychological well-being. There is no denying the critically important role police play in these areas of the lives of those they come into contact with.

- Accountability: Professionals should belong to an organization under the aegis of a licensing authority that investigates and makes records of complaints against its members and can hold them to account for failing to adhere to professional standards, to include barring the individual from continuing to work in the profession. While this is the case within some states, there is no nationwide database that keeps track of officers who have been removed from duty for misconduct—allowing "gypsy cops" to roam from state to state.

- Autonomy: Members of a profession typically operate mostly free from direct, immediate supervisory oversight, setting their own agendas and priorities. Despite the paramilitary structure and regimentation of most police departments, individual officers do exercise a significant degree of autonomy and discretion in their day-to-day work and are rarely under direct supervision.

- Ethical standards: A profession is generally assumed to have a set of ethical and moral standards to which its members are expected to adhere. While most agencies have rules and regulations regarding conduct, and may have mission statements, creeds, or other codes of behavior, there is no authoritative professional association with a common code of ethics for officers nationwide.

- Merit basis: Professionals are expected to continue in their field, become successful, and attract their clients through their reputation and skills as a practitioner, as opposed to being the only available choice or mandated by rule or law. Clearly, there is little the police can do about this element, as the police are the only option when you are the victim of a crime.

- Professional societies: A profession creates organizations of practitioners for the purpose of sharing information and exchanging ideas with regard to emerging challenges, best practices, and training. The police do have many such organizations that promote information sharing, support research, and develop and host training. However, their influence and membership is still somewhat limited.

In order for the police to function properly in American society, they must, above all, be trusted. Personal integrity and trust are the only currency police departments and their officers possess. Without this "buy-in" by a populace that views their power as legitimate and the individual officers as trustworthy, the entire system can begin to unravel swiftly— often with deadly consequences. Sir Robert Peel, founder of the London Metropolitan Police and widely regarded as the father of modern policing, stated clearly that "the ability of the police to perform their duties is dependent upon public approval of police existence, actions, behavior, and the ability of the police to secure and maintain public respect."[6] A recent poll conducted by Reuters[7] found that 31 percent of Americans believe that police officers routinely lie to serve their own interests and that 25 percent were unsure. This number was still higher among black Americans, with 45 percent believing police routinely lie. Members of the black and Hispanic minority groups were also more likely to agree with the statement that police officers tend to unfairly target minorities, with 69 percent of blacks and 54 percent of Hispanics agreeing, while 29 percent of whites agreed.

These poll numbers are disappointing and should be a source of serious concern for police administrators. With such large percentages of people believing that police routinely lie and treat minorities unfairly, police agencies face an uphill battle in obtaining cooperation from their constituent populations, as well as in the arena of public relations. When respondents were asked in the same poll if they believe the police tend to be fair and just, only slightly more than half of all Americans said they did—53 percent—while only 30 percent of blacks agreed with that statement.

The better news for police in the polling data is that while people in general hold the police in lower esteem than they would like, those polled rated their particular local police agencies higher, with 77 percent of whites and 56 percent of blacks saying that they approve of the job being done by their local cops.

It should be noted that the vast majority of Americans have no interaction with the police in any given year, and so their answers are inevitably based on anecdotal information and media reports, which are heavily skewed against the police—if for no other reason than the police simply doing a good job is not "news." Interestingly, while police generally deal with people who are at their worst, and often in situations involving confrontation, the vast majority of people who have *face-to-face* contact with officers feel as though they acted properly. According to the most recent available data, a 2008 Justice Department survey, the percentage of Americans who dealt directly with police and who felt they behaved both respectfully and properly was around 90 percent. For blacks and Hispanics, the numbers hovered around 85 and 86 percent, respectively.[8] These numbers suggest that the effects of negative contact with the police are amplified through word of mouth or media publicity, given the large gap between beliefs about police in the public at large and those of people who have actually had contact with officers.

Still, the police and their leaders need to address these issues of trust, and this will be discussed in the following chapters. In addition, it should be noted that low ratings of police integrity are a problem not simply for police agencies to address. The political authority that the police represent is ultimately responsible for the actions of its enforcement officers and bears equal responsibility to establish the trust and respect required to effectively police its communities. While the police in general would prefer higher approval ratings, they are faring far better than the politicians who control them. Recent polling indicates that only 19 percent of the population trusts the federal government, and 75 percent believe that elected officials place their personal interests above those of the public.[9]

While the public's respect and trust of the police is not at all-time lows, the widespread protests and violence in places like Ferguson, Baltimore, Dallas, and New Orleans are harbingers of a growing distrust of police—especially among inner-city black populations. As is too often the case, the police in many impoverished, minority communities are seen as an outside and oppressive force, rather than as servants and protectors of the community.

Following the widespread racially motivated riots in the late 1960s, police reformers believed much of this perspective was due to the fact that virtually all police officers were white males and so were viewed as outsiders by the minority communities they served. Police administrators hoped that by recruiting more officers from minority groups, they could alleviate this perception. The bad news is that the police force in Baltimore is 44 percent black and 8 percent other minorities,[10] yet the city exploded into two weeks of protests and rioting following the death of black suspect Freddy Gray while in police custody, before any official determination of cause had been made. Clearly, the presence of significant numbers of minority officers is not enough to alter a perception of persecution in some inner-city communities. It is clear that simply adding more minority officers does not immediately translate into increased trust and legitimacy.

Publicity about police abuse of authority and use of excessive force has increased dramatically in recent years. Much of this can be attributed to the ubiquity of smart phones, allowing virtually every citizen the opportunity to record videos of police-citizen encounters and confrontations. Police misconduct can now be recorded, uploaded to YouTube, sent around the world, and be available to the news media within minutes. While malfeasance on the part of police is not excusable, there can be no doubt that the phenomenon of recording and broadcasting an instance of police abusing their authority has the potential to artificially amplify the severity and breadth of the problem. By definition, the millions of police encounters that involve officers helping stranded motorists or caring for the injured, homeless, or mentally ill do not generally make for exciting video. Likewise, the hundreds of thousands of arrests that involve no violence or use of force do not get recorded and uploaded to the Internet. So, does the proliferation of videos showing police misconduct indicate that we are just now starting to see the proverbial tip of the iceberg of a widespread problem, or do the videos simply reflect the fact that the few instances of abuse are more likely to be publicized because of the pervasiveness of smart phones?

The way the various public constituencies view the police depends on numerous factors, not all of which are under the control of police agencies. If an individual feels disenfranchised by an unfair government or society, it follows that he or she will view that government's system of law and justice as inherently inequitable and deliberately designed to prevent him or her from full participation in society. It then follows logically that such people will view those charged with enforcing the laws and policing their community with a great deal of skepticism, if not outright hostility. In a free society, the goal must be to allow all citizens the same opportunities and equal justice before the law; but when either the perception or reality is otherwise, the police will be regarded as oppressors and bullies and may not be able to overcome that perception despite their best efforts.

In the United States, the police function was, in the English tradition, left to each individual community or municipality. Since our nation's founding, policing has remained a decentralized, local responsibility. This was following in the tradition of the local watch and constabulary system brought by colonists from England and was continued as a way to guard against tyranny. A national police force would be large and powerful enough to impose the will of a central authority across the entire nation without regard to local preference or custom. One needs only to look at the history of the FBI and its use as a political secret police force, illegally eavesdropping, blackmailing, intimidating, and otherwise harassing enemies of the incumbent presidential administration, to see that such concerns are well founded.

America has developed from an agrarian society of 13 states and 4 million citizens to 50 states spanning the breadth of the continent and containing more than 300 million people—of whom more than 80 percent live in urban areas. Over the course of two centuries, the police function has evolved and expanded. With each city, town, and state responsible for its own policing, the system has evolved into a web of overlapping agencies, jurisdictions, and responsibilities. Just as with many other institutions, the creation of police forces was not an organized and planned endeavor, but rather an ad hoc affair, resulting in overlapping jurisdictions and problems with information sharing that persist to this day. America is a patchwork of more than 18,000 state and local police agencies, so many in fact that the exact number is uncertain.[11] In fact, to call the criminal justice process in the United States a "system" is a misnomer. The executive function of criminal law enforcement is divided between the police, who conduct investigations and make arrests, and the district or state's attorney office, which prosecutes the accused before the courts. In large urban centers, the cases are then forced through a vastly understaffed, underfunded, and overworked judicial system. With most prosecutor's offices also strained to the breaking point due to lack of resources, the focus of the prosecutors and courts becomes efficiency, not effectiveness, or more bluntly, productivity—not justice. Even though the police represent only the first step in what we call the justice process, they tend to remain the public face for all of the so-called system's failures and faults.

America's police officers have much greater expectations placed upon them today than their predecessors had a generation or two ago. The officer of 1960 was expected to be able to drive, read, write, comprehend basic laws and rules and to mostly obey the law himself. If he was sometimes gruff, vulgar, or violent, it was just part of having a run-in with the cops—and next time you knew to cooperate and not get mouthy. Today, officers are expected to behave as consummate professionals, to deal with defiance, insults, threats, and physical intimidation with stoic detachment. In some ways, they are expected to be superhuman, even though they are quite human and have in many cases only 16 weeks or less of rudimentary training separating them from any other member of the community. Not only does an officer's training not fully prepare him or her for what's expected, in most cases the salary is far from commensurate with the superhuman expectations of the modern patrol officer.

The nature and frequency of police encounters has also changed significantly in recent decades. While the officer of the 1950s might be seen walking the beat or driving past in his squad car, armed with a pistol, a nightstick, and a smile, today's officer often wears military battle dress and carries an array of weapons that would make Batman blush. The officer of the past was a source of reassurance and strength and was called a policeman. Today's officer is feared by motorists, business owners, and children and calls himself a *law enforcement officer*. The officer of the past came to assist when called, looked out for crimes in progress and people in need of help, and sought to rectify nuisances or unsafe conditions on his beat. Today's officers aggressively seek out any minor violation of the law to reach their quota (stated or unstated) of traffic tickets and summonses. As for public nuisances or unsafe conditions, today's officers too often see these things as someone else's responsibility or beneath their station as "not real police work." Advances in technology, the increasingly aggressive drug war, and the political push for ever-increasing revenue from traffic tickets and forfeitures have served to drastically increase the number of negative contacts with police officers.

As stated in the preceding paragraphs, Americans are very disconnected from their government, and as such, there has never been a real national discussion about just what we want from our police; our country has not seriously addressed the issue since the 1960s. We want our police officers to be tough enough to deal with the violent psychopath, the dangerous mentally ill, and the street thug so we don't have to. We also want them to be sensitive enough to deal with injury, death, mental illness, loss, and despair. We want them to treat everyone fairly and without bias or favor. We want them to make our communities safe and orderly for us to enjoy the blessings of liberty, in order to raise our children and live our lives free from fear. Yet, despite the overwhelming importance and nature of the task, we don't talk much about exactly *how* we expect them to do it.

The Reality of Policing

You are 24 years old, a 2-year "veteran" member of the small local city police department, when you receive a call of a deranged man walking down the street smashing car windows with his fists. It is 10:15 P.M. and the call is less than two blocks away; you arrive within moments. You see glass lying on the street, a group of agitated people, with several waving their arms frantically at you. As you exit your car, your heart rate and respiration increase as adrenaline begins to flow into your bloodstream. You stop your car and step out into the night air, as your emergency lights flash on the surrounding buildings and anxious faces. Three people begin shrieking at you all at once, "He's crazy!" "He's going to kill someone!" "He hit that girl over there!" "There he goes!" "Do something!" "*Do something!*"

Remember your training: take care of the injured, call for backup. You quickly look for a girl who got hit and don't see her. You call for backup, not sure if you were understood over the chorus of voices screaming at you. You start moving toward the hulking figure the crowd pointed to as he disappears around the corner. You start to run. Your mind races; do I have the authority to forcibly stop him based on the shouts of bystanders? What if he refuses to stop? Is he armed with a knife or gun? Watch his hands. He is at least 280 pounds and much taller than you—he could knock you out with a single punch and kill you with your own gun.

You round the corner and it's much darker—the streetlights are only on one side of the street and several are out. You are now only 30 feet behind the man, who seems oblivious to your presence. You shout, "Police, stop right there, I need to talk to you!" Unlike in the movies, the man does not run, wheel around with a gun, or turn to attack; he simply hunches his massive shoulders a bit higher around his ears and keeps walking.

Remember, this is *you* who is that cop alone on the street with an obviously irrational and violent man twice your size ignoring your lawful commands. What are you going to do? Picture it through your own eyes, not like watching a screen. You can't call 911—you *are* the police. You can't just let him walk away, because you are obligated by law and department policy to take proper police action. Moreover, several people are following at a safe distance taking a video of your every move. The man's continued defiance both angers and frightens you; he's obviously not afraid of you in the least and that's worrisome. If you don't act swiftly and decisively, the crowd will turn on you; you may face disciplinary action, and your personal, professional, and departmental reputation will suffer. Backup is 10 minutes away—the crowd is murmuring about your inaction—your heart races, your field of vision narrows, your ears ring slightly, your mouth goes dry, and your hands and feet go slightly numb, as your body diverts blood flow to your large muscles and internal organs to prepare to fight. What are you going to *do*?

People like to make reference to police being the ones with the guns, as if that makes them supremely powerful. Unfortunately, bad guys have guns too, and in this case, you don't know if the man is armed, and you can't shoot the man in the back for ignoring you—that's murder. You don't have a Taser because the city council turned down the chief's request for the insanely expensive equipment, and, at any rate, there's a substantial chance it would malfunction or have no effect. You are going to have to physically stop him, but he's a giant who's apparently got a hell of a punch and feels no pain, as evidenced by the blood (possibly carrying hepatitis or HIV) that drips from his clenched fists.

This is the precise moment where the power of the state meets an individual suspected of breaking its laws, and while the power of the state is mighty, it is represented in its entirety by the patrolman on that dark street. He wears a uniform and a badge and carries a gun, but he's just a man—Mrs. Johnson's little boy Billy who grew up and became a policeman. He's the coach of your son's little league team and shops at the same grocery store you go to. Put simply, he's no different than you.

But right now, in our scenario, he *is* you. What are you going to do? It's easy to think of police officers as somehow invincible and fearless, that their training and the few pieces of equipment they carry on their duty belt afford them the power to handle such situations with ease, but that is not true. Your 16 weeks of training at the local police academy does not permit years of study to become a master of jujitsu, able to defeat opponents with a flick of your pinky. Unless the suspect produces a deadly weapon, your gun is nearly as dangerous to you as it is to the suspect—it can be taken away and used to kill you. More than 10 percent of murdered police officers are killed with their own sidearm.[12] You can use your baton or pepper spray to try to even the odds, but how will that look on the video being recorded for YouTube by the assembled spectators? Should you try to protect yourself from injury or death by striking after your commands were ignored or try to protect yourself and your family from a possible lawsuit and public opprobrium by attempting to gain control of the bleeding, angry man with your bare hands?

What if it turns out later that the suspect was deaf and mentally retarded and had run away from a nearby group home after becoming enraged over a dispute with staff? What if the suspect is a war hero suffering from PTSD? What if the suspect is black and you are white? While the YouTube video can be viewed millions of times, paused, and played in slow motion, you don't have the luxury of considering all the possibilities of how and why the suspect arrived at this place, nor of considering his skin color; you have to force him to comply with your directions, place him under arrest, and somehow get a pair of handcuffs on him.

Forty-six seconds have elapsed since you stepped out of your car— *what are you going to do?*

More than 55,000 police officers are assaulted every year, and, since 1961, on average, 131 have died annually in the line of duty.[13] That translates to an officer attacked every 10 minutes and a dead police officer every 67 hours. Police face a thousand different scenarios every single day that involve the potential for violence. The vast majority of police encounters do not result in any use of force, but the potential is always present and necessarily colors everything the officer does. This can make him or her seem gruff, uncaring, or officious. While the nature of policing does not excuse blatant rudeness or wanton arrogance, it does contribute greatly to misunderstandings between police and the public.

Policing is serious business. In my 27 years as a state police officer, I saw 30 members of my agency buried after being killed in the line of duty, and I attended the funeral of at least a dozen others, some of whom were acquaintances of mine. A deputy sheriff with whom I would eat breakfast on occasion in the wee hours of the morning was killed one summer night when he stopped to check on a car stopped in a rural park around 1 A.M. Unknown to the deputy, the car was operated by three young men who had just burglarized a gun and fireworks store just across the state line. They were in the process of moving their loot from that car to another they had staged at the park when they saw the deputy turn onto the access road. They quickly fled to nearby bushes, and when the deputy exited his car and approached the vehicle, they opened fire from out of the darkness that surrounded the patch of the parking lot illuminated by the car lights and the patrol car's spotlight. Seriously wounded, the deputy fell to the ground, as his two attackers jumped in their car, ran over him, and then backed over him a second time, breaking his legs, ribs, and arms and shredding his exposed flesh against the gravel of the parking lot. As he lay helpless and bleeding on the ground, they approached his mangled and bloodied body and, as he struggled to breathe, mocked him saying, "You don't look so bad"; they then took his service weapon and executed him with a single shot to his head.

Every 67 hours, an officer dies, most often alone and in fear and agony. The FBI publishes a summary each year of officers killed in the line of duty.

At approximately 3:15 A.M. on July 22, a sergeant with the Hayward Police Department was shot and killed while conducting a traffic stop. The 48-year-old sergeant . . . requested backup and initiated a traffic stop after observing a vehicle driving erratically. As the sergeant and his partner approached the stopped vehicle, the driver produced a 9 mm semiautomatic handgun and discharged multiple rounds at the officers. The veteran sergeant was struck in the front of his head and also suffered injuries to his front legs/feet. The sergeant, who was wearing body armor, succumbed to the gunshot wound to the front of his head (specifically, his nose/lower forehead area). The backup officer immediately returned fire, striking the subject at least once. The man fled the scene in his vehicle . . . The suspect was found later that day at a nearby hospital with injuries consistent with a gunshot wound. The 21-year-old man, who was under the influence of narcotics at the time of the incident, was arrested and charged with First-Degree Murder.[14]

A 38-year-old police officer with the San Jose Police Department was shot and killed just after 7 P.M. on March 24 while handling a person with a mental illness. The officer responded to a call from a woman who said that her father was threatening to kill himself with a firearm. The officer, a police veteran with 14 years of experience, along with two other officers, positioned themselves in the front of the man's residence. A short time later, one of the officers gave verbal warning that the man in question was standing on a second-story balcony. The man on the balcony immediately fired two shots from a .30–30 lever-action rifle. One round hit the victim officer, who was wearing body armor, in the front of the head, fatally wounding him. Another officer returned fire, killing the 57-year-old suspect who had a history of a mental illness and a prior criminal record, including police assault and a violent crime.[15]

A 47-year-old deputy sheriff with the McHenry County Sheriff's Office (MCSO) died on September 14 from wounds he suffered in an ambush 11 months earlier. Around 1:15 A.M. on October 16, 2014, a man called the MCSO and requested a well-being check on a husband and wife in

Holiday Hills. The wife had called the man indicating her husband was behaving irrationally, and she was afraid he might kill her. Subsequently, the veteran deputy, who had more than 7 years of law enforcement experience, was one of the three deputies who responded to conduct the well-being check at the couple's residence. The veteran deputy and another deputy approached the front door of the residence and noticed a surveillance camera that appeared to be tracking their movements. The deputies knocked on the front door, and a male voice from inside the home asked who was there, but he did not open the door. The deputies responded, "Sheriff's police." The man asked the deputies what they wanted, and they told him they were there to check on his wife's well-being. The man . . . told the deputies that they were not coming in . . . After a long pause, the man said, "Come on in." . . . The man then fired approximately 15 rounds from a .223-caliber semiautomatic rifle through the door. Both deputies were wearing body armor, and both were struck as they sought cover. The veteran deputy was struck in his rear lower torso/back. The other deputy . . . was struck in the rear below her waist (leg). In the meantime, a third deputy, who was situated at the side of the house, heard the gunfire and ran to the front of the house. . . . The deputy behind the parked vehicle fired a round at the subject, but the man maintained his position. The deputy fired approximately seven more rounds at the subject. The veteran deputy who had been struck in the rear lower torso/back tried to get up and get to his vehicle to retrieve his rifle, but the subject shot him in the rear leg, severely damaging his left femur. The subject yelled, "You are messing with an Army paratrooper. I hope you are ready to die. I am." . . . The two injured deputies were taken to local hospitals. The 52-year-old offender, who was under the influence of alcohol and narcotics at the time of the incident, was arrested and charged with six counts of Attempted Murder, two counts of Aggravated Battery, and five counts of Aggravated Discharge of a Firearm. He had a prior criminal record that included a violent crime, police assault, a drug law violation, and a weapons violation. The deputy who was shot in the front of her leg recovered from her injuries and returned to service. The other injured deputy died from the wound to his leg nearly 11 months after the incident.[16]

A 48-year-old police officer with the Cincinnati Police Department was killed during an ambush (entrapment and premeditation) shortly before 9:30 A.M. on June 19. The officer, a veteran of law enforcement with 27½ years of experience, responded to a call reporting a man with a firearm. The officer arrived on the scene at 9:24 A.M. and observed an armed individual arguing with a woman [who was later identified as the individual's mother]. The officer was familiar with the individual and his mother from patrolling the neighborhood. The officer drew his conductive energy device and ordered the individual to show his hands. The individual moved toward the officer and drew a .380-caliber semiautomatic handgun from his waistband. The officer then removed his weapon, a 9 mm semiautomatic handgun, from its holster. The individual fired four rounds at the officer, three of which struck the officer in the arms/hands and in the front lower torso/stomach between the side panels of the body armor he was wearing. The officer fell into the street; he and the suspect wrestled briefly before the suspect gained control of the victim officer's weapon and used it to fire at a probation officer who had arrived on the scene. The suspect then demanded that the probation officer kill him. Another officer arrived, and the suspect and that officer engaged in a gun battle around the officer's car. The responding officer shot the suspect, killing him. The victim officer was transported to the hospital where he was pronounced deceased; the fatal wound was to his front lower torso/stomach. The 21-year-old suspect had a prior criminal record and was under the influence of alcohol and narcotics at the time of the incident.[17]

And on and on it goes . . .

Not all stressful police situations involve the obvious threat of violence. Much of the difficulty in policing stems from the lack of available legal solutions to the problems they are called upon to solve.

An officer is dispatched to the local Wal-Mart parking lot in front of the entrance for an unknown type of dispute. As she arrives, she observes a fire truck with lights flashing, three firemen in full fire-fighting regalia, and about 10 people around a beat-up car parked at the curb in front of the fire truck. The officer exits her vehicle and is approached by one of the firemen who imperiously identifies himself as the chief of the local volunteer fire company. He tells her that the car has a gas leak and that the man at the wheel insists that he is going to drive home with his girlfriend and toddler in the rear car seat. He is animated and angry and says, "You need to do something, there's a baby in that car." As you approach the driver, you see he is a male, about 40 years old, and angrily arguing with a Wal-Mart employee, telling her to "mind her own goddamn business!" and that he's going to "do whatever the f[***] I want!"

The officer approaches the man and asks what is going on. Clad in a classic, stained, white tank-top undershirt (known in police jargon as a "wife-beater") and reeking of cigarette smoke, the man explains that the problem is "these f[***]ing people who don't know how to mind their own f[***]ing business!" While he is talking, two angry employees and the other firemen are chiming in at the officer from the other side of the car about how dangerous the situation is and repeatedly reminding her about the child being placed in mortal danger. Her mind quickly races through available options: Can she arrest the driver for endangering the child? How dangerous is the alleged gas leak? Should she let the man go and risk a complaint from the fire chief to her boss and public oppro-brium from the assembled group? The driver gives every impression that he will react violently to being arrested—how will she get him out of the car? She can't pepper spray him with the toddler in the car, as it would choke the baby. Forcing him out would be very difficult, between the seat belt he's wearing and his much larger size, combined with the danger that he will drive off with the officer's upper body inside the car. She looks under the car and observes a very slow gasoline drip from a fuel line and a small wet spot about 8 inches in diameter. How dangerous is this really? After all, the man is going to be moving most of the time and is not likely to stop long enough for much gas to accumulate. Don't gas leaks occur with some frequency on old cars? She has no memory of a car ever catch-ing fire while driving due to a gas leak.

So here is our officer's choice: tell the man he is free to go, since the dan-ger is so minimal as to not rise to the extent of criminally endangering the child or anyone else or place the man under arrest for a very weak charge of endangering and engage in a physical altercation, which could result in injury to the suspect, herself, bystanders, or possibly even the child that was allegedly endangered in the first place. This is an all-too-frequent situ-ation where the law is not suited to decisively resolve the situation. Our officer in this case finds herself in a no-win position: if the arrest goes bad, she'll likely be faulted for making such a weak, unjustified arrest, but if she releases the man, she will be viewed as incompetent by the firemen and store clerks who think they know the law better than her—and either one is likely to call in a formal complaint against her.

Such situations create tremendous stress and were not what she envi-sioned when she imagined becoming a cop or what she grew up watching on television and in the movies. This is the order-maintenance and problem-solving aspect of policing that is often not covered in police training. This officer knows the law, how to investigate a traffic accident, make an arrest, handle firearms, drive at high speeds, operate a radar, laser, and breath analysis instrument, but nobody ever prepared her for a situation like this.

What Are the Police For?

Just *what* is it that we expect from our police? What is their primary function? Are they supposed to *prevent* crime, and if so, how? Are the police supposed to be primarily law enforcers or keepers of the peace? Should the police attend to all varieties of public nuisances, or are these things the responsibility of other government entities? Despite the fact that police are a fixture of our modern society, there has been very little public dialogue about what is and is not the purview of the police. As a result, police departments tend to cobble together an informal, unwritten policy about the things they respond to. Small departments covering upper middle class or wealthy neighborhoods may respond to lost pets and keys locked in a car or check individual homes while the owners are on vacation, whereas the police in Chicago or New York would never do such things. This is one of the better aspects of local control of policing; the people of the village can decide what they want the police to do for the community and even whether or not they want to have a police department at all.

Numerous studies have demonstrated that the police are generally ineffective at preventing crime, and adding additional police forces does nothing to deter crime. There is evidence that specifically targeted police operations against particular areas of high crime *can* be effective when properly conducted, but the mere presence of police on patrol has no measurable effect on crime rates. So if the police are to engage in crime prevention, they would have to begin to do things which they have not done in the past and for which most officers have not been trained. Police interested in preventing crime would have to work to educate the public about crime deterrence measures at their homes and businesses. They would need to embrace and promote the study and application of crime prevention through environmental design, a technique that seeks to deter crime by creating physical and psychological barriers in the layout of buildings and other public spaces. This would of course require more training and more time spent away from patrol duties and may require the expensive step of hiring additional officers; or could this educational function be carried out primarily by less expensive civilian employees?

Should the police function even be a primary responsibility of the government? We take this condition for granted, yet for thousands of years the responsibility for bringing criminals before the bar of justice belonged to the community at large. Prior to the mid-19th century, if someone committed a crime of theft or violence, it would be up to the members of the community to hunt down the perpetrator. The local sheriff might be available, but he would need to constitute a *posse* of men to locate and take the offender into custody. The term *posse* is well known to anyone who has ever watched American western television shows and films, but it derives from the tradition of the local citizenry being responsible for preserving the public peace. The Latin legal term *posse comitatus* refers to the authority of the county, more specifically all men over the age of 15 who may be summoned by the sheriff to maintain order or apprehend a criminal.

The uniformed, full-time force of police officers that we take as a natural fixture in civilized society has been around only for 150 years or so. When the London Metropolitan Police was formed, the first modern police force as we recognize them today, there were constables and sheriffs in both England and the United States, but they were often not full-time officers and needed the aid of the citizenry to carry out many of their functions. Sir Robert Peel echoed that centuries-old tradition of collective responsibility for policing when he wrote that

> police, at all times, should maintain a relationship with the public that gives reality to the historic tradition that the police are the public and the public are the police; the police being only members of the public who are paid to give full-time attention to duties which are incumbent on every citizen in the interests of community welfare and existence.[18]

In other words, the police are not separate from the public; they are simply members of the whole body of the citizenry whose job is to devote full-time attention to public order, while other citizens still bear some of the responsibility for collective security and order.

The function of the police in a free society is to protect the rights of citizens so that they can exercise their fundamental rights to life, liberty, and property. While police officers can and do enforce the laws of the state, it is not their primary function. Their primary job is *order maintenance*, or more simply, keeping the peace. This is why the terms *peace officer* and *police officer* are often used interchangeably in various states' laws pertaining to the establishment and operation of police forces.

A police officer on patrol may respond to several calls in a single day where laws have been violated, yet not make a single arrest. For example, two acquaintances get into a fight over a basketball game in a park and someone calls the police. The person who threw the first punch is technically guilty of assault and battery. Both men are probably guilty of disorderly conduct for engaging in their shouting, swearing, and fist fighting in a public place. When the police arrive, however, the two stop fighting and both say they do not wish to pursue criminal charges against each other. In all likelihood, the officers will simply take their names and other information for their report and send them on their way.

In this example, the officers accomplished their primary job of keeping the peace and protecting rights. Order was restored to the park for the enjoyment of everyone; the fight, with its potential for injury to the two combatants, was stopped; and everyone involved had their rights respected and protected. The officers *could* have arrested the men, but good officers know that *law enforcement* and making a criminal arrest is simply one *tool* among many they have at their disposal for maintaining order.

Police in a free society should not be continually on the hunt for any- one and everyone who is technically in violation of some law. The key question is whether their activity is infringing upon the rights of others in some way. A person who walks home from a bar because he knows he had too much to drink and then cuts through a public park that closes at dusk is guilty of trespassing. Should a *law enforcement officer* arrest that person? More likely, a good police officer would make inquiry, determine that the person meant no harm, and send him on his way, or perhaps even give him a ride home. The officer's proper concern is making sure the person is not in distress or intending to commit a crime against the property—not strictly enforcing the trespass statute.

One of the most frequent calls received by police on patrol involve *dis- putes*. These disputes come in all forms: domestic, neighbors, landlord- tenant, business-customer, government agency–citizen, motorists, employees, employer-employee, and so forth. Many of them may involve no violation of the law whatsoever, while others do. Still others involve violations of rights but not a violation of the criminal law enforced by the police. These are *civil* matters and are settled between citizens in court through lawsuits. The police are the only governmental agency that is authorized to use force or that holds the real or perceived authority to impose a solution on a problem or dispute. As a result, police can expect to be dispatched to these incidents with regularity, where they are expected to resolve the situation one way or another.

Were the police to make an arrest for everyone who violated a law at these disputes, our courts would become clogged (or I should say *more* clogged) overnight. What's more, hundreds of thousands of normally law-abiding Americans would find themselves very unexpectedly hauled before the bar of justice.

What police do is attempt to resolve disputes while protecting the rights and dignity of those involved. Admittedly, the police often deal with individuals who have no dignity, but they must do their utmost nonetheless. Arrest is a part of the toolkit, but frequently it is better for everyone involved if the officer is able to act as mediator and resolve the dispute before it escalates into violence or further violations of the law. A police officer may have to explain to a customer that he cannot arrest the body shop owner because he did an unsatisfactory job painting his car; he can then explain the customer's options for filing a legal claim or business association complaint against the owner. Likewise, a complainant who, in the heat of the moment, wanted his ex-girlfriend arrested for punching him in the chest may decide after the police calm the situation that he "kind of deserved it" and not want his attacker charged with any violation.

Disputes over property boundaries are a common complaint received by police in rural areas. Since officers do not carry surveying equipment, nor do they have ready access to detailed property abstracts, they generally cannot resolve the issue of who owns a particular piece of land. Yet, police are summoned to resolve such disputes, which can and often do escalate into violent confrontations. Unless the criminal law has been violated by one of the disputants, no enforcement action will be taken. Yet, the officer will interview both parties, advise them of their options for seeking a remedy through the courts, suggest a compromise strategy, compose a narrative of the complaint and the disputants' actions, and create an official record of the event.

Much of what police officers are called upon to do is not specifically designated as their responsibility in either statute or regulation. This is partly because the police are the only governmental agency that is available 24 hours a day and generally accessible with a single phone call to a number everyone knows—911. Officers can expect to be called for malfunctioning railroad-crossing devices, water main breaks, power outages, floods, hurricanes, stranded travelers, downed phone and electrical lines, rabid animals, and medical emergencies. None of these events is likely to result in any type of law enforcement activity. In fact, they are all the principal responsibility of *other* governmental or private entities. Yet, it is the police who will be the first to be called—to ensure public safety and because it is assumed that "the police will know what to do."

All these activities fall under the order maintenance function of the police. If disputes are not attended to once they reach the point where someone feels the need to summon the police, they could likely result in the commission of a crime. At a minimum, they can disrupt the community, place the weak in compromising positions, and in general prevent the involved citizens and their neighbors from enjoying "the blessings of liberty" referred to in the Constitution. The first superintendent of the New York State Police, George F. Chandler, recognized this. Writing in 1922, he said, "Patrolling, settling difficulties, investigation, looking out for unsanitary conditions, and cases of cruelty to animals and children are just as important as the detection of crime."[19]

Some time ago, the American Bar Association laid out a list of objectives that typify those found in police departments:

- Identify criminal offenders and criminal activity and, where appropriate, to apprehend offenders and participate in subsequent court proceedings;
- Reduce the opportunities for the commission of some crimes through preventive patrol and other measures;
- Aid individuals who are in danger of physical harm;
- Protect Constitutional guarantees;
- Facilitate the movement of people and vehicles;
- Assist those who cannot care for themselves;
- Resolve conflict;
- Identify problems that are potentially serious law enforcement or governmental problems;
- Create and maintain a feeling of security in the community;
- Promote and preserve civil order; and
- Provide other services on an emergency basis.[20]

It is easy to see, when these objectives are spelled out in this way, that *law enforcement* is but one of numerous functions performed by the police.

Increasingly, the police function is being handled by private entities. Private security companies handle policing in thousands of private facilities open to the public and within gated communities. While these private police forces can sow confusion and create conflict, they also serve to relieve the public police from the burden of dealing with the thousands of minor incidents that occur in such places every day. Some police agencies have experimented with using civilians or private agencies to handle parking enforcement or even investigation of non-injury traffic accidents. While some argue that this blurs the lines of authority between police and public, Sir Robert Peel and centuries of tradition would not see greater *civilian* participation in policing as anything unusual.

Good Cop—Bad Cop

Corrupt, incompetent, and ineffective police officers exist. There are more than 700,000 police officers in the United States; there is no pool of individuals that size ever created that can ever hope to be free from a certain percentage of bad actors. Despite the best efforts of agencies to weed out those who are unfit, labor laws, union rules, urgent manpower needs, and the limitations of background checks and other screening processes mean bad cops will always be an issue to be dealt with.

Since the shooting death of Michael Brown during a fight with a Ferguson, Missouri, police officer, national attention has become focused on police use of force and most especially when that force is directed at African Americans. A series of deaths of unarmed black males at the hands of police—both legally justified and outright murder—have roiled the nation with protests, sparked the black lives matter movement, and witnessed a 167-percent increase in the numbers of police officers targeted and murdered in ambush attacks—16 during 2016 alone.[21]

Not all bad cops come to the job as deviants; some succumb to the stresses of the job. After personal suffering from exposure to danger, violence, death, injustice, constant threats, and dishonesty, coupled with the often unfair and stifling bureaucratic nature of their workplace, some cops simply break. Some merely become sullen and lazy, others turn to alcohol or drugs, some commit suicide, and some decide to become criminals themselves—either to enrich themselves or to deal out their own brand of justice.

A corrupt police officer is particularly distressing to a free society because of the authority the officer represents. Corrupt police officers have the power to unlawfully imprison someone, to plant evidence, or to use needless and unlawful violence—all under the protection provided by their status as a police officer. While their nature is no more detestable than the city alderman who demands payoffs for city permits, the corrupt officer is more dangerous and represents a physical rather than financial threat to freedom and justice.

Dealing with corrupt and incompetent police officers is one of the most crucial elements of creating and maintaining public trust and is an area in need of reform in many agencies. With thousands of police departments across the country, every one of them has a different approach to dealing with complaints from citizens. These range from prompt, thorough investigations, with a range of penalties for officers found culpable of misconduct, to a dismissive approach with little or no formal investigation. How officer complaints are handled by an agency has a significant impact on the perceived professionalism and legitimacy of the entire force. Even though complainants in most cases never know the outcome of an internal investigation, it is important that they feel their concerns were taken seriously and were formally investigated. Someone who telephones a police department to complain that an officer deliberately violated his or her Constitutional rights should never have the process end with a supervisor on the other end of the phone saying, "I'll have a talk with the officer."

Still, for every cop who is rude or fails to obey the rules, there are a thousand officers who earnestly work every day to help others and improve their communities. Police officers volunteer their time in youth programs, take time to check on the vulnerable and elderly on their beats, find shelter for the homeless, buy a drink from kids at a lemonade stand, and listen to people's concerns. Every day, police officers lock up dangerous criminals without the need to use force, and none of those events goes viral on YouTube. Police officers talk suicidal people off bridges and buildings, deliver babies, administer lifesaving first aid and CPR, pull people from burning cars and houses, find lost children and elderly citizens, rescue people from submerged vehicles and flooded roads, save abused animals, change tires, remove dangerous debris from highways, collect Christmas toys and coats for needy children, raise money and work in the Special Olympics, comfort traumatized or grieving people, and perform countless other acts of kindness and heroism that go largely unseen. Officers also suffer the trauma of watching terrified people die in pain, witnessing horrific scenes of gruesome injury and violent death; handle unattended deaths where the lonely and destitute die unnoticed in their sad homes; see abused and dead children, decomposing human bodies, horrible living conditions, the deranged and tortured mentally ill, the ravages of alcoholism and drug abuse; and confront frightening sociopaths of every stripe that walk mostly unseen among us. Most officers are good people of courage doing a difficult and dangerous job. Some fall short because they should never have become police officers, but where police tactics and agencies fall short of the community's expectations, it is the fault of their leadership that has failed to provide proper training, support, leadership, and discipline.

In my days working patrol, I've witnessed all of the above. I have stood in the lonely, dark, alcohol-soaked rooms, splattered with blood and brains, where the desperate and lonely spent their final moments. I've watched an 18-year-old girl drowning in her own blood after shooting herself with a rifle, because she got pregnant and her boyfriend left her. I've held dead infants; pulled an eight-year-old boy's lifeless body out of a swimming hole; watched a woman with a broken neck die in a ditch on a cold autumn night; told families that their loved ones had died; been in more filthy, smoke-filled apartments and trailers than I can count, refereeing family squabbles and bloody confrontations. I've had four people try to kill me and killed another human being at a domestic dispute. I can vouch for the stresses police officers on patrol are under.

In the pages that follow, there are many criticisms of police training and tactics, as well as the culture that exists in some police agencies. It is important to remember that the United States does not have an entity called *The Police*. There are more 700,000 individuals serving as police officers in more agencies than we can count, drawn from every region, ethnicity, gender, and religion in the country. To paint them all with a broad brush is intellectually indefensible. Every individual officer makes choices that determine whether he or she is a good or a bad cop, and each agency has its own history, traditions, organizational culture, and leadership that determine how its officers behave and how the public perceives them. Failures of police officers to live up to their oaths of office can be attributed to the inevitable bad actors that make it into the police service, but when police agencies fall out of favor with their constituents or engage in widespread violations of civil rights, they do so because of a failure of *leadership.* The criticisms in this book are directed at police and political leadership and not the rank-and-file officers who, by and large, are well-intentioned and quite often heroic men and women who do their very best every day to make their communities better and safer places to live and work.

To Protect and to Serve

This simple phrase has been used by police agencies for decades to succinctly describe their mission and role in the community. As a motto or creed, "protect and serve" casts the officer in a role as sheepdog, protecting the weaker or defenseless members of the community from the wolves who would prey upon them and giving a gentle bite on the leg to any sheep that stray. It also evokes the service ethos that is sometimes lacking in police agencies today.

Unfortunately, our nation's police have tended to evolve from policemen to *law enforcement officers.* This change is not simply in name alone. *Policing,* by definition, means to keep order in a community, to control and regulate by ensuring rules are obeyed, and to make neat and orderly. Law enforcement, on the other hand, connotes arresting people for violations of law—period.

American police should not be law enforcement officers. The police officer of a free society views arrest and issuing tickets as merely one tool among many available to him or her. Mediating disputes, calming tempers, separating combatants, solving problems, and issuing friendly warnings are the tools that good officers use to carry out their primary function of *order maintenance.* The law enforcement officer, by contrast, has only two primary tools: handcuffs and a ticket book.

The drift toward ever more police strictly enforcing ever more laws has served to separate the officer from the community and make police officers an object of apprehension by virtually all citizens, rather than a source of comfort as a strong, caring individual committed to the service and protection of all.

The chapters that follow will trace the historical roots and recent evolution of America's police forces and examine the reasons for breakdowns in police-community relations. We will discuss what the police are doing wrong and what they are doing right, as well as strategies for making improvements. Police culture, race relations, political issues, officer training, use of force, and internal disciplinary policies will be discussed with a view toward creating police agencies that are regarded as trustworthy institutions charged with and dedicated to protect and to serve their fellow citizens.

CHAPTER TWO

The Evolution of the Modern Police Force

> The basic mission for which police exist is to prevent crime and disorder as an alternative to the repression of crime and disorder by military force and severity of legal punishment.
>
> —Sir Robert Peel, 1829

In the modern United States, we take the existence of police agencies and the presence of uniformed police officers for granted, something that has always been a part of life in our country. What most people fail to realize is that, historically, even the concept of the nation-state is relatively new, while the development of organized, professional police forces as a means of maintaining order is a much more recent development.

After the fall of the Roman Empire in the fifth century, western Europe descended into centuries of darkness and chaos. The few governments were loosely defined kingdoms based upon ethnic and linguistic similarities, with little to no administrative infrastructure and no organized group charged with enforcing what few laws existed. Monarchs in the kingdoms of the Visigoths, Burgundians, and the like may have held absolute power in theory, but they had precious little means of exercising that power—for good or ill—on the level of the ordinary peasant, who was left to find his own means of protection from criminals. The map of Europe was drawn and redrawn for centuries into hundreds of large and small kingdoms, duchies, crowns, bishoprics, and principalities.

It was during this medieval period, aptly referred to as the Dark Ages, that the system of feudalism emerged. In simplistic terms, feudalism involved peasants combining together under a powerful landowner who would offer them protection in exchange for a share of their crops or a period of labor or service in wars against other feudal lords. Effectively, the law was whatever the lord of the manor decreed, with enforcement being carried out unevenly; there certainly were no individuals whose primary occupation was enforcing laws or solving crimes.

The legal basis for the nation-state—or what is commonly referred to as a *country*—something most take for granted as the normal state of human affairs from time immemorial, was only established following the Thirty Years' War, with the Peace of Westphalia three-and-a-half centuries ago. A functioning world order of nation-states as we know it would not truly emerge until the 1800s and be completed with the breakup of the multi-ethnic empires following World War I. It would be two centuries after Westphalia before the first modern police force would come into existence.

The system of police we have in the United States today has evolved from the English system brought here by the colonists. In medieval England, laws were enforced under a system known as *frankenpledge*. Groups of 10 men each were organized into *tithings*. These 10 individuals were responsible for the others in their group and for their appearance before the authorities if one of them was accused of a crime. Ten tithings were grouped to make a *hundred* men, and 10 of these were in turn grouped into a *shire*—the precursor to what we would refer to as a county. The crown would appoint someone to oversee the shire—a *shire-reeve*—later to be shortened to *sheriff*. The reeve would have the power to act as judge in many cases brought before him.

Eventually, the power of the sheriff to act as judge was curbed with the establishment of itinerant royal justices. By the 14th century, the franken-pledge system evolved into local constables charged with enforcing laws under the direction of a justice of the peace. These constables, while performing a police function, did not resemble a modern, uniformed police officer; they operated mostly alone, wore no uniform, and performed their duties on a strictly part-time basis. This system continued in various forms well into the 19th century, until the dawn of the industrial revolution and large-scale migration to cities and other population centers.

So it was that when the English began to colonize North America in the 18th century, they brought with them their ancient system of maintaining order. Needless to say, in the beginning, no formal system of policing was required, as the small, intimate nature of settlements made crime rare and easy to deal with. As the population grew, the English model of law enforcement became the norm, with constables and sheriffs investigating crime and bringing the accused before the bar of justice.

Just as in England, the rise of an industrial society led to a need for a different type of police force. The sheriff-farmer, or part-time deputy marshal, simply wasn't capable of dealing with the masses of people and frequency of crime attendant in an urban metropolis. While London's *bobbies* (so-called because of Sir Robert Peel's role in creating the force) did not carry firearms, America's lawmen needed to do so at the outset because of the nearly universal ownership of arms among the citizenry. Because colonial and later republican America had an often dangerous and lawless frontier region, from the first settlements of the late 17th century to the closing of the frontier in the late 19th century, gun violence was an ever-present concern for lawmen. In addition to local sheriffs, the federal government got into the law enforcement business in earnest in the mid-1800s. Although created by the Judiciary Act of 1789, the Marshal Service took on more of a law enforcement role as the country's frontier pushed westward. Territories under U.S. control but without a state government had to rely on the federal marshals to provide law and order.

This tough breed of men who acted as sheriffs or marshals and their deputies in the Wild West are, as we all know, the stuff of legend and helped shape the image of American police as rough, intrepid, gunslingers who always get their man. Once American metropolitan centers reached populations in the millions, the need for a more professional, organized form of policing would become apparent.

Back in England, the teeming masses of people in London, with the attendant urban crime, created unique challenges to the concept of providing the protection of the law to English subjects. By the dawn of the 19th century, London was on its way to becoming the most populous city in the world.[1] The end of the Napoleonic wars in 1815 brought a flood of some 300,000 former soldiers to add to the already swollen ranks of unemployed.[2] In the immediate postwar years, many began to advocate for a professional police to replace the unpaid volunteer constabulary, as they too often proved ineffective and unreliable, for the obvious reason that they were not paid and so rarely prioritized their constable duties above their private affairs. Against the backdrop of rapid urbanization, social conflict, and crime and following a number of official studies and inquiries, the British home secretary, Sir Robert Peel, introduced the Metropolitan Police Act in 1829. The measure passed in Parliament, and in September of that year the London Metropolitan Police was formed and was to become universally regarded as the genesis of the modern police force as we know it today.[3]

Peel's force established a baseline for an organization of professional, fulltime police officers. Sir Robert Peel wanted his officers to be uniformed, so as to distinguish them from the populace. He organized round-the-clock, organized patrols of delineated districts in an effort to deter crime rather than simply investigate after the fact. Sir Robert Peel wanted his officers to be viewed as legitimate and professional to distinguish them from the earlier watchmen who did not command respect and were regarded as ineffective. His men were also given some measure of training and selected on the basis of aptitude and steady temperament. In establishing his new force, Sir Robert Peel promulgated a set of principles to govern the practice of policing. Some scholars dispute the precise wording and origins of the principles as they are known today; however, they can be summarized as follows:

1. The basic mission for which police exist is to prevent crime and disorder as an alternative to the repression of crime and disorder by military force and severity of legal punishment.

2. The ability of the police to perform their duties is dependent upon *public approval* of police existence, actions, behavior and the ability of the police to secure and maintain *public respect*.

3. The police must secure the willing cooperation of the public in voluntary observance of the law to be able to secure and maintain public respect.

4. The degree of cooperation of the public that can be secured diminishes, proportionately, to the necessity for the use of physical force and compulsion in achieving police objectives.

5. The police seek and preserve public favor, not by catering to public opinion, but by constantly demonstrating absolutely impartial service to the law, in complete independence of policy, and without regard to the justice or injustice of the substance of individual laws; by ready offering of individual service and friendship to all members of society without regard to their race or social standing, by ready exercise of courtesy and friendly good humor; and by ready offering of individual sacrifice in protecting and preserving life.

6. The police should use physical force to the extent necessary to secure observance of the law or to restore order only when the exercise of *persuasion, advice and warning* is found to be insufficient to achieve police objectives; and police should use only the minimum degree of physical force which is necessary on any particular occasion for achieving a police objective.

7. The police at all times should maintain a relationship with the public that gives reality to the historic tradition that *the police are the public* and *the public are the police*; the police are the only members of the public who are paid to give full-time attention to duties which are incumbent on every citizen in the intent of the community welfare.

8. The police should always direct their actions toward their functions and never appear to usurp the powers of the judiciary by avenging individuals or the state, or authoritatively judging guilt or punishing the guilty.

9. The test of police efficiency is the *absence* of crime and disorder, not the *visible evidence* of police action in dealing with them.[4]

Although the London police were an arm of the central government, they were still regarded as civilian constables in the tradition of the ancient system of the watch and ward. Subsequent legislation from Parliament requiring local and county police forces left the organization and oversight to local officials, in keeping with the long-established tradition of local control of the police function.[5]

The earliest urban police force in the United States was created in Boston in 1838, with a force of just eight men. It was not until 1859, however, that the force was operating 24 hours per day and fully uniformed.[6] The New York City Police came into being as a unified force in 1845.[7] The organization and proliferation of police forces continued throughout the second half of the 19th century as the country expanded and urban areas grew rapidly. The local control of police function created overlapping jurisdictions, with sheriffs having jurisdiction concurrent with metropolitan police within their county. Later, in the early 20th century, the rise of state police agencies would add another layer of concomitant jurisdiction, creating problems of rivalry and communication that persist to this day.

The early police forces in the United States were, generally speaking, unprofessional and prone to abuse and corruption. While some agencies and officers provided faithful service, corrupt political leaders and party machines used most police departments as a means of dispensing jobs and favors to their supporters. Since educational and training requirements were virtually non-existent, officers oftentimes had a poor understanding of—and little regard for—the laws and the rights of citizens. In 1894, the New York State legislature approved funding for a committee to investigate long-rumored reports of widespread corruption in the New York City Police Department. The committee was chaired by Senator Clarence Lexow, who found that the police were engaged in widespread and systematic bribery, counterfeiting, election fraud, voter intimidation, brutality, and extortion.[8]

In 1896, the journalist and novelist Stephen Crane of *The Red Badge of Courage* fame came to New York to conduct research for a book about New York City policemen. Just as he was beginning his work, he happened to be interviewing three ladies of ill repute near mid-town around 2 A.M. He had just finished his interviews when he escorted one of the women across the street to catch a cable car. As the trolley pulled away, Crane observed two men walk quickly past the two young women he had left on the other side of the road. Neither the men nor the women looked at or spoke to one another. As he crossed the street back to where the women were, he encountered police detective Charles Becker, who was arresting one of the women for solicitation for prostitution, presumably because he knew one of the two women to be a known prostitute.

Knowing that this was a false arrest, Crane dispatched a telegram to Police Commissioner Roosevelt, to which he received no reply. He went on to testify—at great hazard to his personal reputation—on the woman's behalf at her trial and at a hearing with the police department, accusing Becker of misconduct. Crane found himself thereafter harassed and defamed mercilessly by the police department and quickly abandoned his NYPD project, moving on to cover the controversies in Cuba, which would lead to the Spanish-American War.[9] Interestingly, Detective Becker would go on to become the first and only member of the NYPD to die in the electric chair, for arranging the murder of a gambler named Beansie Rosenthal.[10]

The commonly held broad view of the evolution of American policing as taught in criminal justice circles derives from an analysis by George Kelling and Mark Moore, who, in 1988, broke down the history and evolution of American policing into three loosely defined eras: political, reform, and community problem solving.[11] The political era ran from the genesis of American metropolitan policing through the early 20th century. This time period is so called because of the close ties of the police departments with the local political machines. Police officers were advocates for their local ward politicians (to whom they owed their jobs) and would conduct all sorts of activities other than order maintenance and crime detection. Local officers would run soup kitchens, advocate for political candidates, and even run boarding houses for newly arrived immigrants. Although policing tactics varied widely, this era is generally known for a lack of training and widespread corruption, as the police were used as pawns by political machines.

The Twentieth Century

The reform era of the early 1900s coincided with the so-called progressive period in American political life generally. This time period saw the creation of civil service laws, prohibiting local politicians from hiring and firing of police and other government employees at their whim. Applicants were to be hired and promoted based on unbiased competitive and merit-based criteria—making the police (somewhat) independent of politics. It was also during the reform era that the first significant steps toward professionalizing the police were taken.

The most famous of the reformers and innovators of the time was August Vollmer of the Berkeley, California, Police Department. The son of German immigrants and a veteran of the Spanish-American War, Vollmer ran for city marshal over the objection of his family, who saw police work as an embarrassment, and was later appointed as police chief when that position was created in 1909, a job he would retain until his retirement in 1932.

With a mandate from the city to clean up the commercialized vice in the city—gambling, prostitution, and opium dens—he overcame the apathy of his men and efforts to bribe him and greatly reduced the crime rate in the city. Using innovative investigation techniques, Vollmer's men captured two internationally wanted criminals, bringing attention to this otherwise small California city. Vollmer is credited with a host of innovations, including bicycle and motorized patrol, police call boxes for rapid communications, radio dispatch, criminal profiling, and use of fingerprint data collection.

Vollmer also used an intelligence test and a staff psychiatrist to screen applicants, actively recruited college students, employed scientists as "criminalists" to help solve crimes, convinced the University of California to begin a program of study in criminology, and instituted a three-year program of study all of his officers were required to complete. Numerous books and articles he authored helped to spread his ideas, and he was employed to reorganize both the San Diego and Los Angeles police departments. Still, it would be decades before preemployment and in-service training would become standard for police officers in every state.

George Fletcher Chandler, the first superintendent of the New York State Police, established strict preemployment training camps for his *troopers*, the first in the nation, in 1917. Chandler required his troopers to have unimpeachable integrity on and off duty. He went on to found a first-in-the-nation school for police that issued graduates a certificate, backed by a state education department and board of regents, as qualified police officers.

Despite the innovations and progress of men like Vollmer and Chandler, American policing in general remained a sub-profession, often plagued by corruption, brutality, and incompetence. The first time the national spotlight was turned on police practices was in 1931, with the publication of the report of the National Commission on Law Observance and Enforcement, more commonly known as the Wickersham Commission. While the commission was tasked with investigating the effects of and compliance with alcohol prohibition, the commission devoted one of its 14 volumes to the police. The scathing report was damning of the police, beginning with a declaration that the police in general suffered from a "general failure" to detect crime and arrest offenders for serious violent crimes.

The Wickersham Commission chronicled widespread police incompetence, corruption, and brutality, which it blamed primarily on undue political influence over the police and lack of qualified officers and super-visors. The report pointed out that the average tenure of a city police chief was just a little more than two years and that the job was in most cases little more than a sinecure given in return for political patronage and not reserved for experienced police professionals. The investigators even men-tioned the mayor of a major city who announced the appointment of his tailor as chief of police, saying he'd been a good tailor for 20 years and so would be a fine police chief. The lack of competent supervision and quali-fied officers was also blamed on the influence of local politicians who gave police jobs and promotions to their cronies. The commissioners wrote:

> As the patrolmen are directly selected by favoritism because of their parti-san political activities or by civil service examinations, which can only remotely make certain of their qualifications for the discharge of their duties, since they have had no practical experience, have as a rule had nothing more than elementary schooling, are usually without cultural background, and without an adequate sense of the qualifications for the discharge of their duties, it follows that a large part of them are not likely to be and are not competent patrolmen. And from that source must come the commanding officers and nearly always the chief. Inefficient, dishon-est, incompetent patrolmen and those incapacitated by age are too often, by reason of the foregoing conditions, retained on the force, to its prejudice and that of the public to be served. No pains are taken, so far as we can learn from these studies, to educate, train, and discipline for a year or two the prospective patrolmen and to eliminate from their number such as are shown to be incompetent for their prospective duties.[12]

The commission's report recounted widespread use of physically abusive interrogation tactics, known as the *third degree*, where prisoners were beaten or tortured into confessing to crimes, detailing more than a hun-dred instances where false confessions were extracted through physical and/or psychological cruelty.

With local police chiefs appointed at the whim of politicians, the com-mission opined:

> Seeking to avoid repression and to preserve democratic ideals, the people have virtually turned over their police departments to the most notorious and frequently the most dangerous persons in their communities, who do not hesitate to use them for every type of oppression and intimidation. Therefore, their attempt to protect themselves from a powerful autocratic chief of police has served to place them and the government in the hands of unscrupulous cut-throats, murderers, and bootleggers.[13]

While the report created a national discussion of police practices and administration, it was soon overshadowed by events. Prohibition, which had been the reason for the formation of the commission in the first place, was repealed in 1933, and the nation was plunging ever deeper into the Great Depression, turning everyone's attention to the economy and their own personal survival. The depression was still going strong when the United States entered World War II, which was immediately followed by the nuclear age and the Cold War, events that dominated the public sphere through the 1940s and 1950s.

1960s—Riots and Reform

For decades in the south and in northern cities, relations between the police and black communities ranged from poor to abysmal. In the post-Reconstruction south, police were part of the social structure erected to maintain the continued oppression of blacks in the wake of emancipation. In the north, racism persisted at all levels of society, and the police were no exception. A lack of understanding and widespread acceptance of a "benign" prejudice against blacks served to create tensions that flared on and off and finally came to a boil during the civil rights movement.

The decade of the 1960s was turbulent for the United States and indeed much of the world. The United States saw its involvement in the Vietnamese civil war go from one of advisory and economic assistance to full-blown warfare; the civil rights movement, rise of the counter culture and drug culture, war protests, and the women's rights movement all roiled the country. Combined with a rapidly rising violent-crime rate, the government and police were facing a host of challenges. Racial tensions also exploded during large-scale rioting in Los Angeles in the 1965 Watts riots, followed in the subsequent years by racial riots in Newark, Detroit, and Baltimore, with unrest and protests in hundreds of other cities, schools, and universities.

In the wake of the Watts riots, President Lyndon Johnson created The President's Commission on Law Enforcement and the Administration of Justice. The commission's report, titled *The Challenge of Crime in a Free Society*, examined the root causes of various types of crime and the functioning of the criminal justice system and made recommendations for action. In its analysis of the police, the commission found that police officers' behavior had improved since the Wickersham report three decades earlier but still opined that the police generally suffered from a lack of quality officers and leaders.[14]

The commission acknowledged the "commendable zeal, determination, and devotion to duty" of most officers but argued that a majority lacked the education to deal with the legal intricacies and complex social problems facing the modern policeman. At the time of the report, 30 percent of police agencies did not require even a high-school diploma for employment and virtually none required any college education. The commission recommended a requirement that officers possess bachelor's degrees in order to raise the caliber of police and police supervisors and administrators.

Following another summer of race riots in 1967, most notably in Newark and Detroit, President Johnson formed another commission, The National Advisory Committee on Civil Disorders, to look into the causes and solutions for such unrest. The committee did not mince words when it reported that the root causes were "discrimination and segregation [which] have long permeated American life." In its opening paragraphs, the report stated clearly: "This is our basic conclusion: Our nation is moving toward two societies, one black, one white—separate and unequal."[15]

The government and police response to the civil rights and antiwar protests of the 1960s and the new widespread medium of television would cast a new and harsh light on police use of force. Most notable among black leaders, the Reverend Martin Luther King, Jr., led civil rights activists and supporters in boycotts, protests, and marches in several southern cities. Police often met Dr. King's nonviolent protests, modeled after the techniques of Mahatma Gandhi, with unprovoked and shocking violence. In May 1963, infamously racist Birmingham police chief Eugene "Bull" Connor unleashed club-wielding officers, attack dogs, cattle prods, and high-pressure fire hoses on peaceful youths marching in the downtown area. The photographs and video images of these abuses would shock the nation and many around the world.

In 1965, during a protest over voter registration practices in Dallas County, Alabama, a black protester was shot and killed by an Alabama state trooper. To protest the violence, Reverend King's Southern Christian Leadership Conference, along with a student group, organized a march from Selma to Montgomery. On Sunday, March 7, approximately 600 marchers gathered and began their march. As the protesters approached the Edmund Pettus Bridge, which would carry them over the river out of Selma, a force of Alabama state troopers and local police in riot gear confronted them, ordering them to turn back. When this order was ignored, the police fired tear gas and plunged into the crowd, beating the nonviolent and unarmed protesters with riot batons, hospitalizing 50 marchers. Once again, this incident was televised around the world and became infamously known as Bloody Sunday.[16]

In 1964, during what was labeled the *summer of freedom*, civil rights workers were engaged in a campaign across the south to register black citizens to vote. In June of that year, three young volunteers, Michael Schwerner and Andrew Goodman from New York City and James Chaney from Meridian, Mississippi, disappeared outside Philadelphia, Mississippi, and were later found to have been murdered. Schwerner and Goodman were white, and Chaney was black. With the local authorities refusing to conduct a proper inquiry into the disappearance, the FBI orchestrated an extensive criminal investigation and eventually located the bodies of the three men. Autopsies and testimony would later reveal that Cheney had been bound to a tree and beaten with chains before being castrated and shot twice at point-blank range and that Goodman had still been alive when he was buried. The FBI solved the murders, revealing that Neshoba County sheriff Lawrence Rainey was involved and that his deputy, Cecil Price, arranged for the arrest of the three for "speeding" and held them in jail until the lynch mob was prepared. Price then released the three and promptly stopped them again, whereupon they were taken from their car and murdered, with Schwerner and Goodman killed after being forced to watch Chaney's beating and mutilation.[17] The revelation of the involvement of the police in such shocking crime further tarnished the reputation of police—especially those in the states of the former Confederacy.

One of the most shocking revelations of police corruption came with the 1972 Report of the Commission to Investigate Alleged Police Corruption, empaneled by New York City mayor John Lindsay in 1970. The panel, commonly known as the *Knapp Commission*, was created due to the criminality exposed by Detective Frank Serpico, who had spent years first trying to find a precinct where he could be left alone and not participate in the system of payoffs and then trying desperately to get the department brass to do something about the corruption. Finally, he was able to bring media attention to the problem through the *New York Times*. His heroic story was memorialized in the Peter Maas biography, *Serpico*, and the 1973 film by the same name.

The commission's report was shocking in its revelations and devastating to the NYPD. The pages chronicled pervasive corruption involving systematized bribery paid to officers by bookies, numbers runners, pimps, and drug dealers to look the other way. The report told of officers directly involved in drug trafficking and murder for hire and revealed the identity of informants targeted for murder by mobsters. The information in the report indicated that the NYPD itself was, for a period of years, the largest single supplier of heroin in the city.[18]

While the Knapp Commission laid bare the rampant criminality in the NYPD, it stopped short of holding the top echelons of the department and city government accountable. There was ample evidence that the police leadership and individuals in the mayor's office had been presented with accusations and evidence of serious law breaking in the department and had done nothing. Not only had Frank Serpico personally informed police commanders and the head of the department's Internal Affairs Division but the FBI's Bureau of Narcotics and Dangerous Drugs made 69 referrals to the NYPD of specific officers who were "extortionists, murderers, and heroin entrepreneurs."[19] This failure to hold police and political leaders responsible for their complicity in creating, nurturing, or tolerating a culture where such corruption can thrive was seen repeatedly in responses to police corruption scandals.

To a far greater degree than the Wickersham Commission's report, the civil rights movement, revelations of police corruption, and the publication of *The Challenge of Crime in a Free Society* led to a significant effort to reform and professionalize the police. The Omnibus Crime Control and Safe Streets Act of 1968 created the federal Law Enforcement Assistance Administration (LEAA) and allowed the government to assist local law enforcement with grants to pay for everything from new facilities to training programs and public education initiatives. Grants were made available to assist police officers in obtaining a college education and for police research and equipment. Police leaders began to view policing as a profession and as a subject of research and development of best practices.

It was following the chaos of the 1960s, the report of the presidential commission, and the establishment of the LEAA that the era of the professional police officer truly began. States that did not have minimum training standards for their police officers began to establish police officer standards and training commissions and require at least a high-school education for new trainees. Through the auspices of the LEAA, knowledge of policing and new innovations from different regions and departments were disseminated to agencies nationwide.

Colleges began creating hundreds of degree programs in *criminal justice*, where aspiring officers could learn about policing and the justice system in general. Many police agencies began to offer tuition assistance for officers to further their studies on a part-time basis and to actively recruit college-educated applicants. In addition to improving the education of their members, police agencies began to modernize their tactics, implementing new strategies for patrol, studying effective interrogation methods, improving recordkeeping and information sharing, and formalizing rules and regulations for their membership.

The Legal Landscape Changes

During the late 1950s through the early 1970s, a number of landmark Supreme Court rulings would drastically alter the way police conducted business. The Court ruled repeatedly that the protections afforded to U.S. citizens under the Bill of Rights applied equally to the citizens of each state pursuant to the Fourteenth Amendment, which said, "No State shall make or enforce any law which shall abridge the privileges or immunities of citizens of the United States. . . ." Alleged police violations of these interpretations of the Constitution continue to be a source of controversy today.

Search and Seizure

The Supreme Court heard a case in 1961 that dealt with the issue of evidence seized by the police as the result of an illegal search. Without departmental or serious civil consequences for such lawlessness, the police had little incentive not to violate the Fourth Amendment rights of suspects in the hopes of finding some evidence of crime or contraband. The case at issue began in May 1957, when three Cleveland, Ohio, police officers arrived at the home of Dollree Mapp to search for a suspect in a recent bombing,[20] whom they believed may have been hiding in her residence. After consulting with her attorney over the telephone, she denied the officers' entry unless they could produce a search warrant. The officers withdrew and took up positions outside for about three hours and then approached the house again, still without a warrant, this time with 10 to 15 men, forcing open a door and entering. The police found the man they were looking for (who was renting a room from Mapp) and then proceeded to search the entire house, including drawers and a small chest in the basement, where they found "pornographic materials" consisting of a nude pencil sketch and some romance novels.

Miss Mapp was arrested for possession of the "lewd and lascivious materials," subsequently convicted of felony obscenity charges, and sentenced to a maximum term of seven years in prison. She appealed her conviction to the Supreme Court, which—in addition to ruling that the Ohio obscenity statute violated the First Amendment—ruled that evidence illegally seized—as was clearly the situation in Miss Mapp's case—must be suppressed and may not be introduced at trial. The Court's opinion stated, with regard to the use of the evidence unconstitutionally seized:

> If letters and private documents can thus be seized and held and used in evidence against a citizen accused of an offense, the protection of the

Fourth Amendment declaring his right to be secure against such searches and seizures is of no value, and, so far as those thus placed are concerned, might as well be stricken from the Constitution. The efforts of the courts and their officials to bring the guilty to punishment, praiseworthy as they are, are not to be aided by the sacrifice of those great principles established by years of endeavor and suffering which have resulted in their embodiment in the fundamental law of the land . . . use of the seized evidence [would be] a denial of the constitutional rights of the accused.[21]

Dollree Mapp went on to live a colorful life, being arrested in New York City after police executed a real search warrant at her home and found large quantities of heroin. She went on to work with a group that provided legal assistance to prison inmates and started a number of businesses, as well as touring colleges and speaking about her famous Ohio case.[22]

Stop and Frisk

On October 31, 1963, Cleveland detective Martin McFadden, on a downtown beat which he had been patrolling for many years, observed two strangers—John Terry and another man, named Chilton—on a street corner. He saw them proceed alternately back and forth along an identical route, pausing to stare in the same store window, which they did for a total of about 24 times. Each completion of the route was followed by a conference between the two on a corner, at one of which a third man named Katz joined them and quickly left.

Suspecting the two men of *casing a job, a stick-up,* the officer followed them and saw them rejoin the third man a couple of blocks away in front of a store. The officer approached the three, identified himself as a policeman, and asked their names. The men "mumbled something," whereupon McFadden spun Terry around, patted down his outside clothing, and found a pistol in his overcoat pocket but was unable to remove it. The officer ordered the three into the store. He removed Terry's overcoat, took out a revolver, and ordered the three to face the wall with their hands raised. He patted down the outer clothing of Chilton and Katz and seized a revolver from Chilton's outside overcoat pocket. He did not put his hands under the outer garments of Katz (since he discovered nothing in his pat-down, which might have been a weapon) or under Terry's or Chilton's outer garments until he felt the guns. The three were taken to the police station, where Terry and Chilton were charged with carrying concealed weapons.

The defense moved to suppress the weapons as evidence, arguing that they were seized as a result of an illegal search. Though the trial court rejected the prosecution theory that the guns had been seized during a search incident to a lawful arrest, the court denied the motion to suppress and admitted the weapons into evidence on the grounds that the officer had cause to believe that Terry and Chilton were acting suspiciously, that their interrogation was warranted, and that the officer, for his own protection, had the right to pat down their outer clothing having reasonable cause to believe that they might be armed.

The court distinguished between an investigatory "stop" and an arrest and between a "frisk" of the outer clothing for weapons and a full-blown search for evidence of crime. Terry and Chilton were found guilty, an intermediate appellate court affirmed, and the state Supreme Court dismissed the appeal on the ground that "no substantial constitutional question" was involved.[23]

In other words, *stop and frisk* is a step below *arrest and search* and can be justified based upon the behavior of the suspects, the area, time of day, and the experience of the officer, what the courts refer to as the totality of circumstances. Police officers must have the ability to explain exactly what they observed that provided their reasonable suspicion, beyond simple gut feelings or sense that someone just didn't look right.

In the case of *People v. Debour*, the Supreme Court would get much more specific about just what a police officer was permitted to do when it came to stop and frisk. At 12:15 A.M. on the morning of October 15, 1972, Kenneth Steck, a police officer assigned to the Tactical Patrol Force of the NYPD, was working the 6:00 P.M. to 2:00 A.M. tour of duty, assigned to foot patrol in Brooklyn. While walking his beat on a street illuminated by ordinary street lamps and devoid of pedestrian traffic, he and his partner noticed someone walking on the same side of the street in their direction. When the solitary figure of the defendant, Louis Debour, was within 30 or 40 feet of the uniformed officers, he crossed the street. The two policemen followed suit and when Debour reached them, Officer Steck inquired as to what he was doing in the neighborhood. Debour, clearly but nervously, answered that he had just parked his car and was going to a friend's house.

The patrolman then asked Debour for identification. As he was answering that he had none, Officer Steck noticed a slight waist-high bulge in Debour's jacket. At this point, the policeman asked Debour to unzip his coat. When Debour complied with this request, Officer Steck observed a revolver protruding from his waistband. The loaded weapon was removed from behind his waistband, and he was arrested for possession of the gun.[24]

The New York Court denied Debour's motion to have the gun suppressed. He argued unsuccessfully that it was seized unlawfully because the police had no authority to stop him and ask him to unzip his coat. The case eventually reached the Supreme Court, which denied the motion and affirmed Debour's conviction for possession of a weapon.

The Court's ruling detailed proper legal guidelines for police-citizen encounters, creating a four-level hierarchy for such interactions:

Level 1: The police officer has an *objective and credible reason* to approach, only requires a credible suspicion of possible criminal activity.

The officer may ask non-threatening questions such as name, address, what the person is doing or carrying, but must not make the person feel as though he or she is being accused of criminal behavior. The encounter should be brief and free from intimidation or harassment. At this level, the officer may not ask permission to search.

Level 2: The police officer has a *founded suspicion* of criminal activity.

Under the common law right of inquiry, the officer may ask pointed questions that may make the person feel he or she is suspected of a crime. This level of encounter may last a bit longer, but the officer still has no right to pursue or forcibly detain the citizen.

Level 3: Police officer has *reasonable suspicion* of criminal activity.

At this point, an officer has good reason to believe there is criminal activity afoot and that the person he or she is approaching is involved. The officer may forcibly detain the subject or pursue the subject if he or she flees. With justification, the officer may frisk the outer garments for weapons, place the person on the ground, or handcuff the person. This is also known as a *Terry stop*, in reference to *Terry v. Ohio*.

Level 4: Police officer has *probable cause* to believe subject has committed a crime.

The officer may place the person under arrest at this point, using any reasonable force required to do so, in compliance with applicable law. The officer may then immediately search the entire person of the defendant. This is referred to as *search incident to arrest*.

Interrogation and Right to Counsel

In addition to prescribing the bounds within which officers may stop and detain people, the high court also handed down rulings concerning when and how they could interrogate suspects. The first of these cases began in January 1960, when the brother-in-law of a man named Danny Escobedo was shot to death in Chicago. Escobedo was initially arrested by Chicago city police and questioned about the murder, but he refused to make any statements without seeing his attorney. The police refused to permit Escobedo to contact his lawyer; however, he made no statements and was released later the same day. Sometime later, another possible suspect told police during questioning that Escobedo had killed his brother-in-law because he was angry about the way the victim had been treating his sister.

Escobedo was arrested again and again was refused permission to speak to his lawyer. His lawyer came to the police station where Escobedo was being held and was repeatedly refused access to his client. After more than 14 hours of interrogation, Escobedo made admissions that implicated him in the murder. Upon appeal, the Supreme Court ruled that refusing a criminal suspect access to his attorney when he is being held in police custody violates the Sixth Amendment's guarantee of the right to counsel in criminal prosecutions. Danny Escobedo was set free and unfortunately went on to a prolific life of crime that included 12 felony convictions for crimes, including selling heroin, molesting children, and attempted murder.

The Supreme Court would make another ruling concerning police interrogation that is arguably the most famous in its history. The case involved an obscure Mexican American laborer named Ernesto Miranda. In March 1963, Miranda was waiting in his car outside a movie theater in Phoenix, Arizona, for a girl he had been stalking. When 18-year-old Lois Ann Jameson emerged and began walking home from the theater, Miranda kidnapped her at knifepoint, drove her out to the desert, and raped her. He then robbed her of her cash and dropped her off back in town. She described her assailant and his car to the police, who eventually located the vehicle and Miranda at the house he shared with his girlfriend. Miranda was taken to the police station by Officer Carroll Cooley and Detective Wilfred Young, was placed in a lineup, and was identified by the victim as her likely attacker but she could not be certain. After two hours of questioning, he confessed to the crime. Miranda then wrote his confession down on police forms. At the top of each sheet was printed a certification that "this statement has been made voluntarily and of my own free will, with no threats, coercion or promises of immunity and with full knowledge of my legal rights, understanding any statement I make can and will be used against me." The trial took place in June 1963 in Maricopa County Superior Court. Miranda's attorney objected to entering Miranda's confession as evidence during the trial but was overruled.

His case was appealed to the Supreme Court, which ruled that his confession was inadmissible and that the police must inform criminal defendants of their right to remain silent and to have an attorney present. The majority opinion stated, "The atmosphere and environment of incommunicado interrogation as it exists today is inherently intimidating, and works to undermine the privilege against self-incrimination. Unless adequate preventive measures are taken to dispel the compulsion inherent in custodial surroundings, no statement obtained from the defendant can truly be the product of his free choice.[25] As a result of this ruling, today all criminal defendants in police custody must be given a *Miranda warning* prior to any questioning. Unlike on television, the rights are not rattled off to the defendant as he or she is being handcuffed and bundled off to a police car. They are usually read from a card and then only if the suspect is about to be interrogated. The rights are read from a card so that there can be no mistake made, and the card itself can be introduced into evidence at trial, along with testimony from the officer that he or she read the exact text printed on the card to the defendant prior to questioning. If a defendant is not going to be questioned, the rights do not need to be read at all.

Ernesto Miranda was retried without his confession and convicted.[26] He was paroled in 1972 and made a living by selling autographed Miranda cards for $1.50 and working as a delivery driver. He was stabbed to death in January 1976 in a bar fight; the perpetrator invoked his Miranda rights upon arrest and was never convicted of the murder.[27]

The standard Miranda warning follows this basic format:

> You have the right to remain silent. Anything you say can and will be used against you in a court of law. You have the right to talk to a lawyer, and to have a lawyer present while you are being questioned. If you cannot afford a lawyer, one will be appointed for you before any questioning if you wish. You have the right to exercise these rights at any time and not make any statements or answer any questions. Do you understand each of these rights as I have explained them to you? Having these rights in mind, do you wish to talk with us now?

That same year, the Supreme Court had extended the right to counsel to indigent defendants in criminal trials. The tale began when, in June 1961, a burglary occurred at the Bay Harbor Pool Room in Panama City, Florida. Money was stolen from a cash register, along with coins from a cigarette machine. A witness told police he had seen Clarence Gideon leaving the building in the early morning hours with a bottle of wine and money in his pockets. (It's not clear how the witness knew Gideon's pockets were filled with money.) Gideon was subsequently arrested and charged with the crime on the basis of this evidence alone. The judge denied Gideon's request for a court-appointed lawyer to defend him because, at the time, Florida law allowed for appointed counsel only in capital cases.

Gideon was convicted and sentenced to five years in prison. While incarcerated, Gideon researched the law in the prison library and petitioned the Florida State Supreme Court for a writ of habeas corpus, arguing that the Fourteenth Amendment made the Sixth Amendment's right to counsel applicable to the states and that his trial was thus unfair. The Supreme Court ruled in Gideon's favor, ordering a new trial in which Gideon was found not guilty.[28]

From Professional Police Officer to Crusading Warrior

The police had a whole new set of rules to go by, and the job of policing was becoming more complex. While the rise of the professional police officer was an improvement, there were some unintended consequences. Police became more and more detached from their communities; sealed off in their squad cars, they became enigmatic and more focused on law enforcement than community service. The 1960s saw the advent of new "scientific" methods of policing and measuring results focused on numbers of arrests and tickets. Police officers who viewed themselves as professional crime fighters had little use for dealing with the mundane problems police are called upon to address. In 1966, President Johnson declared a "war on crime," saying to Congress, "The front-line soldier in the war on crime is the local law enforcement officer," called repeatedly for "battle," and closed by telling the assembled lawmakers, "The war on crime will be waged by our children and our children's children."[29] The Nixon Administration echoed the same theme. In a 1971 speech, Nixon's attorney general, John Mitchell, said, "If there is one area where the word 'war' is appropriate it is in the fight against crime. We must declare and win the war against the criminal elements which increasingly threaten our cities, our homes, and our lives."[30]

Then in 1972, President Nixon declared the war on drugs. This was a continuation of the government's string of "wars" on communism, poverty, hunger, and crime. The drug war continues to this day and has done more to damage police-citizen relationships and to distort the criminal justice system than any other phenomenon. While drug abuse is unhealthy and carries with it societal costs, it is an intimately personal activity, and efforts to eradicate the possession of contraband necessitate the most intrusive of police actions, trying to discover what you are carrying in your pockets or bag or what you are doing in the privacy of your home. The war on drugs fundamentally changed the relationship of the police officer with the public.

The war on drugs would continue to escalate through the 1980s and be attended by increasing violence from drug cartels made wealthy by drug prohibition. Their growing savagery and firepower eventually resulted in police responding by obtaining the same sophisticated weaponry to counter the drug traffickers. After the terrorist attacks of September 11, 2001, the federal government would declare a global war on terrorism, which would unleash a torrent of federal funds for police agencies across the country to obtain military-grade weapons and surveillance equipment. The government, as part of its efforts to instill a pervasive fear of terrorism, would actively promote the idea of police officers being on the frontline of a war for the very survival of human civilization being fought inside the United States. All of these elements would combine with growing government omnipotence and the proliferation of laws to transform police officers into law enforcement warriors—alienating them from the very community they serve.

CHAPTER THREE

From Neighborhood Patrolman to Law Enforcement Officer

Go about with the idea of helpfulness and friendliness that wins the
confidence of the people . . . Never hesitate to render assistance of
any kind, and let nothing be too much trouble which you can do for
the people you come in contact with.
>—Colonel George F. Chandler, New York
>State Police, Bulletin #1, 1917

They [police officers] made a mistake. There's no one to blame for a
mistake. The way these people were treated has to be judged in the
context of a war.
>—Attorney for the Hallandale, Florida Police Department,
>after they raided the wrong house and arrested
>its occupants at gunpoint, 1999

Throughout recent history, children in the United States have generally
been taught that police officers are your friend and to seek them out if you
are frightened or in trouble. The police officer of your parents' and grand-
parents' day was, depending on where they lived, either a friendly local
known to everyone or a neighborhood beat cop strolling along the street
and chatting with local residents and shopkeepers. He was called a *policeman*. The policeman knew the people in his town or on his beat, who the
hoodlums were, which couples would fight with each other when they
were drunk, and was aware of any problems that cropped up, from a big
hole in the sidewalk to trash being dumped on a vacant lot. If he was a
good cop, he was approachable and took the time to listen to people's
concerns, and his presence made people feel safe. He was tough as nails

with any bad guys or punks causing trouble, but he had a smile and a kind word for children and passersby.

This, at least, was the idealized version of the policeman. The revelations of the Wickersham and Knapp Commissions, among others, would reveal incompetence, malfeasance, and outright corruption in large and small police agencies alike. Oversight and supervision of officers were often severely lacking, as was proper training. Nevertheless, police were generally respected and did their jobs more or less to the satisfaction of the communities they served.

This image began to change during the civil rights movement of the 1960s. As black citizens began to agitate for equal rights under the law, the established order in the south fought back, in many cases using the police to violently break up peaceful protest marches and aggressively enforce Jim Crow segregation laws. In northern cities, blacks became more keenly aware of institutionalized racism and their seemingly intractable position of inferiority in society. America's nearly all-white male police forces began to seem like a symbol of oppression in many black communities.

While the problems of racial discrimination and disharmony were far bigger than the police force in any given community, the police were—then as now—the face of the government's laws and perceived legitimacy. As the growing racial tension across the country exploded into large-scale and often deadly riots in major cities, including Los Angeles, Detroit, and New York, the federal and state governments began to examine the causes and search for solutions. In 1967, the federal government created the National Advisory Commission on Civil Disorders, which issued a 426-page report the following year on the causes and solutions. The report made recommendations from expanding welfare to addressing unemployment, segregation, education, and other societal shortcomings. The commission addressed police-community relations as well as police training and response to civil disorders. Among the report's recommendations with regard to police were the following:

- Review police operations in black communities to ensure proper conduct, and the elimination of abrasive practices.
- Provide more adequate police protection to ghetto residents to eliminate their high sense of insecurity, and the belief of many Negro citizens in the existence of a dual standard of law enforcement.
- Establish fair and effective mechanisms for the redress of grievances against the police, and other municipal employees.
- Develop and adopt policy guidelines to assist officers in making critical decisions in areas where police conduct can create tension.

- Develop and use innovative programs to ensure widespread community support for law enforcement.

- Recruit more Negroes into the regular police force, and review promotion policies to ensure fair promotion for Negro officers.[1]

While these are all fine recommendations, some would require significant amounts of money to implement, and many would have required a radical change in thinking and approach to policing. Such things are easy to suggest on paper, but trying to change large city police departments and their massive, moribund bureaucracies is another matter entirely. In order to change tactics, reform the disciplinary process, create programs to improve community relations, and recruit more blacks, you would have to change the thinking and outlook of police administrators who have been in policing for decades. These leaders would in turn need to have the ability to implement changes over the objection to and apathy of the political apparatus, the police administration, and the rank-and-file members. Turning a bureaucratic organization around without broad-based support has been likened to turning the *Titanic* with a canoe paddle.

Still, some changes were made in tactics, public relations, and minority recruiting, but it would be years before significant modifications would begin to show up in the police culture. The creation of the federal Law Enforcement Assistance Administration in the 1960s would make large sums of cash available to police agencies to improve the education and training of their officers, and, as standards slowly improved, the *professional* police officer emerged. More and more police leaders began to realize that good police officers needed to be more than just tough; they needed to have an ability to empathize and understand others' viewpoints and be able to communicate effectively with people from widely varying backgrounds and cultures. Where some departments used to exclude college-educated candidates, they now began to seek them out—but this too would be very slow in coming.

With improved training and equipment, coupled with national attention to the rising levels of violent crime, police began to fashion themselves as professional crime fighters. Then, as now, the rhetoric from the government was warlike; from the ongoing Vietnam War to the war on crime, the war on poverty, and later the war on drugs, the soldier mentality began to seep into the marrow of America's police officers. Police would become less corrupt and more efficient and agile but also increasingly less approachable and more distant from those they served.

More than anything else, the war on drugs, officially decreed by President Nixon in the early 1970s, would work to transform not only the self-image of the police but the relationship of the police with the communities they serve, bringing officers into ever-increasing conflict with citizens. The prohibition of a class of intoxicants and an official government policy of aggressive enforcement inevitably resulted in an exponential increase in police contacts and intrusiveness. Whereas the policeman of the 1950s was concerned about your intention to commit a crime against someone else's person or property, the cop of the 1970s wanted to know what you had in your pockets or your car. This new reality meant that the police became interested if you had a plant or powder in your house that was for your own personal use but that the government had decreed you were not allowed to possess. Regardless of anyone's opinion regarding drug prohibition, this change in government policy translated into a much more intrusive police apparatus by default.

Despite the war on crime and the war on drugs, violent-crime rates continued to climb through the 1960s, 1970s, and 1980s. By the 1980s, the vast black market created by drug prohibition was turning both increasingly sophisticated and violent. The public were terrified; some areas of America's cities had been likened to war zones, where people lived behind barricaded doors and iron bars. During the 1960s, American culture was substantially de-civilized, as violence and criminality were celebrated in the popular culture.[2] This cultural phenomenon, combined with the surge in young adult males courtesy of the baby boom, caused violent crime to go through the roof. Between 1960 and 1991, the violent-crime rate in the United States increased by more than 370 percent.[3] Violent crime became a hot topic among politicians from the national level right down to the local city council. Throwing the book at criminals was a sure way to win votes, and it of course fell to the police to do the dirty work of getting tough on crime.

The surge in crime was very real, and the police paid the price along with the public. Police officer line-of-duty deaths surged throughout the 1960s, rising from 110 in 1959 to 240 in 1974.[4] These numbers of police dead had only been seen once before—during the years of alcohol prohibition. When the police are given marching orders by their government to fight a war on crime and drugs and they are dying and being assaulted in numbers not seen in a generation, they become too busy—and too cynical to deal with petty neighborhood problems or noncriminal issues of any kind. The police officer was becoming a soldier, fighting to "take back the streets" in places like the aptly nicknamed Fort Apache—the 41st NYPD precinct in the Bronx—and deadly neighborhoods in south-central Los Angeles and Detroit's Virginia Park.

While riots and unchecked street crime declined somewhat by 1980, the overall crime rate continued to rise, as the drug prohibition black market flourished and profit potential continued to increase. When crack cocaine was introduced in the mid-1980s, allowing virtually anyone an entry into the drug-dealing business because of its cheap price, the crime rate, which had begun to decline slightly, rose sharply as dealers competed for business in this hot new commodity. Foreign drug cartels, most notably from Columbia and run by efficient and brutal drug lords such as Pablo Escobar, turned cities like Miami into free-fire zones where the cartels fought for high-level dominance in the underground market for drugs. The city of Miami's morgue had to lease a refrigerated truck during most of the decade to store the overflow of murdered corpses.[5]

The incredibly lucrative trade in black market narcotics made it possible for the cartels and their minions to purchase increasingly deadly weaponry. Gone were the days of the punk with a "Saturday night special" .38 caliber revolver. The new drug entrepreneurs carried the Israeli-made 9-mm Uzi submachine gun or Kalashnikov AK-47 assault rifle. With money and guns flooding the underworld, the police began to clamor for newer and better weapons to be able to counter the threat.

Outgunned

On April 11, 1986, FBI agents from the Miami Field Office dispatched multiple two-man teams to search for a pair of serial bank robbers who had committed five armed robberies in the area over the past six months. Fourteen agents were deployed in an area with a large concentration of banks in southwest Miami in an attempt to locate the robbers or their vehicle en route to another robbery. The suspects were William Mattix and Michael Platt, two Army veterans with no criminal record prior to their Miami crime spree, which had already claimed one life and left three others with gunshot wounds. One of the FBI teams spotted the pair in the car they had used in a previous robbery. With the aid of a second car, they attempted a stop of the suspects, which resulted in the suspects' vehicle crashing into a tree. The moment their vehicle came to a stop, Mattix opened fire on the agents with a shotgun, wounding one agent. Eight agents immediately converged on the scene as a wild gunfight erupted. The agents, armed mostly with revolvers, were facing the two killers who were armed with a .223 Ruger Mini-14 semiautomatic rifle, a shotgun, and several handguns.[6]

By the time it was over, two agents were dead with five more wounded, three of them seriously. Nearly all the rounds fired at the agents came from Platt, as Mattix was knocked unconscious for most of the gunfight when he was shot in the head and neck in the opening moments of the battle. Platt was shot five times by the agents *before* he inflicted the fatal wounds on Special Agents Benjamin Grogan and Jerry Dove as they attempted to reload their six-shot revolvers. Platt also shot four of the five wounded agents after he was wounded. Both Platt and Mattix were ultimately killed in the gunfight.[7]

The ensuing investigation made clear that, despite their numerical advantage in both guns and men, one man with a Mini-14 had seriously outgunned the eight agents. Moreover, despite inflicting numerous wounds—one that would eventually prove fatal—the agents' weapons lacked adequate stopping power to end the suspect's aggressive actions when he was hit. Of the 10 men involved in the gunfight, Platt accounted for fully one-third of all rounds fired, and his rifle caused every significant wound to the agents.[8] In the aftermath, police agencies across the country got national attention for a problem they had been complaining of for years—that they were often at a severe disadvantage in firepower when confronted by deadly criminals. Agencies nationwide followed the FBI's lead in obtaining semiautomatic pistols for their officers, as well as obtaining some more powerful weaponry to have on hand when dealing with suspects known to be armed and dangerous.

Following the same pattern as alcohol prohibition 60 years earlier, drug dealers and other criminals were killing police officers, drugs were flooding the streets, and President Reagan had made fighting the drug war a central theme of his administration. Police departments were getting a steady supply of new and improved weaponry and being trained in drug interdiction—how to spot drug users and couriers during traffic stops as well as techniques for carrying out narcotics investigations. Meanwhile, the Drug Enforcement Administration (DEA) grew steadily in size as well as in its budget allocations. Since its inception with President Nixon's Executive Order in 1973, the agency has grown from 1,500 agents to nearly 5,000 while its budget has ballooned from $75 million to more than $2 *billion* annually.[9] Even the military was involved in fighting this war against illicit substances.

Then, during President Reagan's last year in office, another crime would shock the nation. On the night of February 26, 1988, a young New York City patrolman named Edward Byrne was seated in his patrol car outside the home of a witness in an upcoming trial of a major local drug dealer. The witness had received death threats and his house had been firebombed. At around 3:00 A.M., a car pulled up and, as one man tapped on the passenger side window of the police cruiser, a second man, armed with a .38 caliber pistol, crept up to the driver's side window and fired five bullets into the 22-year-old officer's head. It would soon be learned that the assassination of the officer was a contract murder ordered by the local drug lord Howard "Pappy" Mason from his jail cell. The killers had been to the house three times before but found two female and later a black officer on post, and waited until a white officer was on duty protecting the home. Pappy Mason was intent on sending a "message" to the NYPD that he was untouchable and could get to anyone.[10] Instead, the gambit backfired, as the police and city declared all-out war on the drug trade and its operators. The murder shocked the country and served to harden the resolve to continue the war against drugs. All four men involved in the murder were apprehended and convicted.

While the crime rate did not begin to drop right away, the police and city made steady progress. Rudy Giuliani would become mayor of New York in 1994 and preside over an unprecedented drop in all categories of crime—with violent crime cut in half and murders by an incredible 67 percent.[11] But it was the murder of Eddie Byrne that galvanized the city and shocked the political and police establishment into taking decisive action—actions that were praised for many years from some quarters but have come under intense scrutiny and criticism in recent years— more on that later.

While the drug war had been in full swing since being declared by Richard Nixon, President Reagan would take it to the next level— declaring that the flow of illegal narcotics into the country was a threat to national security. In his remarks at a 1982 speech at the Justice Department, Reagan even invoked the words of a French soldier at the desperate World War I Battle of Verdun, saying, "There are no impossible situations, only people who think they're impossible."[12] In the last year of his administration, Reagan created the Office of National Drug Control Policy (ONDCP), whose head was christened "drug czar" by the media. President Clinton would later raise the ONDCP chief to a cabinet-level position.[13]

The Military Joins the Drug War

A year earlier, Congress had taken up debate on a role for the military in combating the black market in drugs. They passed into law the Military Support for Civilian Law Enforcement Agencies Act,[14] which permitted American armed forces to provide assistance to local law enforcement inside and outside the United States. This included the assignment of Navy and Coast Guard vessels to work with police and the provision of military equipment to police agencies.[15] Reagan's secretary of defense, Caspar Weinberger, resisted the use of military for law enforcement on grounds of both principle and practicality, saying, "Reliance on military forces to accomplish civilian tasks is detrimental to both military readiness and the democratic process."[16]

In 1986, President Reagan signed the Anti-Drug Abuse Act, providing $1.7 billion to build new prisons and to provide for drug education and treatment. The bill also contained provisions for new mandatory minimum sentencing for drug offenses.[17] It was this bill's provision for long sentences for possession of small amounts of crack cocaine that would become a major factor leading to increasing racial disparity in the prison population. The war was getting bigger and more expensive every year and causing the U.S. prison population to explode.

As with all previous attempts at prohibition, the resulting black market created tremendous profit potential, and the harder the police and federal government squeezed, the more profitable drugs became. The result was the rise of the colossal Columbian drug cartels, flush with narco dollars, that would bring increased violence within the drug underworld and lead to a virtual civil war in that country, as the government—pressured and funded by the United States—fought a mostly losing battle against the heavily armed and vicious gangs that ran the drug trade. While the United States assisted Columbia, it also provided funds and DEA agents to Mexico to fight the drug lords there. In 1985, an event would take place that would further galvanize the government and the public in their war against drugs.

On February 7, 1985, DEA special agent Enrique "Kiki" Camarena was abducted on the street as he left the DEA offices in Guadalajara, Mexico. The kidnappers took him to the home of a notorious drug kingpin named Rafael Caro Quintero, where, over the course of the next 30 hours, Camarena was brutally beaten, tortured, and interrogated about DEA operations in Mexico. Several days after his disappearance, his battered corpse was discovered; the autopsy would reveal that Camarena's skull, cheekbones, nose, jaw, and windpipe had been crushed. All his ribs had been broken, and a hole had been drilled into his skull with a power drill. Camarena had also been injected with amphetamines to keep him conscious during his torture.[18]

The killers were eventually brought to the United States, tried, and convicted of the murder. Numerous high-ranking Mexican government officials were implicated in the kidnapping and murder but were never brought to justice. The gruesome crime infuriated both the police and the public nationwide in the United States. Camarena's photograph would appear on the cover of *Time* magazine, and the story would be made into a television miniseries. The violence caused the government to redouble its efforts at drug interdiction, although its efforts had proved to be an abysmal failure for more than a decade. The widespread media coverage of every sensational gangland killing, the murder of Agent Camarena, the increasing involvement of the military, and the steady drumbeat of bellicose rhetoric and fear mongering from the government all served to amplify the feeling that America's police were indeed engaged in a "war" against drugs and crime. To be fair, this feeling was not entirely unwarranted. Drug dealers, violent gangs, and ordinary street thugs were increasingly armed with powerful firearms, including semiautomatic and fully automatic pistols and rifles. The police clearly needed an upgrade in their available firepower to deal with the threat. They would get it—and then some.

Section 1208 of the 1990 National Defense Authorization Act (NDAA) permitted the Department of Defense to provide surplus military equipment "suitable for use in counter-drug activities" to domestic police departments across the country. The section preamble read, "Secretary of Defense may transfer to Federal and State agencies personal property of the Department of Defense, including small arms and ammunition."[19] This section was later replaced by Section 1033 of the 1996 NDAA and gave the program the name it is known by today. Since its inception, the Defense Department has transferred some $5 billion in military hardware to local police.[20]

This program garnered little to no public attention until the outbreak of rioting in Ferguson, Missouri, following the shooting death of Michael Brown. As the violence spun out of control, area police responded with officers dressed in military camouflage, tactical vests, combat rifles, and armored vehicles. The police were accused of using heavy-handed tactics and behaving like an invading military force rather than a domestic police agency. The riots sparked a debate about the perceived *militarization* of America's police departments and the propriety of the 1033 program. President Obama later issued an Executive Order to create a review board to examine the 1033 program and make recommendations.

The review board's report was completed in May 2015 and included numerous recommendations to improve the program, including better record keeping and tracking of the equipment. The panel also recommended prohibiting the transfer of certain equipment, including tracked armored vehicles; weaponized aircraft, vehicles, or vessels; .50 caliber or larger firearms and ammunition; and grenade launchers. The authors of the report recognized that, while the 1033 program had serious flaws, the police do, at times, have a need for more sophisticated weapons and equipment in order to protect themselves and the public from a criminal actor or during times of civil unrest or natural disaster, saying that police agencies "rely on Federally-acquired equipment to conduct a variety of law enforcement operations including hostage rescue, special operations, response to threats of terrorism, and fugitive apprehension. Use of Federally-acquired equipment also enhances the safety of officers who are often called upon to respond to dangerous or violent situations; being improperly equipped in such operations can have life-threatening consequences, both for the law enforcement personnel and the public they are charged with protecting."[21]

As the working group correctly stated, there are many legitimate uses for military-grade equipment for domestic police. Many of the so-called armored personnel carriers that were seen in Ferguson were nothing more than Bearcat vehicles. These 8,000-pound bullet-resistant armored trucks have been in use by police departments for a very long time and provide a safe haven for officers in transit or on the scene of a situation where they may come under attack. They allow officers to safely approach an armed individual barricaded in a structure to initiate negotiations or make observations, and they allow officers to remain safe from deadly gunfire or other projectiles such as bricks or firebombs. The mere existence of an armored vehicle like a Bearcat, or a much larger mine-resistant ambush-protected personnel carrier, does not by itself mean a department has become militarized. The issue is the nature of the circumstances in which it is deployed.

Police should have access to whatever equipment they may need to deal with the threats they face. Departments are not militarized by simply having access to some military-grade equipment but rather by the development of a combat-focused mind-set and the resulting use of excessive force. It would be foolish to suggest that police departments should not possess the same firearms that millions of other citizens possess, to include shotguns and semiautomatic rifles—or what the media refers to as *assault rifles*. There is also a need for access to specially trained tactical teams to deal with unusual but highly dangerous situations, such as barricaded subjects and hostage situations, but it is not necessary for every small town department to have a Bearcat and a group of officers calling themselves a SWAT team.

Police agencies rightfully place a great deal of attention on officer safety and survival, but this sort of training needs to be balanced with training that assists officers in their more frequent role as problem solvers and peacekeepers. Police on patrol walk the line between civilization and mayhem; they wear a uniform that indicates to everyone what and who they are, while those who would do them harm hide among the rest of us, wearing ordinary clothing, with their intentions as unknown as their identity. Because of the fact that officers have to be prepared for a violent assault at all times, it is easy for a warrior mentality to dominate. Shifting from fight-or-flight mode to refereeing a neighbor dispute or dealing with someone's 10-year-old child that they cannot control is difficult at best and is rarely addressed in training.

Enter the Terror War

The U.S. response to the September 11, 2001, terrorist attacks was a military one from the beginning. Just a little over a month after the Twin Towers fell, American forces began pounding targets in Afghanistan, which had harbored Al Qaeda for years. U.S. Special Forces troops with friendly rebel forces in the north initiated a ground war and quickly vanquished the Taliban regime. At home, President Bush declared a "global war on terrorism," a war with no countries, no borders, no clear objectives, and no criteria for victory. The war in fact did not even have a defined enemy; it was a war declared against a tactic rather than an adversary. The spigots of government money were opened wide and everyone had a chance to cash in on this new "war." To date, the federal government has spent more than $4.8 *trillion* on the global war on terrorism,[22] fighting a nameless, stateless enemy who has spent perhaps a few million dollars and killed fewer than 100 Americans in the United States since September 12, 2001.

The federal government created yet another massive bureaucracy called the Department of Homeland Security (DHS), consolidating the alphabet soup list of intelligence agencies under one department head. The nation's airport security was taken under federal control and an army of some 55,000 uniformed, unionized, federal "security officers" was created. These are the sometimes rude folks who make you take you shoes off and get them x-rayed and have your crotch fondled for the ostensible purpose of catching terrorists. The results have been predictable; the Transportation Security Administration has never caught a terrorist and virtually every time they are tested, they allow weapons and explosives past their checkpoints.[23] It wasn't long before the nation's police were enlisted in the war and offered cash and equipment to join in. George Bush made a speech to a joint session of Congress shortly after the attacks, in which he said the police were needed to help fight the war and talked about the police shield he carried that was given to him by the mother of a fallen officer at the World Trade Center.

The DHS would become the ultimate cash cow for police agencies all over the country. Police departments that had never had a Muslim resident in their jurisdiction or even a hint of terrorist threat were showered with money and urged to get into the fight against what was portrayed as an imminent threat to the existence of our country. The DHS has doled out more than $34 billion to local police agencies[24] for the purchase of all manner of terrorist-fighting equipment. The problem is that virtually none of these agencies outside of a few large metropolitan areas will ever have to respond to a serious terrorist attack. Fargo, North Dakota, has a population of 118,000, averages two homicides per year, and has never had a terrorist attack. But that did not stop the local police from acquiring military rifles and combat helmets for every patrol car, as well as a quarter-million-dollar armored vehicle.[25] Bossier Parish, Louisiana, has a similar population and in 2014 had one negligent homicide, one rape, and one robbery.[26] Still, the department felt it wise to acquire an armored personnel carrier with a mounted .50 caliber machine gun, which the local sheriff referred to as a "war wagon." The purchase was part of Operation Exodus, a plan to prepare for a potential terrorist attack or rioting.[27] Exactly what juicy terrorist target lies in that mostly rural county in northwest Louisiana is not clear.

The sleepy little town of Keene, New Hampshire, approved the acceptance of a federal grant to purchase a Bearcat despite the fact that the town has a population of 23,000 and has had a total of two murders since 2004.[28] The police department in the little city of Hoover, Alabama, purchased a Bearcat in 2016 with monies confiscated in drug raids. Hoover averages just over one murder per year, but the police chief cited the need for the vehicle to respond to active-shooter situations.[29] Jasper, Florida, police—all seven of them—who had not investigated a single murder in more than 10 years, felt the need to acquire M-16 rifles for each of them, leading one newspaper to headline its story, "Three Stoplights, Seven M-16's."[30] The Carroll County sheriff's office in Georgia even has four grenade launchers.[31]

The stories of small local departments acquiring military weapons for which they have no demonstrated use are legion. Since the outcry about militarized police at Ferguson, the issue has received much more attention, and such acquisitions are receiving more scrutiny. The Cato Institute commissioned a public opinion survey, showing that 54 percent of Americans believe that police using military equipment "goes too far," while the remaining 46 percent agree with its use as "necessary for law enforcement purposes."[32] Cato has called for the end of all transfers of military equipment to domestic police agencies.

Militarization is a creeping phenomenon that manifests itself in the overemphasis of the warrior role for police. To be fair, police officers must fight and at times find themselves at "war" with an individual suspect or a particular group of acutely dangerous criminals. Police also must have access to certain advanced tools and weaponry to deal with unusually dangerous situations. But dressing cops as soldiers and constantly emphasizing the warrior mind-set subtly pushes an officer's thinking toward that of a soldier and not a civil officer of the law, charged with safeguarding the rights of the people. Former New York City police commissioner Raymond Kelly expressed this thinking clearly; when he was asked about his hiring of a retired general as a deputy commissioner, he said, "We are at war, and we have to be able to defend ourselves in a variety of ways. . . . The military experience is really perfect for what we have to do."[33] Ray Kelly also told the television news program *60 Minutes* that his police force was capable of shooting down an aircraft if necessary. When questioned about the comment from his police commissioner, Mayor Michael Bloomberg arrogantly told the reporter, "The New York City Police Department has lots of capabilities you don't know about, and you won't know about them."[34] The NYPD has in fact morphed into a global enterprise with a multimillion-dollar intelligence headquarters and offices in several foreign capitals such as London and Tel Aviv. NYPD personnel have even flown to military bases, including Guantanamo Bay, to conduct interrogations of terror suspects.[35] Mayor Bloomberg has said, "I have my own army in the NYPD."[36] This sort of thinking can affect the mind-set of an entire organization; officers of the NYPD Street Crimes Unit formerly referred to themselves as *commandos*.[37] It was these commandos who were responsible for the infamous 1999 shooting of Amadou Diallo, an unarmed immigrant who died in a hail of 42 bullets fired by four undercover officers.

New York is, at least, a city that faces a very real threat from terrorists, given its global name recognition, economic importance, and population density. But police departments nationwide are getting in on the act as soldiers in the frontline defending the "homeland." The DHS has set up a network of 78 fusion centers across the country, where representatives from law enforcement agencies, first responders, FBI, military, and DHS intelligence officers operate to gather information on citizens. According to the DHS, their purpose is to serve as "focal points for the receipt, analysis, gathering, and sharing of threat-related information between federal, state, local, tribal, territorial, and private sector partners."[38]

While, on the surface, this seems to be a common sense approach to addressing many of the problems of information sharing among police agencies, it also enhances the perception among some police that they are directly engaged in some sort of existential struggle—a war. The rhetoric of war is everywhere since the 9/11 attacks and has affected the police as well as the politicians who control and direct them. This should not be understood as a call for the elimination of fusion centers; police agencies and emergency responders have long needed to become more adept at information sharing, and the fusion concept is a wise step. However, the involvement of the federal government and its military and intelligence apparatus have the potential to turn them into the nucleus of a national police and intelligence force with far too much information about law-abiding citizens and intrusive spying capabilities ripe for abuse. More-over, since most places in the United States face no serious threat from international terrorism, the fusion centers spend most of their energies gathering intelligence to fight the drug war or in some cases conjuring up terrorist boogiemen to justify their existence.

As an example, in 2009, the Missouri Information Analysis Center dis-tributed a report that described "militia" terrorists as "usually supporters of former presidential candidates Ron Paul, Chuck Baldwin, and Bob Barr."[39] Ron Paul was a sitting U.S. congressman from Texas and Bob Barr a former House member from Georgia, but if someone supported their presidential campaign they were to be targets of suspicion by the police. The report also advises that such terrorists are also known to display symbols such as antiabortion bumper stickers, the Navy Jack, and the Gadsden "don't tread on me" flag.[40] It is just this sort of purely unethical attempt at placing political opponents under criminal suspicion that makes these arrangements dangerous.

The Texas fusion center, known as the Texas Joint Crime Information Center, put out a call to all agencies, stating that it was "imperative for law enforcement officers to report" any activities of lobbying groups, Muslim civil rights organizations, and antiwar protest groups in their areas.[41] The call to provide a domestic intelligence agency with any and all informa-tion on the lawful activities of political groups or activists is chilling. For-mer FBI agent Michael German said of the revelation:

> The Texas fusion center's bulletin shows an unhealthy disregard for consti-tutional rights and democratic processes. . . . It demonstrates the lack of professionalism that exists at fusion centers and the severe lack of over-sight at the state, local and federal levels. According to its website, North Central Texas Fusion System bulletins are disseminated to thousands of people in over a hundred different agencies, and this report directs law enforcement officers to "report" on the political activities of advocacy

groups. The web of connections it weaves—drawing parallels between Muslim civil liberties groups, lobbying organizations, peace activists, hip hop bands, a former congresswoman and even the U.S. Treasury Department—would be comical if not for the real consequences that these organizations and individuals might face.[42]

Fusion centers in cities and states far from any real terror threat are equipped with sophisticated special compartmented information facilities. These expensive bunkers are secured against all forms of eavesdropping and electronic surveillance and are typically used by military intelligence personnel and the CIA for performing work with information classified above the top secret level. Police agency members assigned to these centers are granted top secret special compartmented information security clearances to view federal and international intelligence data—furthering the image of the police officer as a frontline soldier in the terror war.

To be clear, states *should* have a way of coordinating the efforts of law enforcement and emergency responders to address pervasive crime problems, natural disasters, or a sudden and unexpected event or threat such as a terrorist incident. It is the constant talk of war and the unrealistic emphasis on terror that poses the problem in terms of the orientation of police agencies toward a warrior mentality. On its website, the fusion center in Oklahoma touts the attack on the Murrah Federal Building *twenty-one years* ago as one of its reasons for being, and states that it "monitors the world for events that may have an effect on Oklahoma."[43] Given the last and only major act of terrorism in that state's history occurred more than two decades ago, and was carried out by a domestic white supremacist, it is unlikely that a car bombing in Iraq or a U.S. drone strike in Pakistan will impact the good folks of Oklahoma. The Idaho state fusion center lists combating terrorism as its first mission, and the Montana center's director referred to the sharing of terrorist threat information as a valuable function of the Montana Analysis and Technical Information Center.[44]

Since the September 11, 2001 terrorist attacks, a total of 61 Americans have died in foreign terrorist events on U.S. soil, while 53 have died in events outside the country. By contrast, the City of Chicago alone recorded 741 murders and more than 3,000 shootings *just in 2016*—none of which were terrorist-related.[45] That is 1,215 percent more deaths than have been caused by terrorism in the United States during the past fifteen years. Nationally, the numbers place the likelihood of being killed by a terrorist at 1 in 3,500,000 *including* the unprecedented number killed on 9/11. To put that in perspective, here is a short list of things much more likely to kill you: hitting a deer while driving (1:2,000,000), being crushed by furniture (1:1,500,000), drowning in your bathtub (1:950,000), industrial accident (1:53,000), natural disaster (1:450,000), murder by a non-terrorist (1:22,000), traffic accident (1:8,000), cancer (1:540).[46]

So, living in the United States, you are nearly four times more likely to drown in your bathtub than be killed by a terrorist, 438 times more likely to die in a car accident, and more than twice as likely to be crushed to death by your own home furnishings.

None of this is to minimize the potential dangers of a terrorist attack using a weapon of mass destruction or another on the scale of 9/11. But the September 11 attacks were a failure of intelligence exploitation and information sharing between the FBI and CIA, not of local law enforcement. Despite the diminishing threat of terrorism, it remains a concern for local police, as most attacks come from individuals motivated by religious or political ideology, and as such may be likely to come to the attention of local authorities, who should be on the lookout for any such information. The fear of terrorism however far outweighs the actual threat—which is of course the entire point. The terrorists receive much of their assistance in this regard from the American media and federal government which deliberately and continuously over-hype the terror threat for their own ends; the media for ratings, and the government for justification for expanding its power and ever-increasing expenditures.

The constant refrain of warfare and terrorist threats affects the police as much as the general public; creating a sense of impending doom and constant danger, thus reinforcing a warrior mentality. A simple Internet search of "police are frontline in war on terror" yields 1.6 million hits. What police actually are is an invaluable resource of eyes and ears that can spot potential terrorist actors or planners. Terror attacks are vanishingly rare compared with other forms of violent crime. Police are not (or at least should not be) in a "war" on terror any more than they are in a war on drugs or crime; they are simply a part of the never-ending struggle to contain and control violence and disorder so that Americans can enjoy their freedom in relative peace and safety—and by and large they are successful in that endeavor. Police officers *should* be trained in the characteristics and methods of terrorists, be on the lookout for suspicious activity, be aware of possible terrorist targets in their patrol areas, and take all reports of potential terror seriously. They should *not* view themselves as frontline soldiers in an existential battle for the future of human liberty under siege from endless threats of limitless violence. Such a mentality can only lead to extremism, as it has in the highest levels of our government and national security apparatus; witness the lawlessness of the NSA domestic surveillance program, drone assassinations by presidential decree, and carte blanche wiretapping authority from the secret Foreign Intelligence Surveillance Act court.

A textbook example of a police officer's role in combatting terrorism occurred in 2009, when a Chicago police officer observed a man in a city park running his young children through what appeared to be military maneuvers, including rolling on the ground into firing positions. The officer had received training in counterterrorism and reported what he witnessed. The officer ultimately was part of a criminal case against the father—David Coleman Headley—for his involvement in the 2008 terror attacks in Mumbai and in planning a further attack in Denmark.[47]

Officers must be alert to the possibility of terrorist attacks just as they are to the ever-present danger of other violence in their work. In May 2015, Gregory Stevens, an off-duty Garland, Texas, police officer was working as a security guard at an event where cartoons of the Muslim prophet Mohammad were being displayed. Alert to the possibility of violence, as previous displays had prompted widespread riots across the Muslim world and even murder by Islamic terrorists in Holland, the officer was able to defeat two attacking terrorists single-handedly. Officer Stevens was taken under fire by both assailants armed with military rifles and wearing body armor and took both men down with only his sidearm, thus preventing them from entering the crowded venue and carrying out a mass murder.[48]

Given the rarity of terrorist attacks, it is not productive to tell police officers they are frontline troops in some sort of war, in the way Special Operations or drone pilot assassins are aggressively seeking out suspected terrorists to kill. Terrorism is simply a new and rare form of danger police must be aware of and prepared to protect the public from.

Shock Troops

When police officers are up against heavily armed, barricaded persons or know in advance that they will be conducting a high-risk arrest or search warrant execution, they turn to specially trained and equipped police units. These units are generally known by the acronym made famous by the LAPD and the television program by the same name—SWAT—for special weapons and tactics. In practice, they are known by dozens of different names, such as emergency response teams, special operations units, or NYPD's Emergency Service Unit. These entities came into being in response to the rising tide of violent crime and riots of the late 1960s. Police officers were dealing with increasing numbers of ambush attacks, snipers, and heavily armed and fortified criminal and subversive gangs, such as the Black Panthers, the Weather Underground, and the Symbionese Liberation Army (SLA). The 1966 mass shooting at the University of Texas was a turning point in the mind of the public. Charles Whitman barricaded himself at the top of the clock tower on campus and proceeded to shoot 46 people, killing 15, while the police struggled for more than 90 minutes to gain entry and end the rampage.[49] SWAT-type units are a necessity when regular patrol officers encounter situations that outstrip their capabilities and equipment needs. In effect, they serve as an alternative to having every officer armed to the teeth and prepared for open warfare.

In recent years, however, these units have proliferated, and they are used routinely by many agencies to conduct low-risk searches and arrests. In 1983, only 13 percent of American towns with populations between 25,000 and 50,000 had a SWAT team; by 1995, that number had increased to 80 percent. The number of raids increased at more than double that rate, rising from 3,000 to 50,000 in the same time period[50]—an increase of 157 percent. These sorts of specialized teams were originally intended to deal with people like Charles Whitman, heavily armed bank robbers like the SLA, and other extreme situations. Today, however, they are habitually employed to carry out raids on alleged drug dealers, including low-level marijuana sellers, and even against individuals suspected of nonviolent offenses such as credit card fraud, gambling, or tax evasion. In fact, today, SWAT teams are deployed for barricade and hostage incidents—the purpose for which they were created—only 7 percent of the time.[51]

These paramilitary units are sold to the public as needed to respond to mass shootings, terrorist attacks, or hostage situations. These events are, however, exceedingly rare, and, like any other tool obtained at great cost, SWAT teams need to be utilized to retain their funding and relevance. The result is that in many places these units are overutilized and are engaged in outrageous overkill in their use of force, all too frequently resulting in injury and death. The *Capitol Times* of Madison, Wisconsin, reported in 2001 that there were *nine* SWAT teams within Milwaukee County alone.[52] When reporters questioned police about the need for such overkill, they gave answers such as, "Because of some of the things nationally, and some locally, mostly at the schools" and "[for] Drug searches and stuff."[53]

In 1999, Hallandale, Florida, residents Edwin and Catherine Bernhardt were visited by the local SWAT team, which smashed down their front door late one evening. Catherine was immediately thrown to the floor and held at gunpoint, while Edwin ran downstairs in the nude to see what was happening. He was subsequently handcuffed, forced to put on a pair of his wife's underwear, and taken to the police station, where he spent a number of hours in lockup, until the police realized they had invaded the wrong house.[54]

This is not simply a local police phenomenon; the federal government's enforcement agents all get in on the act. The issue first garnered widespread attention in 1992 following the federal government's attack on the Randy Weaver family at Ruby Ridge, Idaho. Weaver was wanted for sawing off a pair of shotguns for an informant who requested the service at the behest of the government. When the family dog caught the scent of agents surveilling the Weaver residence from the woods, Weaver's 14-year-old son believed the dog had spotted a bear and unwittingly followed it toward their position. One of the agents shot the dog dead, then killed the boy, and later wounded Weaver and a family friend. During the ensuing siege lasting several days, a government sniper shot Weaver's wife, Vicki, through the head while she was standing, unarmed, and holding her infant daughter. In the end, Weaver was acquitted of all charges brought against him, save for his failure to appear on the initial gun charge. The government was eventually required to pay damages to Weaver in the amount of $100,000 and to pay each of his surviving children $1,000,000 each.[55]

Nearly all of the federal government's executive departments have armed enforcement agents and "tactical teams" for carrying out paramilitary raids—generally on unarmed and nonviolent suspects. The U.S. Marshal Service conducted a SWAT raid, complete with automatic weapons, on the Gibson guitar factory in Nashville, Tennessee, in August 2011, because they were suspected of having purchased "endangered wood" from Madagascar.[56] The Internal Revenue Service has its own tactical teams that conduct aggressive raids against small businesses, terrorizing employees and pointing automatic rifles at officer workers.[57]

Rather than being utilized only in high-risk situations, SWAT teams are routinely—and primarily—used for executing marijuana and drug search warrants, regardless of any known risk factors. Seventy-five to 80 percent of all SWAT callouts are for search warrant executions.[58] These paramilitary units are even used for patrol duties in some high-crime areas. Before shutting down the program due to numerous lawsuits, the Fresno, California, police's SWAT team patrolled the streets of poor, mainly minority, neighborhoods, dressed in military gear and conducting illegal stops, searches, and entries. Their invasive tactics were summed up by one officer who said "It's a war" and another who said "If you're 21, male, living in one of these neighborhoods, and you're not in our computer, then there's something definitely wrong."[59]

On November 21, 2013, Benjamin Burris had been experiencing marital difficulties and was staying at a local hotel, when his employer became concerned and requested that the county police check his welfare. They were apparently concerned that Burris may harm himself, although they informed the police that he had made no statements about hurting himself or others. The Albemarle County Police responded to the Comfort Inn in Charlottesville, Virginia, in an effort to locate Burris. As Burris was departing to go on a hunting trip, two officers spotted him getting into his pickup truck and approached him.

Burris informed the officers repeatedly that he did not wish to speak with them. As two more officers arrived, Burris started his truck and prepared to leave, when an officer ordered him to shut off his truck and place it in park, which he did. The officers then placed a tire-deflating stinger device behind his rear tires and surrounded his truck with police cars to prevent him from leaving. Burris had his hunting weapon in the rear seat in plain view with the action open, and he informed the officers that it was unloaded and he merely wanted to leave and go on his hunting trip to Montana. The officers detained him in the parking lot for more than two hours, repeatedly trying to cajole him into exiting his truck. Despite the fact that they had no legal right to detain him, the officers at that point decided to contact Burris's doctor and wife to attempt to obtain an emergency custody order for a psychiatric evaluation. They made contact with the wife and convinced her to go to a judge to obtain the order, which she did. After *another* 90 minutes, the officers had the order in hand and called for the SWAT team. Despite having a key to the truck provided by the wife, the team's operators stormed the truck, detonating a flash-bang grenade, smashed the driver's window, and yanked Burris out onto the pavement, causing significant injury to his hands. He was handcuffed and transported to the hospital and forced to undergo a psychiatric evaluation.[60]

The Burris case is illustrative of well-meaning police gone completely off the rails. Checking on the man's welfare is a legitimate function; the police should have concern for a citizen who may be going through great difficulty and might harm himself. A free society, however, dictates that, absent some reasonable suspicion that he has violated the law or is mentally ill to the point he poses a serious threat to himself or others, he is free to leave and go about his business. The officers wildly overstepped their authority by detaining Burris without cause for hours and by attempting to have a baseless order issued to arrest him. This was then followed by an unnecessarily violent assault by paramilitary officers against a man who had complied with every order given to him by police for the entire three-and-a-half-hour standoff.

SWAT teams are a necessity for police; there are simply too many instances where street officers find themselves outgunned or require specialized equipment to deal with threats to themselves and the public. These teams must be highly trained and disciplined, but every department does *not* need one. A tactical team can be put together on a regional basis to save considerable waste and allow for the members to be properly trained and drilled in both tactics and doctrine. These teams should be used sparingly and not for routine arrests or warrants where there is no indication of significant risk. There are far too many SWAT units that are created simply because some money was made available for buying equipment and the officers enjoy dressing up like soldiers. There is a world of difference between a highly trained, disciplined, tactical unit, deployed for specific, legitimate purposes, and a group of hyped-up cops with some surplus military gear and rudimentary instruction.

Former New Haven, Connecticut, police chief Nick Pastore turned down offers of military hardware from the Pentagon. In an interview with the *New York Times*, Pastore said that dressing cops like soldiers, "feeds a mindset that you're not a police officer serving a community, you're a soldier at war. I had some tough guy cops in my department pushing for bigger and more hardware. They used to say, 'It's a war out there.' They like SWAT because it's an adventure. If you think everyone who uses drugs is the enemy, then you're more likely to declare war on the people."[61] Chief Pastore did not disband his tactical unit but put an end to the use of SWAT several times per week, reducing the number to about four times per year. As Pastore put it, "The whole city was suffering trauma. We had politicians saying 'the streets are a war zone, the police have taken over,' and the police were driven by fear and adventure. SWAT was a big part of that."[62] Sheriff Rick Fullmer of Marquette County, Wisconsin, disbanded his SWAT team in 1996, saying, "Quite frankly, they get excited about dressing up in black and doing that kind of thing. I said, 'this is ridiculous.' All we're going to do is get people hurt."[63]

A great majority of police misconduct stems from a pervasive lack of adequate training. I have personally sat at a table with a local deputy sheriff as he went through every page of our state's penal law to prove to me that "Grand Theft Auto" was a legitimate criminal charge, when it was, in fact, a video game that he played or perhaps something he remembered from watching CHiPs or Adam-12 episodes as a kid. These shows took place in California, where stealing a car falls under a statute by that name.

Many states use the term *larceny* rather than *theft* and may or may not have separate laws for the theft of a vehicle. In Pennsylvania, it is called "unauthorized use of automobiles and other vehicles," while in Texas it is called "unauthorized use of a vehicle" and in Georgia stealing a car or anything else is called "theft by taking."

Police officers are often not properly trained in how to safeguard the rights of citizens, and this does those officers a great disservice. Training focuses mainly on asserting authority and overcoming resistance to that authority. Obviously, this is an important aspect of police training, but recruits should be indoctrinated with the primary focus being on the safeguarding of rights. The problem arises because of the fact that officers need to jealously guard their personal and legal authority for their personal safety and in order to be able to carry out their assigned function and, because they have not been taught that upholding rights is their highest duty, they reflexively view any challenge to their authority as both impudent and dangerous. Officers also tend to feel that they will have their authority diminished if they admit to being in error when challenged rather than understanding that such behavior is the hallmark of a true professional and an individual of personal integrity.

Police officers who do not understand or respect the limits of their authority are becoming the subject of numerous Internet videos. Many times, these are well-intentioned men and women who are unexpectedly confronted by someone who refuses to cooperate with their polite request for information or identification. Where knowledgeable officers would realize where their authority ended, poorly trained officers will dig in their heels against this challenge to their authority and escalate the situation. A perfect example is a video brought to my attention courtesy of the Rutherford Institute, which shows a Hollywood, Florida, officer along with a caseworker from the Department of Children and Families attempting to interview a man at his place of business concerning a phone tip that he was abusing his children. The officer is polite and asks for the man's name and then for identification, which the man refuses to provide, stating that he wishes to not speak with them and that he will not produce his children without a warrant, to which the state worker replies, "We still have to speak to you." The dialogue continued:

Officer: "Do you have your ID?"
Citizen: "I don't need my ID."
Officer: "Yes you do Sir."
Citizen: "What crime am I suspected of committing?"

Officer: "Child abuse and neglect. I tell you that's why we're here to conduct an investigation [*sic*]."

Citizen: "Well I'm telling you if you have a warrant—unless you have a warrant, I don't want to speak to you or you. You said you're investigating something, right? Okay, well my, my rights are at that time I can be silent. I do have an attorney if you'd like to speak with him."[64]

At this point, the conversation is over; the man has invoked his Fifth Amendment right to remain silent and his Sixth Amendment to have an attorney represent him. The man's right to an attorney is legally attached, and the officer should have simply asked for the lawyer's contact information and left to speak with him.

Officer: "This what's gonna happen, we're getting allegations that something's happen to children [*sic*] . . . yes, allegations, allegations. So we need to speak with you reference these allegations [*sic*]."

Citizen: "I don't want to speak to you."

Officer: "Ok, your name is Richard?"

Citizen: "I don't want to give you my name."

Officer: "Well I'm conducting an investigation so I need your name."

Citizen: "If you're conducting an investigation then I have the right to remain silent."

Officer: "You have the right to remain silent, but you have to give me basic identifiable information [*sic*]."

The officer then goes on to tell the man he must come outside with him and that refusing to provide his name is "obstructing his investigation." The situation continues to deteriorate as the officer forces his way through the hallway door and informs the man again that he is obstructing the investigation. The officer then calls for backup and tells him to "turn around and put your hands behind your back," which the man refuses to do, asking why he is being arrested. The officer then says he is "being detained" for "obstructing my investigation." Unfortunately, by my reading, there is no such statute under the Florida criminal law. The officer then proceeds to debate the law, the meaning of probable cause, and the Constitution for several minutes with the business owner. After a few minutes, the man begins to walk away from the officer when the officer physically seizes him and orders him repeatedly to "get down on the f[***]ing floor!" A second person picks up the dropped cell phone and records the officer helplessly flailing away at the larger man's back, kicking his legs and yanking on his shirt, as the man keeps asking the officer why he is hitting him. In a few moments, three additional officers rush in and slam the man to the floor and handcuff him.[65]

The officer in the video is most likely a decent person who believes he is doing what is right. He is aiding a state worker in conducting a lawful investigation into an allegation of child abuse. The officer is very polite and businesslike during (almost) the entire interaction and has probably conducted dozens of proper investigations and arrests. It is unlikely that he set out to violate the law or anyone's Constitutional rights when he left for work that day and is most likely a sincere individual. The problem is the officer doesn't have the slightest understanding of what he's talking about and is completely ignorant of the applicable laws. Because he does not understand either the laws of his state or the Fourth, Fifth, or Sixth Amendment to the Constitution, he proceeds to press ahead and illegally detain, assault, and arrest the man for some sort of imagined "obstruction," which was nothing more than refusing to provide the officer with identification and asking for legal representation. The only thing the citizen *was* guilty of was "contempt of cop."

This is a classic, but not unusual, case of an unexpectedly uncooperative citizen confounding an officer who does not have a firm grasp of the law, resulting in the officer reacting inappropriately to the perceived challenge to his authority. Had he been properly trained, he would have known that, lacking any evidence of a crime other than a phone tip, he had no legal justification for detaining or requiring the citizen to identify himself. The officer would have known that the Fifth Amendment allows a suspect to remain silent, that the Sixth Amendment guarantees his right to an attorney, and that he could not continue to question him once he was (illegally) detained without an attorney present. A properly trained officer would also understand that physically seizing and handcuffing the man, without any probable cause to believe he had committed any crime other than irritating the officer, was a violation of his Fourth Amendment rights.

Proliferation of Laws

Sixty years ago, a police officer would set out on patrol in a squad car or on a foot patrol and wait to be called on the radio or by a passerby. The officers would be on the lookout for problems, ranging from a broken traffic signal to suspicious characters on the street who got nervous when they approached. If they stopped a car, it was because the operator did something egregious, driving straight through a stop sign without slowing down or speeding so fast anyone looking could see. Perhaps they'd stop a car with a headlamp or taillight out after dark. The cops might tell some local kids to go home or stop hanging around the street corner, and they'd check the alleyways at night for burglars or other criminals looking to steal someone's property or hurt an innocent person.

Today's "law enforcement officers" set out in a car with a mission to write tickets or summonses to keep from getting in trouble with their sergeant or lieutenant and to keep open their opportunities for advancement or special assignments. They will mentally calculate the date: how many "numbers" they have for the month and how many they need to meet or exceed their quota. Now, of course, almost every police agency will say that they don't have a quota, and many do not. Many more, however, have informal quotas: *precinct averages*, *benchmarks*, *performance goals*, *objectives*, *targets*, and other euphemistic references to what is essentially a quota.

The reasons for this vary from place to place but boil down to three main causes. First is the fault of police leadership. Police work is extremely difficult to evaluate from a supervisor's point of view. A sergeant's officers work almost entirely out of sight, leaving only what the supervisor sees on paper to evaluate the officer, and that boils down to their reports and their "numbers." Good officers don't necessarily make a lot of arrests or write a lot of tickets. Yet, some excellent officers make a significant number of arrests because they are proactive and particularly good investigators. The type of arrest and the surrounding circumstances are what makes one officer better than another. While one officer might arrest someone for a mid-level crime by fortuitously stumbling across a fleeing suspect and saying, "Hey, you," another officer might have spent days, asking around her beat, interviewing neighbors, talking with other officers, and come up with the perpetrator through solid police work and tenacity. Numbers on a page don't reflect the difference. Still, the easiest way for a supervisor to evaluate the officers under his or her command is to just tally up numbers, as if police officers were factory workers being judged by their output of a product.

The second reason is the push by municipalities all over the country to use tickets and summonses for petty local ordinance violations as a way to raise revenue. This practice was cited as one of the most salient causes of the rioting in Ferguson, Missouri, after the Michael Brown shooting. The mostly poor population had been under constant scrutiny from the police, who were churning out as many summonses as possible under pressure from the city manager and the police chief.[66] This type of effort to raise revenue is an abuse of the police and the judicial system, and it is no surprise that it creates resentment, especially when those targeted are those who can least afford to pay the often exorbitant fines.

The third reason is expansion of laws at every level of government. This is driven in part—in places like Ferguson—out of a desire to find a way to increase revenues without raising taxes and partly out of the general growth of government and the things it has taken upon itself to regulate and to police. Where the police officer of the past was interested in keeping order in his neighborhood and being on the lookout for robbers and burglars, today's officer is looking for someone who doesn't have a seatbelt on or is talking on his phone in the car or even for people who haven't mowed their lawn properly. Take for example the recent widespread phenomenon of police shutting down lemonade stands being run by small children.[67] Police across the country are frightening little boys and girls and threatening their parents with arrest for engaging in an all-American ritual of childhood. This is due to the proliferation of laws that are also shutting down bake sales for lack of health department permits and other aspects of community life. This reflects the shift from policing to law enforcement. A *police officer* would buy a cup of lemonade from the children and talk with them and their folks for a few minutes. The *law enforcement officer* sees a violation of *the law* and moves swiftly to put little Billy and Suzie and their parents back in their place. Mind you, there are few officers who are so callous and robotic that they would even dream of making an issue about a lemonade stand. But the fact that there are now enough such incidents to attract the attention of the national media speaks volumes about the transformation police have undergone.

These laws continue to grow in number. California and several other states have outlawed smoking in cars when minors are present in the vehicle, giving police yet another reason to stop cars and demand information. Talking on a cellular telephone while driving is illegal in every state, but more laws are sure to follow. Research has already been conducted demonstrating that talking with a passenger in the vehicle is at least as distracting as talking on a mobile device.[68] This could be a prelude to banning conversation in cars, leading to still more police stops. We are forcing our police to hide in bushes with binoculars to catch adult citizens who didn't buckle up and wonder why people are losing respect for officers. Police leaders should begin to fight back against laws that place them in conflict with their communities and that require them to arrest or interfere with the free movement of citizens when they are in the privacy of their own automobiles. It should be noted, however, that there is little police administrators can do to combat these trends.

Police or Law Enforcement

The creeping militarization of the police is a part of a larger phenomenon of the growing size and reach of government. The drug war and the war on terror have served to foist upon the police establishment the responsibility for policing the private lives of every citizen. In a country where everything is the business of government—from what you have in your pockets, to the Web sites you visit, what you write in your emails, and whether you talk on a phone while driving—everything is also the business of that country's police. The violence of the black market in drugs, the growing involvement of the military and intelligence apparatus in policing, and the over-hyped fear of terrorism combine to create a siege mentality among police, who in some cases have begun to view themselves more as soldiers than police officers. These laws and political pressures have caused the drift from policing to law enforcement and are generally outside the control of police agencies.

Some police leaders have begun to push back. In 2003, the organization Law Enforcement against Prohibition was founded and today has grown to more than 3,500 members. The group works to educate the public and politicians about the failed police war against drug abuse and the toll it has taken on society, civil liberties, and police agencies. After more than four decades and a trillion dollars, we are no closer to "winning" the drug war than we were during the Nixon Administration.

The reality is that police work involves the constant threat of violence and that there are vicious and deadly individuals in society whom we expect police to deal with. Because of this, officers need to be prepared mentally and physically to defend themselves and others and to have the ability to become a warrior when it is called for. They must also, however, be able to change from one mode to another and realize that fighting is only one small part of their job. Again, this is a very difficult thing to do: being constantly prepared to fight for your life while dealing courteously with angry or disrespectful people or shifting your mind-set from issuing a traffic ticket to plunging into a bar fight. For the human psyche, this behavior is difficult and fraught with stress. Moreover, this is something that is rarely, if ever, addressed in police training.

Police must be trained to understand each role they play, how to play it, and how to cope with the mental strain it causes when continuously shifting from one to the other. Today, too many officers are being imbued with the idea that the warrior ethos is central to policing, when the spirit of guardian and caretaker is much better suited. Much police training occurs after leaving the academy either formally or informally in the field or in thousands of outside training courses provided by state or local entities. While states have specific standards for the basic training of police officers, there are no such standards for the training of thousands of SWAT teams in weapons, equipment, and tactics. Many departments simply purchase the military gear and play at being a paramilitary warrior using an ad hoc collection of training manuals, things they've seen in movies, or tactics passed on from an officer who was once in the military.

One popular trainer, who appears at seminars nationwide, is Lieutenant Colonel David Grossman, head of the "Killology" Research Group. Colonel Grossman is a former professor of psychology at the U.S. Military Academy at West Point and the author of several books. His insights on the warrior mind-set and the psychology of violence and killing have great relevance for the military and some application in the realm of policing. His delivery to police special operators is, however, deeply troublesome: "Cop says, 'gunfight, bad guy's down, I'm alive!' Finally get home at the end of the incident and . . . they all say, 'the best sex I've had in months.' "[69] As someone who has had the misfortune to take a life in the line of duty, I can attest that, in the hours immediately following such an event, sexual intercourse is not the first priority. Grossman also says,

> You ever hear the old saying, it's gotta get worse before it gets better? Oh it's gonna get worse folks. We are at *war*! And you are the front line troops in this war! And folks, I want you to understand something; when they come to murder the children, the individuals who tried to disarm our cops will be hunted down, and across the nation they will be attacked, they will be spit on, they will be driven deep into their slimy little holes, and they'll never come out again. Folks, there ain't nobody in Mexico right now complaining about militarization of police, you understand? There ain't nobody in Russia complaining about militarization of police. In the very near future you will be vindicated. The bad news—the wolf is at the door, very bad times are coming. The good news—you have job security, eh? Because the world desperately needs what you have to give.[70]

Yes, America's police officers must be prepared to fight and to kill when necessary. The only way for them to protect the public they serve is to be prepared and capable of using force—up to and including deadly force. That is the ugly reality of policing and one that many people are not able or willing to comprehend. The warrior component of policing is important and must not be ignored. Police who are properly trained and prepared to use force when it is both legal and necessary make more effective and competent officers. What needs to change is that police must learn from the start that they play a number of roles and each one is as important as the others. As Superintendent Chandler told his first troopers in 1917,

> A physician aims to save life and cure disease; a lawyer helps people out of trouble; a clergyman tries to make people better; a soldier fights for his country in time of war. These are fine professions, all of them. They are professions of service.
>
> The service a State Trooper renders to his community is an auxiliary to all of these and his duty in a measure embraces the work of these four great professions.
>
> You who wear the uniform of the [police] must be ready to render first aid pending the arrival of the doctor; you must maintain the law which the lawyer expounds; you must instruct people to do right, and if the need arises, you must fight.[71]

The next generation of police needs to view themselves as guardians of the people and of their rights. They should be taught that they are *police officers* and not law enforcement officers and that the role of police officers is to safeguard the community in which they serve. Today, to do the things we expect of them, officers must be warriors, but they must be warrior-philosophers in the tradition of Marcus Aurelius.

They should understand the difference between a warrior and a fighter; not everyone who fights is a warrior. A true warrior operates upon a strict code of conduct and fights only as a last resort. He never fights for personal gain or for pleasure but for his fellowman and for what is right and true. Police officers should be warriors not simply in the cause of justice but in the battle to preserve peace and harmony in the community, to be vigilant, to protect, to guide, and to provide aid and comfort.

It should also be understood that for every video of a cop violating someone's rights or a SWAT team engaged in absurd overkill, there are thousands of police interactions that involve no violence and no misconduct. These incidents of malfeasance featured on YouTube and the evening news are not acceptable but they do not represent the everyday reality of police contacts.

In short, it is not a warrior mentality *per se* that is the problem but rather a misunderstanding of the true way of a warrior and the neglect of the other roles played by police officers. In their training and assimilation, they should be indoctrinated not with the mind-set of simply a fighter or soldier but to embrace their role as a blend of warrior, doctor, clergyman, and lawyer—a protector, champion of the law, upholder of justice, and a voice of reason and caring.

CHAPTER FOUR

The Consequences of Eroding Respect

Our Government is the potent, the omnipresent teacher. For good or for ill, it teaches the whole people by its example. Crime is contagious. If the Government becomes a lawbreaker, it breeds contempt for law; it invites every man to become a law unto himself; it invites anarchy.

—Justice Louis Brandeis

On December 2, 2016, the director of the U.S. Justice Department's Civil Rights Division, Vanita Gupta, delivered an address to the University of North Carolina Center for Civil Rights Conference. Gupta took the opportunity to characterize police misconduct as "long-standing and systemic," calling police practices "broken systems—plagued by unlawful practices and tainted with bias."[1] While her own numbers failed to bear out the tenor of her remarks, which cast police as brutal racists—she cited arrests of 580 police officers for civil rights violations, or just 0.0008 of American police, and 23 suspect police departments, or roughly 0.001 of all police agencies nationwide—she nonetheless made important points about the significance of fairness and the *perception* of fairness in the justice system generally. For us to examine the causes of discontent with the police and *the system*, generally, it is necessary to go beyond an examination of police tactics alone.

To be sure, police in some jurisdictions have employed shortsighted, foolish, and even unconstitutional tactics in their efforts to combat street crime. Regardless of whether these abuses represent a truly significant number of police officers, the perception created when they are exposed can indeed be devastating and have grave impacts far beyond the offending officer or agency's jurisdiction.

Too Many Laws

As stated, the job of the police is maintaining order and safety, while safeguarding the rights of their fellow citizens. Police officers should make arrests and write summonses when it is reasonable and necessary to do so, not merely because they can. People generally do not spend much of their time thinking about the police or what they should be doing but have a general idea that they should occupy themselves looking for persons who have committed or are about to commit a crime and maybe write some traffic tickets along the way. What happens in too many communities is that the police become a mechanism for generating revenue for the municipality. The town or city passes dozens of ordinances for "offenses" such as parking in arbitrarily chosen wrong places or wrong times, feeding the homeless (yes, that's a real offense), wearing saggy pants, pumping your own gas, or being in a public park after dark, to name just a few. Then outrageous fines are attached to these heinous acts, and the local police are pressured to write as many summonses as possible for these violations. The local court plays along and money is made.

We live in a society where almost every human activity is governed by a law of some sort. There are so many traffic laws and they are so strict in their wording that any cop will tell you that you can stop almost any car, any time you want. Roll through a stop sign at 1 mile per hour at three in the morning on a deserted street, have a bulb out, touch a painted line with your tire, have a crack in your windshield, drive too fast, drive too slow, have the wrong color sticker in your window, have something dangling from your rearview mirror, have a broken side mirror, have a swinging license plate: the list is endless. Depending on where you live, you can get arrested for drinking a beer on the sidewalk in front of your house, putting up a clothesline, or capturing rainwater in a barrel.

Our federal government has promulgated so many tens of thousands of laws that no one is even able to accurately count them—and most of them require no intent on the part of the offenders for them to be guilty. With most crimes, assault, theft, murder, and so on, the perpetrator has to have *intended* to do what he or she did. Taking someone's coat that looks just like yours, killing a roadside pedestrian because you suffered a heart attack, or slapping someone in the face accidentally while gesturing in conversation is not chargeable as larceny, murder, and assault because there was no intent to cause the harm. Attorney Harvey Silvergate published his research on federal laws and estimated that the average American citizen commits as many as three felonies per day that he or she is completely unaware of.[2] Add to this your state laws and regulations, and a mountain of local laws, and we are approaching a society where citizens can be arrested at will.

Following the example of our federal government, and with the licentiousness brought on by the drug and terror "wars," Americans have become over-policed. While we don't necessarily need fewer police, we need laws that don't encourage police to interfere with or limit the freedom of their fellow citizens—and we need police who are trained to recognize when they are being asked to behave as law enforcers rather than police officers. Some months ago, I was taking a hike in a wilderness area owned by the county. It was intended to be a county park, but they put up a sign and a few picnic tables near the lake a few years back and never went further with the project due to lack of funds. To get to the lake and the wilderness beyond, you need to drive several miles along a narrow country road, park, and walk about a half mile on a dirt trail. As I was approaching the lake at the end of my hike, I observed the same two young lovers I had seen on the way in, fishing along the shore and enjoying a picnic lunch. This time they were chatting with a police officer dressed in the now ubiquitous style of external battle-dress armor emblazoned with "POLICE," festooned with radio, microphone, magazine carriers, flex cuffs, special forces–type subdued patches, and the obligatory fingerless gloves and shaved head with perched sunglasses atop. Upon closer inspection, I found he was a state conservation police officer, who proceeded to escort the two out of the park and detain them at length while he finished arresting them for catching and releasing 4-inch sun fish without having purchased a license from the state to do so. Even having spent the better part of three decades as a police officer, I was sickened by the sight of two perfectly innocent and seemingly friendly young people, enjoying an afternoon by a lake in an abandoned county park, being detained and ticketed by a cop dressed as though he was on a combat patrol in Fallujah. It seems there is nowhere you can look without coming across a police officer. What's worse is that everyone who sees a police officer becomes fearful—not just criminals—because we instinctively realize at some level that we are *all* subject to arrest.

Police are the face of the laws and policies made by the government. As the government becomes ever larger and more intrusive, so too will the police forces employed to ensure compliance. As our Constitutional protections have dwindled and the government claims jurisdiction over our private affairs, the arrogance of government officials has grown exponentially. Government employees do not generally view themselves as servants of their fellow citizens but rather as a special class chosen to dictate to their fellow citizens in whatever petty domain they rule. Just go to your local motor vehicle department or county clerk's office and stand in the wrong line or make a mistake on your paperwork and see how you are treated.

The arrogance that comes with administrative authority now permeates every level of government. A far too typical example is Town Councilman Michael Wolfensohn of the little suburban town of New Castle, New York. When he discovered two 13-year-old boys selling cupcakes in a park in his town without having paid him fees in tribute, he immediately telephoned the local constabulary to put a stop to it.[3]

A local police officer—an armed government agent—arrived promptly, telephoned the boys' mothers, dispatched them from the park, and shut down the renegade operation. According to one boy's mother, the young man was crying and terrified he might go to jail or have a criminal record. The two friends were doing a brisk business and hoping one day to open a restaurant together. His mom said, "I am shocked and sad for the boys. It was such a great idea, and they worked hard at it but then some town board member decided to get on his high horse and wreck their dreams."[4] Of course, the boys could have reopened their business if they paid Michael Wolfensohn $350 for a two-hour permit and showed him proof of $1 million of insurance coverage.[5]

Use of Force—The Rodney King Affair

Just past midnight on March 3, 1991, the California Highway Patrol began a high-speed chase with a white Hyundai sedan that was observed speeding and refused to stop. Officers from the LAPD later joined the chase, which ended in Lake View Terrace. Inside the car were two black male passengers, Bryant Allen and Freddie Helms, and the driver, Rodney Glenn King. King was drunk and was running from police because a DUI would have been a violation of his parole on a previous conviction for robbery.

Once the vehicle was stopped, the occupants were ordered by police to exit the car and lie face down on the ground. Allen and Helms complied, but King refused to exit the car. A few moments later, King stepped out of the car, patted the ground, waved to the overhead helicopter, and grabbed his buttocks—refusing commands to lie on the ground. King was shot with a Taser to no effect. Several officers attempted to gain control of King by rushing him and using open-hand tactics, getting him to the ground.

The gigantic King was able to easily peel the officers off him and then stood and charged directly at Officer Lawrence Powell, who struck him with his issued baton.

A nearby resident had awoken to the sound of police sirens and began filming the incident just after King was Tasered. The video, blurry in places, shows King's attack on Officer Powell and the subsequent attempts to subdue King. The video shows King actively resisting arrest for several more minutes, rising to his knees and attempting to crawl away. As he does so, several officers beat him with their batons, as they continue to order him to lie down. Eventually, after the police struck some 56 baton blows to King's body and kicked him in the head and body six times, he was grabbed and handcuffed by the officers.[6]

That video would change policing in Los Angeles and the entire country in the months and years to come. After trying to turn his video over to the LAPD, George Holliday, the citizen who shot the original footage, took it to a local TV station, which edited out the first, somewhat blurry portion of the video that records King's attack on Officer Powell. The national news media played the video in a nearly continuous loop around the clock, universally referring to King as a "black motorist" and the police as "white police officers."

Facing intense political pressure, the Los Angeles county district attorney eventually indicted the officers involved on charges of assault. At trial, Sergeant Stacy Koon and Officers Lawrence Powell, Theodore Briseno, and Timothy Wind testified that they believed King to be under the influence of PCP because of his incredible strength and imperviousness to the Taser and painful baton strikes. They further testified that they were following their training in attempting to strike King in his joints and extremities to gain compliance. Combined with the testimony and the first-ever public showing of the entire video of the incident,[7] the officers were acquitted of all charges.

Unfortunately for the City of Los Angeles, the trial venue had been changed at the request of the defense, and the verdict had come from a courthouse in mostly white, upper-class Simi Valley and with a mostly white jury. Despite the fact that even King's lawyer did not view the case as racially motivated,[8] LA's inner-city black residents, already embittered by the LAPD's tactics and having been whipped into a frenzy by a year of media coverage about the innocent "black motorist" beaten by the "white police officers," vented their outrage at the verdict by beginning a rampage of violence and destruction in riots that would last for three days. By the time order was restored by police and National Guard units, 53 people had been killed and more than 2,000 injured, and 7,000 fires had destroyed businesses and property worth in excess of $1 billion.[9] Rodney King would later file suit against the city and be awarded $3.8 million in damages.[10]

Following the riots, the U.S. Justice Department would file civil rights charges against the officers. After their trial in March 1993, Sergeant Koon and Officer Powell were found guilty and sentenced each to 30 months in federal prison. Officers Briseno and Wind were acquitted.

Regardless of any racial motivation on the part of the officers involved, many LA residents saw the video as vindication of what they had been claiming for years, that the LAPD routinely used excessive force when dealing blacks and other minorities. While the beating is shocking to watch, it raises questions as to just exactly what police are supposed to do with actively resisting suspects who are not affected by electronic or even pain compliance techniques. The Rodney King arrest began the modern discussion of police and race that has culminated in the current war against the police beginning under the Obama Administration and its open hostility toward police institutions.

The Christopher Commission

In the wake of the Rodney King affair and the devastating rioting that followed, the city created the Independent Commission on the LAPD, commonly known as the Christopher Commission, after its chairman, Warren Christopher (who would later become President Clinton's secretary of state). The commission was charged with conducting a top-to-bottom investigation of the LAPD, its training, policies, practices, use of force, and disciplinary process. Not surprisingly, the commission found that a relatively small number of officers were responsible for the vast majority of instances where excessive force was used during the course of an arrest. During the five-year period from 1986 to 1990, there were 1,800 complaints made against officers for use of excessive force or improper tactics; of that number, 1,400 officers had only 1 or 2 complaints, while 183 officers had 4 or more, 44 had 6 or more, and 16 had 8 or more—with 1 officer having 16 such complaints in his record.[11] During the same time period, there were 6,000 officers involved in use-of-force incidents. Analyzing the numbers reveals that, of the 8,450 sworn officers in the LAPD at that time, *3 percent* of them were responsible for generating 71 percent of the excessive-force complaints.[12]

This is a common finding in research and in real-world police supervisory experience; a very small percentage of personnel account for the majority of citizen complaints as well as other problems. It is a maxim in police administration that 90 percent of your problems come from 10 percent of your people. I have seen from years of experience that misconduct and corruption cannot flourish in an organization that takes organizational integrity seriously. The Christopher Commission reviewed transcripts of messages sent between officers via their in-car (MDT) computers wherein officers would talk openly about beating people and being eager to become involved in a shooting incident. Clearly, there is a serious problem in an agency where officers feel comfortable transmitting such things on a recorded system or when officers *want* to be involved in a shooting. Officers in a healthy police organization view violence as an unfortunate last-resort necessity in their work and a shooting as something they hope never happens.

A contemporaneous survey conducted by the LAPD itself revealed that around 25 percent of officers believed that racial prejudice existed in the department and that it contributed to negative interactions and use of excessive force. The commission also found blatantly racist comments made between officers on the MDT system, which, while not indicative of pervasive racism, makes it apparent that the atmosphere in the department was one wherein officers felt they could make such comments with impunity.[13] Other findings included individuals serving as field-training officers who had been disciplined for excessive use of force, a pervasive *us versus them* mentality, lack of disciplinary measures for misconduct, officers with long histories of misconduct receiving promotions, and woefully inadequate investigations into charges of excessive force.[14]

The commission laid the blame for the problems with the supervisors and administrators of the LAPD, and rightfully so. A department that is properly supervised and disciplined would not tolerate the sorts of behavior the commission found. The report quoted recently retired assistant chief Jesse Brewer, who described lack of attention from management as being "the essence of the excessive force problem" in the LAPD:

> We know who the bad guys are. Reputations become well known, especially to the sergeants and then of course to lieutenants and the captains in the areas. We know the ones who are getting into trouble more than anyone else. But, I don't see anyone bringing these people up and saying, "Look, you are not conforming, you are not measuring up. You need to take a look at yourself and your conduct and the way you're treating people" and so forth. . . . The sergeants don't, they're not held accountable so why should they be that much concerned. They know that some of these officers who do generate the most complaints are also the ones who make a lot of arrests and write a lot of tickets and so forth and the sergeants, I have a feeling that they don't think that much is going to

happen to them anyway if they tried to take action and perhaps [they will] not even be supported by the lieutenant or the captain all the way up the line when they do take action against some individual.[15]

These words could be used to describe the root of most problems that appear in a police agency anywhere in the United States. Accountability begins at the top; administrators need to hold supervisors accountable for the actions of their subordinates, and they must support first-line supervisors who take disciplinary measures against their subordinates. A head-in-the-sand approach is a certain recipe for eventual problems. Police officers are no different from other humans; they will tend to conform to the dominant culture within their organizations. If the culture is one of professionalism and strict accountability, most officers will work hard to comply. Likewise, when the atmosphere is permissive, and discipline nonexistent, officers perhaps not previously so inclined may slide off the rails—especially those working in high-crime areas, where the stresses are enormous.

Police do, however, have a legitimate need and legal authority to use force in order to effect arrests or to protect themselves and others. This fact is often lost in discussions about police use of force. Force is the central defining aspect of the police officer; he or she is charged with maintaining order and enforcing laws and is the person called whenever things begin to spiral out of control or an emergency takes place, specifically because police officers have the authority to use force to regain control of a situation—even if they don't necessarily exercise that power. When a police encounter results in the use of physical force against a suspect, critics tend to point to what is often a relatively minor underlying offense or the age and condition of the suspect: "He was just selling untaxed cigarettes" or "She's just a teenager." Once a police officer has placed someone under arrest for an offense, he or she is obligated by law and his or her department's rules to take the person into custody and process that person into the legal system. A point of distinction here: a person is under arrest when a police officer says "you are under arrest." That is not the same thing as being "in custody," which means that an officer has physical control, that is, handcuffs, on the person. When an officer arrests someone for a minor crime and that person then fails to comply and resists or fights with officer to avoid custody, *that defendant*— not the police officer—has escalated the situation far beyond the original alleged offense.

Should a suspect feel the arrest is unwarranted, he has the option of making a complaint to the department, telling his side to the judge and having his case reviewed by the prosecutor's office and ultimately a jury for validity. Resisting arrest is a serious crime in and of itself, and the officer has no way of knowing whether the suspect is armed or whether his intention is simply to escape or to injure or kill the officer. Moreover, because a police officer wears a visible sidearm, every fight with a suspect is a gunfight on some level. As stated previously, more than 10 percent of murdered police officers are killed with their own sidearm. So when someone who fights with the police is legally shot and killed, he did not die because he had a headlight out or he sold a joint; he died because he engaged in the crime of resisting arrest and assaulting a police officer and because he either brandished a weapon or made movements indicative of someone reaching for a weapon.

Often, the use of force can appear inappropriate, given the situation, context, and demeanor of the suspect. The endless videos of such situations rarely contain any context whatsoever. The problem for a police officer comes at the point when someone refuses to be taken into custody. A 180-pound teenage girl under arrest for disorderly conduct may be relatively calm by the time someone trains his iPhone on the confrontation, leaving the viewer unaware of the outrageous and obscene behavior that she was engaged in moments earlier. The officer now *has* to take the suspect into custody, and if she refuses to cooperate, force will have to be employed. Whether the officer takes her to the ground, uses pepper spray, baton strikes, or uses a Taser, it will appear shocking on camera—at least to people unaccustomed to seeing violence in their daily lives. Yet, the officer has no other option but to use force. If the suspect is calm enough, there may be a few moments when the officer can try to explain and reason with the suspect, but then no other option exists. If the suspect is still out of control or the officer is surrounded with hostile onlookers, there is no time for anything but decisive action; this is an unfortunate but central part of the job of policing—some people simply will not comply regardless of the professionalism or respectfulness of the officer.

I had the unfortunate experience of having to arrest a couple in their late 60s in the lobby of my station one afternoon. I was interviewing the husband and wife along with my recruit, whom I was training. The woman was small and frail and wore a colostomy bag, while the husband was of average build. We had dealt with them earlier in the day because they had been harassing their neighbors, and while I believed we had successfully resolved the issue without incident, the two came to the station essentially to yell at us for not arresting the neighbors. I tried at length to have a conversation, but the woman kept yelling with the husband interjecting here and there. Eventually, the volume and obscenities reached a

level that could no longer be tolerated, as we were in a larger public facil-
ity with many members of the public passing by, and I instructed them to
leave. They repeatedly refused my direction to leave the premises and
continued shouting and cursing. I warned them that I would have to
arrest them if they did not leave or quieted down and talked. This warning was also ignored several times. Eventually, I informed them that they
were under arrest, to which the husband replied, "F[***] you I am,"
punched my partner in the gut, and ran for the parking lot. The little old
lady took a swing at my jaw, but I was able to catch her bird-like forearm
between my index finger and thumb. So there I was, a six-foot tall, 200-
pound man holding a little old lady around both wrists with my fingers,
dancing around trying to somehow gingerly subdue her without injuring
her or damaging her colostomy bag and tube, while she continued to
curse and kick at me.

When she was finally secured to the bench inside the station unhurt,
my recruit returned with the old man in handcuffs and bleeding from an
abrasion above his eye. The recruit had chased him into the lot and, also
being careful not to hurt him, had tried to grab his arm rather than tackle
him. Unfortunately, the man pulled away, lost his balance and fell, scrap-
ing his forehead on the pavement.

This incident occurred two decades ago, but imagine the headlines if a
YouTube video was possible then: "Elderly Couple Arrested and Beaten for
Complaining to Cops." Neither of us wanted to arrest either one of them
and in fact did everything we could to avoid it, yet once it became necessary it created a very ugly scene, which would have immediately appeared
to a YouTube viewer to be an act of bullying or brutality. This is just one
small example of the no-win scenarios police find themselves in every day.

Power, Authority, and Legitimacy

The police, as stated, are merely the manifestation of the power of the
state. It is the state that makes law and compels citizens to obey the laws
through the police. In an ostensibly free society such as ours, sovereignty
rests with the people, who in turn express their will in government
through their democratically elected representatives. The state and the
police have *power* because they have guns and a military to back them up,
but a free republic cannot function when government power is required
to maintain order.

A government official such as a police officer operates under a grant of
legal *authority* from the state. An officer has the authority to pull over a
speeding driver or take physical control over someone he or she has

probable cause to believe committed a burglary. A well-equipped police force has both the power and legal authority to enforce laws and make arrests. This, however, is also not the way the government of a free people operates.

A government of free people maintains order through the citizenry's voluntary compliance with the laws. The people make the law through their representatives so they in turn generally obey since they had a hand in crafting the rules. This is what makes a government *legitimate*. A government that has the power to coerce and cow its people into compliance out of fear may be able to maintain law and order, as in a dictatorship, but it is not a legitimate government. Likewise, a government established without the people's consent can create laws and police and so grant legal authority to police and other officials it appoints, but if the foundation of those laws is an illegitimate government, then so too will the authority of the officials so appointed be regarded—as illegitimate. More generally, the legitimacy of a government and its laws can be roughly approximated by the degree to which the citizenry feels an obligation to obey those laws voluntarily.

Should the government begin to lose its legitimacy in the eyes of the public or a large constituency, then the police, as the enforcement arm and public face of the government, lose their legitimacy as well by default. Should a particular police department employ tactics that are regarded as intrusive, officious, and illegal, they risk losing legitimacy in the estimation of their constituents. Once the police or the government is no longer viewed as a legitimate authority, peace and order can rapidly begin to collapse; people feel free or even obliged to break the laws and to vent their anger against symbols of the illegitimate authority.

This is what is happening in many inner cities across the country. While most protesters and activists have only a vague notion of what precisely they are angry about, they have a shared belief that the entire "system" is rigged against them. They rail against generalized grievances and demand remedies without definition: "institutional racism," "income inequality," "social justice," "economic justice," and other nebulous evils and nostrums. While one can argue the validity of the proposed remedies and the cause of the problems, there *is* an inherent unfairness built into our criminal justice system.

The Environment

Police officers operate in the widest possible variety of environments: wide-open mountain ranges, prairies, deserts, forests, college campuses, big cities, ports, little villages, sprawling suburbs, ghettos, industrial wastelands, mining towns, gated communities, and swamplands. They deal with every color, class, religion, age, political viewpoint, job, career, disability, illness, and personality. The vast majority of attention and criticism of the police that has arisen in the past several years concerns police officers' tactics in predominantly black communities—and mainly in those communities that are economically poor in character. While there are good and bad cops everywhere, the protests and criticism are largely focused on urban police agencies and their interactions with black citizens.

Police in the inner-city ghettos—whether black, white, or Latino in character—are faced with an unimaginable tangle of intractable social pathologies. Poverty, violence, routine murder, drug addiction, theft, fatherlessness, filth, disease, chaos, indolence, hopelessness, bitterness, and rampant antisocial behavior ravage these areas. The good people of these neighborhoods get caught up in the crossfire, both figuratively and literally, between cops and bad guys and between rival bad guys.

The police officers patrolling these areas are almost exclusively the newest and least experienced officers in the department, because seniority buys cops a ticket out of the deadliest and most difficult neighborhoods. This creates serious difficulties for young officers, who have received minimal training and absolutely no training on how to deal with a clientele as just described.

The police leadership gets demands from the politicians to "do something" about the rampant crime and above all to prevent the disease from creeping into other neighborhoods. Politicians want low crime rates to attract business and tourism and leave it to the police to wade through all the social problems for which they have neither the training nor the resources to alleviate. So police leaders devise strategies and pass them down to officers on the street. Unfortunately, these strategies can be overly aggressive, and officers without adequate training and supervision are unable to apply them properly. Often, incompetent or poorly trained supervisors simply boil down every tactic to the simplest denominator—numbers. Police officers go out to aggressively target bad guys to help the people of a neighborhood but wind up sweeping up very minor offenders and innocent people in their net. The drug war is the primary culprit for the vast majority of police contacts that go wrong or result in some sort of injustice. Without the ability or incentive to arrest people simply for personal-use intoxicants they may carry in their pockets, the police would have neither incentive nor justification for stopping such vast numbers of individuals and subjecting them to invasive questions and searches, which can and do lead to angry or violent confrontations.

"Broken Systems"

It is important to remember that the police are only one component of the justice system. Police officers can accuse people of crimes and hand them off to the prosecutor's office, but that is where their authority ends. Police do not keep people locked up for months awaiting trial for nonviolent offenses, prosecute people they know are innocent, or impose sentences on those convicted of crimes. In fact, the justice system was designed to quickly correct any mistakes or abuse by the police. A police officer makes an arrest for what he or she believes is a crime committed by a particular person. That defendant is then arraigned before a judge where the charges are read to him and his rights are explained. The judge determines if the accusations and supporting documents are sufficient to support the charge and asks for a plea. The defendant generally pleads not guilty—or the judge enters the not-guilty plea on his behalf—and the case is adjourned to a later date. The judge can either release the defendant upon his own recognizance or require that he post bail. The prosecutor's office receives the paperwork associated with the case and reviews it to ensure that the defendant is being accused of all the elements that make up the particular crime and that there is enough evidence to at least provide probable cause to believe that the defendant committed the crime. They should review the officer's written notes, police reports, witness statements, accusatory instruments, and any physical evidence and then talk with the arresting officer for more detail. They should interview witnesses and victims and begin preparing to try the case in court, prepare a reduced charge in light of the facts of the case, or ask for a dismissal or different charge because the police were in error.

This, however, is not what happens. Most prosecutors' offices are severely underfunded and understaffed. Most assistant prosecutors have dozens of cases on their desk and could never begin to perform due diligence on them all. So, rather than seek the truth, their goal eventually becomes to get rid of as many cases as possible as quickly as possible. If individual prosecutors have far too many cases to handle, that goes doubly for judges. What most laypeople don't realize is that criminal trials are a relative rarity. First, trials take a tremendous amount of time, for the attorneys involved to prepare their cases, to present the case to the grand jury for felonies, to summon a jury pool and conduct the jury selection process, to pay the jurors, to provide them with meals, and days and days of the judge's time while more and more cases pile up.

What actually happens is the police make an arrest and perhaps the defendant goes to jail in lieu of bail. The case file goes to the court clerk and prosecutor's office and is placed at the bottom of the gigantic pile of pending cases. The larger the town or city, the longer it will take to reach that file—anywhere from a week or two to six months. Only then will the prosecutor take a quick look through the file as he is sprinting into the courthouse hoping to get through as many files as possible that day. Now, the prosecutor doesn't want a trial and the judge *really* won't like the prosecutor if he forces the issue, so the defendant is offered a "deal" or plea bargain; if the defendant agrees to plead guilty to a lesser charge, the prosecutor will drop the more serious charge and make a sentencing recommendation to the judge. The question of guilt or innocence never enters into the equation. The goal is to meet with the defendant and his lawyer, get a deal, rush out in front of the judge, bang the gavel, and toss another file into the out basket.

It is at this stage that the system really breaks down. A guilty defendant gets offered a deal simply for the convenience of the court and prosecutor and so often escapes justice, robbing his victims of the justice they sought through the legal system. Much worse, if the defendant is innocent, neither his appointed attorney nor the prosecutor is interested: they just want to "get rid of" the case and definitely don't want to go to trial—they don't get paid enough, nor do they have the time for that kind of work. So the innocent man sits before a prosecutor who offers a plea to a lesser charge, with less time in prison, for a crime he did not commit. Should he refuse the deal, he is threatened with far harsher treatment: prosecution for every possible offense, recommendations for maximum sentence, or even legally tenuous prosecutions of his loved ones for alleged conspiracy or abetting. This is essentially a threat to punish the defendant for refusing to cooperate in his own wrongful conviction. The defendant is then forced to choose between a much-shortened prison term or the possibility of a long sentence and other calamities—for a crime he did not commit. So we wind up with a system where the guilty go free and the innocent are punished, not all the time, but far more frequently that the public is aware; but for the family, friends, and acquaintances of those caught up in the gears of the justice system, it is well known.

Even those with limited education or intelligence can sense something is wrong when their brother's best friend is locked up in a violent county jail for months because he jumped a turnstile six months ago, and couldn't make bail or scrape together the money to pay the fine, while at the same time the criminals who created the financial collapse of 2008 walk away without so much as a tongue-lashing from the judicial system. A middle class or wealthy person charged with a minor crime can hire a decent lawyer and stay out of jail while the charges are pending—either because he is a "respectable" citizen with long-term employment and a mortgage to pay and so is trusted to return to court or because he can afford to post bail. Then, even if the process drags on for a lengthy period, he can generally have the charges reduced to a noncriminal offense, pay a fine, and put the matter behind him. For those with limited financial resources, the experience of being charged with a minor offense can be much different. Consider this example from the Justice Department's report about the situation in Ferguson, Missouri:

> We spoke, for example, with an African-American woman who has a still-pending case stemming from 2007, when, on a single occasion, she parked her car illegally. She received two citations and a $151 fine, plus fees. The woman, who experienced financial difficulties and periods of homelessness over several years, was charged with seven Failure to Appear offenses for missing court dates or fine payments on her parking tickets between 2007 and 2010. For each Failure to Appear, the court issued an arrest warrant and imposed new fines and fees. From 2007 to 2014, the woman was arrested twice, spent six days in jail, and paid $550 to the court for the events stemming from this single instance of illegal parking. Court records show that she twice attempted to make partial payments of $25 and $50, but the court returned those payments, refusing to accept anything less than payment in full. One of those payments was later accepted, but only after the court's letter rejecting payment by money order was returned as undeliverable. This woman is now making regular payments on the fine. As of December 2014, over seven years later, despite initially owing a $151 fine and having already paid $550, she still owed $541.[16]

In the mid-1990s, I was a state police officer living in a village that had a local police department. This village had a law that between November and April, between 12:00 and 6:00 A.M., residents were required to park their car on either the even-or the odd-numbered side of the street, corresponding with the date. The purpose of such laws (for the benefit of readers from warmer climates) is to facilitate snow removal in the event of such precipitation. There were no signs on my street indicating this fact, and I parked directly in front of my house most days year-round. Then, one day, I began receiving tickets for violating the village ordinance on alternate street parking. I researched the state traffic laws and learned that the village is required to post signs about such a law only at the entrances to the village. I then went to the police station and asked for a copy of the law, whereupon they opened a drawer and produced a yellowed, stained, threadbare piece of paper with the ordinance printed on it. From the age of the paper, I became suspicious, and obtained a copy of the village code. Sure enough, the current village code had no such provision for alternate street parking, and the numbering system in the code book was totally different from that of the ordinance the police were enforcing. The current village code had superseded the old code more than a decade earlier and in fact contained not a single ordinance pertaining to parking, which meant that the police were enforcing a law that had ceased to exist during the Reagan Administration. I was understandably outraged by this fact, as well as by the fact that whenever I got one of these bogus tickets, it was not snowing, nor was there any snow on the streets; when it did snow, I parked in my cramped driveway like a good citizen.

I took my handful of illegally issued tickets, pleaded not guilty, and dropped them off at the courthouse. When I appeared in court—to the shock of the judge who usually saw me with handcuffed defendants in tow—I submitted a lengthy motion to dismiss the charges based on the fact that I had not violated any existing law as well as on numerous other grounds in furtherance of justice; for example, I wasn't interfering with snow removal, I had no other tickets, and the fine to be paid was printed right on the ticket, allowing no leeway for circumstances, among others. I was advised that the court would review my motion, and the case was adjourned.

Several months went by, and I never received a trial notice or indication of how the court ruled on my motion. About the same time, I realized my car's registration was about to expire, and I had not received the customary renewal notice in the mail from the DMV. Again suspicious, I checked my registration and learned that it had been *suspended* for "failure to pay fine" to the village court. In order to be suspended in that way, the village has to send a sworn statement to the state DMV that the person has been fined by the court after a guilty plea or conviction at trial and did not pay. Enraged, I went to the village offices and demanded to speak to the village clerk, who I learned had transmitted the false document to the DMV. He suavely and arrogantly told me that there was nothing I could do about it and waved aside my assertions that the village was enforcing a nonexistent law, that the court ignored my motion, and that a village of this size, under state law, was not entitled to suspend registrations for unpaid tickets.

By late that afternoon, the tickets were dismissed and my registration restored. How you ask? I left the clerk's office and went down the hall to the office of the mayor and informed him I was going to return with a felony warrant of arrest for his town clerk for filing a false document with the state, and was going to inform the local area newspaper of the arrest and that the village had been extracting untold sums of money from residents with tickets based on a law that did not even exist. The village attorney telephoned shortly thereafter and advised that, after consideration of the facts and circumstances, the village had opted to "forgive" my summonses and dismiss the charges.

After tremendous inconvenience and frustration, I was able to get a small measure of justice, although I should note that my complaint to the judicial district office overseeing the court was ignored. The reason I received justice where other village residents did not was not because I was white but because I knew the law and had the time, resources, and education to research applicable laws and criminal procedure and was a person of some "respectability" and so wasn't simply ushered out of the village hall by the scruff of my neck when I came to argue for my rights. A poor person, struggling to get by, working two jobs, and who didn't own a suit, would likely have gotten precisely nowhere with his claims— black or white.

People treated in this manner by the justice system are not likely to view the government as a legitimate authority. They certainly aren't going to view the police who write the tickets and summonses in the first place as having any proper moral authority for their actions. When people suffer such treatment, they look for an explanation: why me? What did I do? It seems impossible that everyone could have such an experience and so they are likely in this case to attribute it to some personal characteristic, such as being black, or in my case, because I was a trooper. (Local cops often harbor a jealous dislike of state police.) However, the woman in Ferguson would be wrong to think that—it happened because she was *poor*. A person with a decent income and permanent address would simply have not fallen into the situation; she would have paid the absurdly high fine, grumbled a bit, and moved on—whether she was black or white. A poor person can't afford to pay $150 because she parked her car on a piece of asphalt the local politicians deemed off limits, perhaps during certain days of the week or hours of the day, or, more likely, in the fervent hope that people *would* park there to in turn be fleeced for cash. In these examples, the woman would have been better off spending five days in jail for her parking violation. That would have been two arrests, one day less jail time, and $1091 less lost income than she got for being unable to pay her initial ticket. This illustrates that the ticket is not about "justice" in the remotest sense of the word; it is simply a means of making money.

The problem with the so-called justice system is that it is mainly focused on raising revenue for the government. Aside from serious felony crimes, the courts mainly deal in money changing. Many crimes that some may think of as significant are treated chiefly as ways for courts to extract money from the accused. This varies widely from one state or jurisdiction to another, but the general trend nationwide is local jails filled to capacity and local sheriffs begging the courts not to sentence people to jail terms. While you may think that someone arrested for assault and battery or stealing a car is going to be sent to jail for his crime, what nearly always happens is the assistant district or state attorney will meet with the accused and offer to reduce the charge to a noncriminal offense such as disorderly conduct, trespass, or harassment. The defendant then pleads guilty and is assessed a steep fine, often accompanied by a heavy surcharge or some other such fee payable to the state government, which is essentially a tax for getting arrested. The defendant is then released and given a set time in which to pay the fine. If he fails to pay on time, the court will issue a warrant for his arrest, dispatching the police to act as debt collectors for the court. Once back before the court, the judge can either release the defendant with another promise to pay (likely leading to another warrant for the cops a few weeks or months later) or commit him to jail pending satisfaction of the fine.

Another nationwide trend is for states to charge defendants for their own public defender, probation supervision, and even room and board while in jail. This helps to ensure that the poor are treated much more harshly than other defendants in the legal system. Once again, for those with the money to pay, things go much easier. New York University's Brennan Center for Justice and the National Center for State Courts conducted a survey of all the 50 states' court systems and found that in 43 states offenders can be billed for the services of a public defender; 44 states can charge offenders for their own parole and probation supervision; 41 states allow inmates to be billed for room and board while in jail; and every state except Hawaii can charge defendants for the costs of electronic monitoring.[17] These monies are then used to pay for the cost of operating the court and even for amenities like the employee fitness center at the Allegan County, Michigan Courthouse.[18]

This results in cases like that of Jared Thornburg of Westminster, Colorado. He was ticketed for making an illegal left turn, went to court, and got a lesser charge with $165 worth of fines and fees. Thornburg was unemployed and homeless after losing his oilfield job following an injury and so had no way to pay the fine. One day, before starting a new job at a fast-food restaurant, Thornburg was arrested for not paying the fines, which had since increased to $306. As a result, he spent the next 10 days in jail.[19]

Kyle DeWitt of Ionia, Michigan, spent three days in jail as a result of catching a fish out of season. Originally sentenced to a fine of $155, which he could not pay, as he was broke and homeless, he was arrested for failure to pay and jailed for three days, still owing $215.[20]

Tom Barrett was a homeless man who had just landed a subsidized apartment with a monthly rent of $25, which he paid for by selling his plasma at the local blood bank. He stole a $1.29 can of beer from a convenience store and got arrested and then went to court with no lawyer because he could not pay the $50 fee for a public defender. The court sentenced Barrett to 12 months' probation and to wear a monitoring device that would verify he was not drinking any alcohol. He was required to pay a $50 set-up fee, $39 per month to a private probation company, and $12 per day for the device. Unable to pay such costs, he spent a year in jail for the theft of the single can of beer.[21]

While these are just anecdotal stories, they illustrate the absurdity of charging desperately poor and indigent defendants large sums of money as punishment. A $500 fine might teach a middle class college kid a lesson about smashing a beer bottle on the sidewalk, but for a poor person trying to get by or better himself, it's a ticket to a life of hiding from the police and chronic unemployment. I do not advocate simply allowing those who steal or otherwise break reasonable laws to walk away without punishment, but a system that is centered almost entirely around squeezing every possible dime from those caught violating the law is inherently unfair and ripe for abuse and corruption.

Another method commonly used by the courts is to suspend the driver's license of individuals who are delinquent on their fines. In this way, people can be arrested on a warrant for failing to pay their fine, but even if and when they are released, they cannot pay the fine because they can't drive to a job to earn the money. One survey in the state of Florida revealed that 85 percent of the courts used this as a tactic for extracting monies from defendants.[22]

Author Matt Taibbi perfectly captures the cynical nature of an urban courtroom in his thoroughly researched book *The Divide*. He recounts the story of a young man named Andre Finley with no criminal record who was one of 20,000 New York City residents to receive a summons for riding a bicycle on the sidewalk. Andre is at his third appearance in court because the police didn't show up for the first two court dates.

The judge was about an hour late. A hundred people who had been told to appear at nine had to wait an hour just to hear His Honor, a walrus-looking old man with a shiny bald head and a long handlebar mustache, give a speech that he clearly thought was funny about the proceedings

ahead. "Get your wallets ready!" he cracked. "We take Visa and Master-
card here, but no American Express!" . . . Fifty dollars, a hundred, twenty-
five. Minute after mindless minute, fine after fine. "Just like a lemon," said
Finley, "They just keep squeezing and squeezing."[23]

As Taibbi points out, one can imagine the collective frustration and
wasted time of appearing three times in court, waiting for 15 total hours,
just to try to get a break on a fine you cannot afford to pay. America's
urban courtrooms are packed full of such defendants, and while poor
whites and others receive the same treatment, the court is held locally, so
when black folks look around the courtroom, they see mostly black and
brown faces.

So many people get caught up in the web of fines and warrants for nonviolent and petty offenses that New Jersey began a program to try and
lower the numbers (and still collect as much money as possible), called
the Fugitive Safe Surrender Program, where thousands of people line up
at locations across the state to turn themselves in on outstanding warrants
for failing to pay exorbitant fines. The state sets up an express-lane-style
makeshift court, with judges and prosecutors on hand, and bargains with
the offenders for lesser fines in exchange for closing the cases and rescind-
ing the warrants. This provides a way for people wanted for failure to pay
to resume their lives, and although they are still being essentially shaken
down for money, they can get out of it without spending time in jail in
most cases. There is clearly something wrong with a justice system that
has thousands of "fugitives" in every major population center who are
merely ordinary folks who broke minor laws and whose only real offense
is being too poor to pay money as punishment.

Jail and Bail

On May 10, 2010, Kalief Browder was walking home with a friend after
attending a party in the Bronx, when they were stopped by police officers.
A man had reported being robbed nearby and was riding with the officers
and had said it was Kalief and his friend. They consented to be searched,
and when nothing was found, they were shown to the man in the car,
who then changed his story and said that the two were not the ones who
robbed him that night but had done so a week earlier. Kalief would be
charged with robbery and sent to jail, as his mother could not afford the
$3,000 bail. Kalief was 16 years old and would spend the next 3 years and
9 days behind bars, having never been convicted of a crime. Kalief would
appear in court more than 30 times as the prosecutor's office requested

and received one continuance after another, with excuses no better than "people not ready" or the assigned prosecutor was on vacation. He was a small kid and was beaten by inmates as well as the notoriously violent guards. He would spend much of his time in a cell 12 feet by 7 in solitary confinement and attempt suicide at least twice.

Eventually, after Kalief's high school class had long since graduated, the prosecutor admitted that they had no case, and, besides, the alleged victim had moved back to Mexico, and so the boy, now a young man, was released. But Kalief never recovered from his ordeal. He suffered from severe PTSD as a result of the psychological damage of those years in jail, the solitary confinement, and the beatings. He tried attending college and had his ups and downs, even becoming a minor celebrity for his troubles, appearing on television programs such as *The View* and receiving visits from celebrities like Jay Z. Sadly, Kalief's demons got the better of him, and in June 2015, at the age of 22, he committed suicide.[24] Kalief's story sparked calls for bail reform by New York's mayor and helped to fuel a growing movement to repair at least the pretrial portion of our justice system.

The problems with the system of bail as a means to secure a defendant's appearance in court is exacerbated by overly aggressive policing, since so many innocent people tend to be caught up in urban police dragnets. The concept of bail is logical on its face: require a defendant to post a significant amount of money to the court as assurance that he will reappear when required, and if he fails to do so, the money is forfeit. The problem with bail as it is used today is that it is often used as a means to keep a defendant locked up until trial or to keep a dangerous offender off the street until trial. Bail was never intended for that purpose. Too often, a judge will set bail in a case, resulting in a very poor or indigent defendant being sent to jail for the entire duration his case. In small or rural districts, this is not such a serious issue, as the case may be adjudicated within a matter of a few weeks. However, in large metropolitan areas, such as New York, Chicago, Los Angeles, and any one of the hundreds of large American cities, an inability to make bail can result in months or even years of detention for a defendant accused but never convicted of an offense. If the defendant is employed, even a short stay in jail for an inability to pay bail is likely to result in a loss of employment, leading to further inability to pay bail or fines.

Prosecutors can also abuse bail as a means to bully defendants into a guilty plea. The Eighth Amendment guarantees all citizens the right to a speedy trial, and states' criminal procedure laws generally require the state to be prepared to go to trial in a misdemeanor case in around

90 days and somewhat longer for felonies. In practice, however, the prosecution may wait until the trial date and request a continuance of some small, reasonable amount of time, say 10 days. This will delay the trial by as much as two or three months, given the massive volume of cases in the system. Then, three days later, the prosecutor will file that she is ready for trial. So the 90-day clock has been reset, and although the defendant will now spend additional months behind bars, only three days will tick off the clock because the prosecutor's filing stops the clock even though time marches on for the incarcerated defendant. It is not uncommon for defendants to spend far more time in jail awaiting trial than they would have received as a sentence *if* they were found guilty. On any given day in the United States, there are more than half a million people locked up in local jails in pretrial detention.[25] Prisoners who had jobs or were looking for work are now without income and unable to support loved ones for the duration. Innocent defendants may lose not only their job but custody of their children and other hardships. Those locked away before trial are not able to fully participate in preparing their defense and are in fact suffering punishment without having been convicted of a crime. America's jails are dark, dirty, deadly places that no innocent person should have to suffer for even a day.

The right to bail for noncapital offenses goes back at least as far as the Statute of Westminster of 1275, which denoted which offenses could be eligible for bail.[26] The purpose of requiring any bail set to be *reasonable* stems from the long fight against English monarchs' prerogative to jail their subjects without showing any cause, to allow the accused to participate in preparing their own defense, and to prevent the imposition of imprisonment upon those falsely accused. Bail and prohibitions against excessive bail were further codified in the English Bill of Rights in 1689. These traditions were adopted by the American colonies in such famous documents as the Virginia Declaration of Rights and later incorporated into our Constitution in the Eighth Amendment.[27]

The legal debate surrounding the system of bail centers around two main points: whether there is an absolute right to bail and what constitutes *excessive* bail. The Eighth Amendment merely states that bail cannot be excessive, but it does not state whether it must be granted at all or under what conditions, and neither does it define what constitutes *excessive*. The federal government's Bail Reform Act of 1984 allowed for denial of bail, following a hearing, for defendants who are shown to be a likely danger to the community if allowed to remain free pending trial. In upholding a challenge to that law, the Supreme Court ruled that there is no absolute right to bail and that legitimate concerns about public safety and the integrity of the judicial process may be taken into consideration when deciding whether to set bail.[28]

Having stated that there is a need for bail reform, there is also a serious problem of offenders committing further offenses while out on bail. Many defendants are dangerous individuals with demonstrated records of habitual criminality or violence. Releasing such people on bail once the police have managed to gather enough evidence and find and arrest them is often unwise. Moreover, in my experience, knowledgeable criminals know that the period they are on pretrial release is a sort of free pass to commit any crimes of an equal or lesser severity to the one they are awaiting trial on. Once the defendant reappears on the original charge and now has two or three more cases pending, the prosecutor is now looking at three times the work he had before the defendant was released on bail. The prosecutor is still facing the same time and resource constraints discussed earlier and so will just "bundle" all the charges together and offer the same plea deal that was going to be proposed for the first offense— meaning no conviction or punishment of any kind for the crimes committed while free on bail.

So bail reform needs to be done carefully and with common sense. Individuals accused of petty or nonviolent offenses, who have no serious criminal record, should be released while their case is pending, with bail that they can afford or on their own recognizance with certain restrictions and requirements, such as being placed under pretrial supervision. Those charged with violent crimes, who have a history of failing to appear, absconding, long records of recent criminal activity, and those who are shown to be likely to pose a threat to victims or witnesses should simply be held without bail. Perhaps judges could be required to hold brief hearings wherein the strength of a case is reviewed; witnesses, physical evidence, admissions of guilt, and prior convictions for similar behavior could be presented by the prosecutor if seeking to deny bail to the defendant.

Unless and until the Supreme Court rules on criteria for determining what constitutes *excessive bail*, the states need to begin addressing the problem. But the problem begins with too many laws being enforced far too aggressively by the police, and in many jurisdictions, by police officers making bad arrests. For example, Tyrone Tomlin of Brooklyn, New York, was a construction worker just off work when he ran into some friends outside a local shop. He chatted for a minute, went inside, and purchased a soda, which the clerk wrapped in a paper bag and then handed him a straw. He emerged onto the street to find narcotics detectives shaking down his friends, asking them if they "had anything on them that they shouldn't" and asking permission to search them, which they proceeded to do at length. After finding no contraband on anyone, Tomlin was handcuffed. When he asked why he was being arrested, the detective showed him the straw he had carried out of the store. Tomlin was charged with possession of drug paraphernalia; the supporting documents indicated that the officer's training and experience made him aware that straws are commonly used for packaging heroin residue.[29] Straws are also far more commonly used for drinking beverages—especially when they are clean and in the possession of a sweaty construction worker walking home covered with dirt and concrete dust and who also is in possession of a cold soda pop.

The prosecutor offered him a deal, that he plead guilty and serve a 30-day sentence. Tomlin pleaded not guilty—because he was not guilty and because he didn't want a new conviction on his record. Because Tomlin had past felony convictions for auto theft and drug possession, the court ordered a $1,500 bail, which there was no way for him to afford, and so off to Rikers island he went. He returned to court a week later for a discovery hearing, wherein the prosecution is supposed to turn over all their evidence. They had none but again pressured Tomlin to plead guilty and get a 30-day sentence, which he again refused since he was not guilty of any wrongdoing. Before he could make it back to court for another hearing, Tomlin was severely beaten by a group of inmates while in the shower in retaliation for not getting off the phone earlier when some punk ordered him to. Back in court, with a lumped-up head and one eye swollen shut, the lab report on his criminal straw possession was available and indicated no illegal substances were present; the date of the report was ironically the same day of his previous court appearance and well before he received his brutal beating in jail.[30]

What do you suppose Tyrone Tomlin, everyone he knows, and everyone who hears his story will think about the police who arrested him for no good reason and put him through that meat grinder? Clearly, there are problems other than the police in Tomlin's ordeal: prosecutors and judges who don't review the validity of an arrest, judges who don't consider the totality of circumstances before setting bail, overburdened courts, lack of adequate time for public defenders to meet with their clients and prepare for arraignment, and jails that are unsafe and inhumane. But it is the police who will get the blame for all of it. Even if an officer made a *valid* arrest of Tomlin for some minor offense and the case had gone the way it did, the police would still be the face of "what happened to Tyrone." Police officers who make arrests like the Tyrone Tomlin straw caper need serious retraining, quick termination, or transfer to a post directing traffic.

The idiocy of that arrest and the subsequent ordeal suffered by its victim will spread hatred of the police through a network of dozens if not hundreds of people, as Tomlin's friends and coworkers share the story with their friends and family, and so on.

On the other hand, even after the wrongful arrest, had Tyrone's bail been set at $100 so that he could pay or had the judge asked where and if he was working and if he would promise to appear when required, he would have been free all those weeks his case was pending. He would have been able to go to work every day to earn a living and the case would have been dismissed—and he wouldn't have been brutally beaten by a group of thugs, naked in a cinderblock shower in one of the darkest holes in America.

As of this writing, New Jersey has just become the first state to eliminate the use of cash bail and bail bonds. Instead, judges utilize a risk assessment process to determine whether the offender poses a serious flight risk or danger to the public. Those who do not fall into that category are to be released without bail. Reforms of this type have been implemented in smaller jurisdictions, such as Washington, D.C., and Cleveland, Ohio, but New Jersey will be the first statewide experiment in such sweeping reform.

The System

The police are only one part of a broken system of justice in the United States. The prosecutorial team is overworked and understaffed and too often cares far more about conviction and clearance rates than it does about truth or justice. Courts are overburdened with far too many cases as a result of far too many intrusive laws, far too many arrests, and sentencing is often arbitrary and unfair—for both perpetrators and victims. The so-called correctional system, where those convicted are sent to be warehoused, is nothing more than a terrifying, violent black hole, which virtually guarantees that inmates will leave more vicious and bitter than when they went in; fully one-third are rearrested within six months and more than two-thirds within three years.[31] It is the police, however, that act as the intake into this impenetrable and inscrutable world of American justice, and any carelessness or overly aggressive tactics on their part feed too many people—and often the wrong people—into the system. The police can do nothing to reform the rest of the system, and there is little they can do to convince the government to end its failed crusade against marijuana and drug use. The police can, however, exercise due diligence and strict professionalism when it comes to deciding whom to arrest, making certain they have the right person and ensuring all leads are followed to eliminate other possibilities. Police agencies that engage in the dragnet approach to stopping and frisking every person they don't like the looks of and conducting 15-minute investigations and making slapdash arrests of people who meet only the barest definition of probable cause need new leadership and a top-down overhaul of their training and supervision.

The police officer on the street is for the most part a well-intentioned person trying to do his or her best in what are often impossible circumstances. Policing in American ghettos is a soul-crushing experience, and the police are generally doing what they think is best to minimize the violence and chaos. Sometimes, their methods are ill conceived and sometimes they are applied without enough reflection, and this is a failure of their leadership. Police administrators must provide better leadership and training for their officers and first-line supervisors. They need to understand the critical element of legitimacy and how to cultivate and maintain it within their communities.

The root of the problem is a pervasive attitude at all levels of government that the citizenry, whom they are ostensibly supposed to serve, are a nuisance and beneath the station of any petty government official. Anyone who questions the propriety of government actions or talks about the principles of liberty is, by definition, a "nut" or "whack-job." When you see the disdain with which we are treated by government clerks and bureaucrats, it is clear that there is no longer a culture in the civil service generally that honors the notion of *service*. The police, as a profession, need to be the guardians of those principles of liberty and service and ensure that they act as a bulwark against not only crime and disorder but against unreasonable government intrusion and against any of their own number that fail to live up to the standards of police in a free society.

CHAPTER FIVE

The Police and Racial Conflict in America

Pigs in a blanket—fry 'em like bacon!
—Black Lives Matter Protest, St. Paul, Minnesota, August 29, 2015

Poor relations between police agencies and minority communities have been an intractable problem in many cities for more than half a century—and far longer in many instances. While the true function of American police officers is to act as guardians of the people's liberty and safety, historically police have at times been used as a tool of politicians to control others or to promote their own self-interest. Police brutality—when publicized in the national media—is nearly always combined with accusations of racial bias. This chapter will examine the sources of conflict and the successful and unsuccessful efforts made by police agencies to bridge the gap of trust and respect that too often separates the police and the citizens they serve.

The American republic was founded upon a set of ideals, a concept entirely new in the history of modern states. These radical ideas included the principle that governments were formed by men for the purpose of protecting their people's right to life, liberty, and property—*not* to dictate to the people or exploit them for the benefit and glory of the government.

No one can deny that it was truly a glorious chapter in human history. The words of the Declaration of Independence and the Constitution echoed across the globe and made America and then the rest of the western civilization more prosperous, healthy, and safe than anyone could have even dreamed two centuries ago. Black Americans played an active role in the American Revolution, fighting with George Washington and other Continental Army generals. With black citizens in bondage or only one step from it, the words of the revolution had special meaning for them. The American Revolution was and remains a beautiful ideal. The Marquis de Lafayette, who fought with General Washington, put it most eloquently: "Humanity has won its battle; liberty has a country."

Sadly, but perhaps inevitably, that dream was not realized for everyone, and Southern slavery persisted for decades. The problem with human ideals and our efforts to implement them is that doing so requires *humans*. We humans are seriously flawed when compared to our ideal selves. Humans have shortcomings, limitations, weaknesses, fears, superstitions, vices, prejudices, and jealousies. Black Americans, whether slaves in the South, or freedmen in the North, did not share fully in the promise of the revolution. Immediately at its birth, "liberty's country" fell short of its promise to humanity and compromised on the issue of slavery. A host of political and socioeconomic realities combined with those human weaknesses to deny freedom for most blacks. This was a terrible tragedy. Imagine if those first Americans could have found a way to achieve freedom and legal equality for *all*; what an even greater example to the world it could have been.

But enough cheerleading for American ideals. American ideals are great, but the reality of their attainment has been a long and often tragic story of disappointment. The story of America, while great in its sweeping notions of human liberty and dignity and its many contributions to the world, is also a story filled with unfairness, oppression, tragedy, corruption, racial bigotry, discrimination—a *human* story. I believe America remains a great country because it was founded upon great ideals and not race or religion—anyone can be an American.

Black and White in Modern America

It is a fundamental truth that those in positions of power will always seek to safeguard their status; this is a natural and universal human characteristic. So it has been throughout the centuries; each race and class has endeavored to defend its place in society. There are some major hurdles that Americans as a people need to get over before getting past issues of race. First is the notion that *black* and *white* are monolithic groups or even *races* of people. These are simply artificial constructs created long ago to divide people into groups.[1] When I fill out forms, I check "white" or "Caucasian" for my race, but it has no meaning for me. My personal ethnic background is mix of German, English, Dutch, American Indian, and maybe Italian. I don't view myself as "white" either; I'm me—an

American, not a German, or my father's son, or part of any ethnic, racial, or religious tribe. I've never been in a room with a large number of dark-skinned people and shared a knowing glance or wink with another "white" person in the room.

Obviously, the experience of being black is necessarily different; African Americans are in the minority and can be immediately recognized as a member of their "race" by the color of their skin. There is also the long history of oppression that cannot simply be erased and is part of the culture of memory for black citizens. The tragedy is that every new generation of Americans born since 1965 have it within their power to largely put an end to the white-black divide, and we all live in the best possible country in the world in which to accomplish it. We live a country of ideals—we have a shared set of fundamental values that empower everyone.

Before discussing the issue of the police and race relations, it is important to establish what the terms *racism* and *prejudice* mean. Prejudice or *bias* is something *everyone* has; all of us carry preconceived notions about not only people of other ethnic origins but about everything from the water quality in South America to teachers, truck drivers, and lawyers. Many common prejudices are positive in character; for example, Hispanics are very family oriented, Asians are superb students of math and music, Jewish people are excellent businesspeople. Some are even socially acceptable to express publicly, while others are not. These concepts come from our personal experiences, from people we meet and the entertainment and the news media. Racism, on the other hand, implies that one believes his or her race to be superior to—and has a right to dominate—others, and further, in our modern discourse, it means the racist possesses an utter disdain and even hatred of other races. While racism may be based upon a host of negative prejudices, they are *not* the same thing.

White and black folks alike, if they are honest, must admit harboring some prejudices about one another. Hopefully, they are a mix of positive and negative biases rather than all negative. Intelligent, decent people, however, are capable of recognizing their prejudices and setting them aside when making important judgments and decisions about policy or individuals. Most of us have encountered or heard stories of people who have been pleasantly surprised to discover that they like someone even though that person is white, or black, or a cop, or a lawyer, or a member of some other ethnic group or profession.

Scientific research has demonstrated that our brains are hard wired to be prejudiced;[2] it is how we survived as a species all these millennia. Early humans lived together in tribes and clans in order to survive. To stay safe, our ancestors needed to be highly attuned to any *other* that could potentially pose a threat. Those best adapted were more likely to survive and so the primeval or *reptilian* parts of our brain have developed to instinctively fear and distrust anyone whom it recognizes as an *other*, that is, apparently different in some way. There is no more obvious difference between humans than our entire skin being a different color. Even though our modern brains have evolved and grown an entire cerebral cortex over our cave-dwelling ancestors' more primitive brains, we still need to create mental shortcuts to make sense out of the billions of pieces of data that flood our minds every single day and keep ourselves safe. For the caveman, learning that animals on four legs or people from another tribe who look different may be deadly is something that must be accomplished quickly—or he will swiftly be eliminated from the gene pool. His subconscious mind rapidly establishes a reflexive understanding that four legs or a different face equals danger. His brain creates a shortcut for protection, so he's instantly on guard when he spots a four-legged creature or lighter-skinned human out of the corner of his eye, at least until he realizes it's just a small fox or a man from a friendly tribe.

These ancient shortcuts have stayed with us, and we create new ones all the time; they are what psychologists refer to as *heuristics*. Dark alleys aren't safe; taxi drivers know good places to eat; pit bulls bite; women/men all cheat; snakes are dangerous; black people are natural athletes; fire is hot; white people can't dance; lawyers lie; Jews are shrewd businesspeople—the list goes on. We use heuristics to make decisions about things when we don't have enough information at hand. Suppose I'm thinking about whether I should invest in a real estate deal. I may know little about the real estate business, so my decision will be based upon a heuristic created from whatever examples my brain can quickly cobble together. If I've had luck in past investments or know someone who made money investing in real estate, I'm likely to jump in. The opposite is true if most of my exposure to investing has been negative. Most of my judgment is not based upon the relevant facts because I don't have the time, inclination, or capacity to evaluate the particular investment opportunity before me.

The discussion of the roots and causes of prejudices and racism could fill volumes. For our purposes, it is important to understand the difference between the two and that all decent people from all walks of life and occupations should be capable of recognizing their biases—both positive and negative—and ensure that those biases do not cloud their judgment when it comes to specific situations and individuals.

Americans born after 1965 grew up in a country where racial equality was the law of the land and where racial bigotry was rejected, or at a minimum largely out of fashion. This does not mean that prejudice has been eliminated and, most likely, it never will be. There will always be ignorant people who let their prejudices cloud their judgment. People of any race or color who are ignorant or unintelligent will always turn to tribalist behaviors to make themselves feel relevant through their membership in a racial or ethnic group and espousing their greatness or superiority. We witness this behavior all the time in our daily lives: visceral hatred of rival sports team fans; first shift versus second shift animosity; "anchor" store mall employees looking down on the small store employees—the list goes on. The great actor Morgan Freeman gave perhaps one of the most insightful and succinct methods for effectively reducing racism. "Stop talking about it," he said. "I'm going to stop calling you a white man, and I'm going to ask you to stop calling me a black man."[3] Maybe that's a good place to start.

Do the Police Target African Americans?

On July 17, 2014, New York City police officers responded to a report from their lieutenant that a known seller of untaxed cigarettes—*loosies* in street parlance—was operating in the Staten Island neighborhood of Tompkinsville. Within a few minutes, the suspect, Eric Garner—a black male—lay dead on the sidewalk.[4]

The immediate area of Garner's arrest had been the site of 646 calls to 911, 3 complaints to the department's Web site, and some 98 arrests in the months leading up to that July day. The area of Bay Street had been a scene of chronic disorder and complaints from local residents about individuals selling untaxed cigarettes and drugs. These contraband dealers were intimidating to passersby and would often engage in disorderly behavior and get into fights with one another. Because of all the complaints, it was an area the police were keen to clean up, and they had begun to focus on enforcement.

As Ramsey Orta, a friend of Garner, took cell phone video, two officers arrived and approached Garner to arrest him for his sale of untaxed cigarettes. The now-infamous video that was shown thousands of times on television did not contain the 2 minutes prior to the physical confrontation. During that time, the officers were calmly talking with Garner and trying to convince him to submit peacefully to arrest. In the unedited video, Garner, who weighed nearly 400 pounds and is larger than both the officers combined, is seen ranting, gesturing wildly, and shouting

obscenities as he defies the officers' requests for his identification and telling them he will not allow himself to be arrested.

As backup units arrive, the two officers move in on the giant, and one
of them climbs on his back, wrapping his arm around Garner's neck as
they take him to the ground, while he continues to resist. Within about
25 seconds, Garner is cuffed and face down on the sidewalk, having just
stated "I can't breathe" nine times. (It should be noted here that a person
who cannot breathe is not physically capable of saying those words.) As
this is taking place, hostile onlookers can be heard shouting at police, and
Orta narrates, calling the police officers "niggers." The officers can then
be seen turning the unconscious Garner onto his side and leaning over
him, tapping his shoulder for a response.[5]

Emergency medical personnel arrive shortly and tend to Garner, who
never regained consciousness. The autopsy performed on Garner's body
would find that his death was caused by a combination of the compres-
sion of his neck by the officer and Garner's obesity, asthma, high blood
pressure, and diabetes.[6]

Garner's death sparked outrage from many quarters, claiming that the
death was somehow racially motivated. New York City mayor Bill De Blasio
commented about how he and his African American wife had warned
their son about the "threat" posed by police officers, saying, "Because of
the dangers he may face, we've had to literally train him . . . in how
to take special care in any encounter he has with the police officers who
are there to protect him."[7] Garner's last words, "I can't breathe," became a
rallying cry at protests around the country. In the end, a grand jury would
hear all the evidence and refuse to indict the officers involved for any
criminal wrongdoing.

The death of Eric Garner is instructive for a number of reasons. First,
he was not approached or targeted because of his race. The responding
officers went to his location because they were ordered to do so after
Garner was recognized as a known criminal. Second, his alleged offense
was seemingly minor—not a crime of violence or private theft. Third, he
defied lawful orders from the police, resisted arrest, and subsequently
died as a result. This case provides an example of where the debate over
police and their behavior should focus: not on race but on public policy
and strategies for dealing with disorder.

The two responding plainclothes officers look like kids, sent to deal
with a giant of a man who was seen as part of a larger problem of crime
and disorder in and around the Bay Street area. They went there and
approached Garner not because he was a black man but because they
were sent to deal with his alleged illegal activity. Garner was angry

because he believed he should be allowed to freely sell untaxed cigarettes, and, in this particular instance, he mistakenly believed the cops were there to harass and blame him for a fight that had just occurred and which he had broken up.

From the point of view of the officers, they do not have the option of walking away. They cannot consider the race of the person they are confronted with; if Garner were white, the officers would not have had the choice of simply saying "since you're white, we'll give you a break" and simply drive off. The officers were required to take action and were confronted with a literal giant who is angry and defiant. Regardless of the petty nature of his offense, they are committed to the situation and dealing with a potentially dangerous individual. Garner's friend, calling them niggers, and other hostile onlookers also confronted the officers. Were the officers to do nothing, they would face severe criticism from the dozens of residents and business owners who had been demanding action to clean up the disorder in the area, not to mention discipline from their superiors. So here we have a common situation where the police are not only caught between the law and a citizen but between department and government policies and the public, and between citizen complainants and citizens conducting illicit business in their neighborhood. On top of that, the officers are simply ordinary human beings in a tense and frightening confrontation.

An unbiased look at what occurred shows absolutely no evidence of racial bias. Had Garner been white, the police still would have been forced to take action against him and been equally afraid of an angry, defiant, and gigantic white man. Had Garner not been morbidly obese, with a laundry list of severe health problems, the altercation would almost certainly not have been fatal. Even if Garner believed he was not guilty of any crime, common sense and the New York State penal law required him to obey the officers and argue his case later.

The legitimate debate in the Garner case, as in many others, is whether the police department's strategy for cleaning up Bay Street was wise or whether New York City's government should have created the black market for cigarettes by enacting massive local taxes, thereby making the product unaffordable for its many poor consumers. A sign posted at the street memorial for Garner read "Stop the war on poor people." What are police to do? Ignore the hundreds of 911 calls from citizens? Simply walk away when confronted with suspected offenders who are morbidly obese and defiant?

A police officer standing on the sidewalk and in that confrontation is frightened and on stage in front of dozens of onlookers—perhaps millions if anyone has a cell phone. The reputation of the police department is on the line and any show of weakness will encourage others to defy their authority in the future. Even a police officer who holds a negative bias toward black people does not have the time or ability to contemplate the race of his opponent; those two officers had no option available other than to arrest Garner, because he was *not* going to comply. They needed to somehow subdue him without getting crushed, getting disarmed, or falling through the plate glass window Garner was standing in front of—not to mention the very real possibility of a hostile member of the crowd attacking them with fists, knives, or firearms. When people are experiencing the physical and psychological effects of the fight-or-flight response, their ability to process higher-order thinking is severely impaired and they do not have time to contemplate their personal opinions and preferences—racial or otherwise.

Watching the video, it's clear that Eric Garner died because he fought with police and because of his physical condition and ailments. The arriving EMTs also failed to take any swift action to aid Garner, to restore his respiration, or provide him with oxygen. He should not have died as a result of the mere scuffle, and he certainly should not have died over selling loosies. Those who portray Garner's death as indicative of police brutality and racism are seeing what they want to see. The term Garner kept repeating was *harassment*, believing the police had no right to interfere with the illegal cigarette and drug sales in the area. For whatever reason, Garner seemed to believe that the police had no legitimate authority to enforce such laws against him.

The Garner case is particularly instructive because of all the real issues. The officers present that day had no intention of killing or even injuring Garner. The argument rather should be about whether they should have been there in the first place or arresting him at all—but they had no option at that moment in time. That question is far above the pay grade of the two hapless officers faced with the raging Garner on that tragic summer afternoon. Could the officers have used pepper spray or a Taser if they were so equipped? Yes, but people in Garner's condition can easily die from the use of either of those methods as well. But the notion that if Garner had white skin the officers would have simply wished him a pleasant afternoon and driven away is absurd.

Freddie Gray was a Baltimore resident with a long rap sheet of mostly drug offenses. A black male living in a black neighborhood, he found himself on a street corner around 8:30 in the morning on April 12, 2015, after having attempted to get breakfast at a takeout joint that was closed. He was not engaged in any criminal activity and was carrying only a small folding knife. Nevertheless, upon the approach of police officers, he ran away. The police then gave chase, assuming he must be up to no good if he was fleeing. He was caught, arrested, and placed into the rear of a police transport van.[8] Gray rode in the van for a total of 30 minutes as the van made four more stops before arriving at the police station. The police there found him comatose in the back of the van and immediately called for an ambulance, and Gray would die shortly thereafter due to his spinal cord having been 80 percent severed at his neck.[9] Despite a department policy to seat belt prisoners in transport, neither Gray nor most other prisoners were belted when being hauled away in transport vans. It is apparent that Gray suffered his fatal injury while riding in the back of the van, either by intentionally running into the walls or by falling after standing up—he had been loaded into the van on the floor in a prone position. The state's attorney, Marilyn Mosby, also an African American, filed murder charges against the van's driver and manslaughter charges against two of his supervisors and another patrolman and charged two officers with felony assault, along with a host of lesser charges for all six policemen indicted. There was no indication of any intent on the part of the police to injure, let alone kill, Gray, yet Mosby pressed ahead with her prosecution.

Mosby lost the first and strongest case against the driver of the van and was caught withholding evidence; she tried to hide a statement from a passenger on the other side of the divided van who testified that he heard repeated banging coming from Gray's side. Mosby refused to back down after the failure of her first case and put two more police officers on trial. After both of those officers were found not guilty, she finally dropped the charges against the remaining three cops. A disbarment complaint is currently pending against her at the Maryland Attorney Grievance Commission, charging her with misconduct in the matter.[10]

The national media and rioters in Baltimore portrayed this case as an example of police targeting blacks for death and police racism. What is fascinating is that the Baltimore Police Department has a majority of minority officers, and three of the officers charged were black, as was the presiding judge, the defense attorney, and the prosecutor. Riots tore the City of Baltimore apart—fanned by the city's African American mayor, Stephanie Rawlings-Blake, who "gave those who wish to destroy a space to do that."[11]

Again, the Freddy Gray case could be instructive if leaders would look at the real cause of the problem—which is not racism. As in the case of Eric Garner, the question is why the city police were driving around looking for someone to arrest on a trumped-up charge of having a folding knife. The answer, ironically, is the initiative created by none other than the state's attorney Marilyn Mosby. According to the *Baltimore Sun*, the officers were there because "they were part of a daily narcotics initiative" as a result of a request from Mosby's office to a Western District commander to target that corner for "enhanced" attention. That translated into orders from the commander to officers—including Lieutenant Brian Rice, the highest-ranking officer who faced charges after Gray's death—to produce "daily measurables." This goes to the heart of the problem in policing: trying to find a way to measure productivity and results too often is reduced down to a numbers game and leads to officers to making questionable arrests to meet the demand for numbers from their supervisors.

Whether or not any police use of force is truly motivated by racism, even the perception that police are abusive toward any particular constituency should be cause for concern for police administrators, as it can rapidly erode the perception of the police as legitimate authority figures. The issue of race in America has become so toxic that people in the public eye tend to avoid it at all costs. For more than two decades, the issues of racial profiling and differential treatment of minorities have dominated headlines concerning police conduct. Separating fact from myth and political hyperbole requires a strong constitution and a hard look at data. Further complicating the issue is the extent to which factors outside the control of police agencies affect the data and the perceptions of community members. Because of the racial environment in the country, generally, any perceived abuses of African Americans by the police tend to take on exaggerated meaning as a symbol of real or perceived racial discrimination.

Are there police officers who are racist? Of course there are; police are human beings, and humans are prone to a very long list of failings and character flaws. Police are also made up of 700,000 individuals drawn from every region, socioeconomic background, ethnicity, and religion in the country, working at anywhere from 16,000 to 18,000 different agencies. The idea that they are a monolithic group who all share the trait of bias or racism against blacks has no basis in fact. Still, pseudoscience that presents disparities in numbers and percentages as proof of causation is rampant.

The issue of racial bias in policing is plagued with political agendas and bad science. A 1998 report on police brutality and accountability in the United States by Human Rights Watch stated in its summary: "Race continues to play a central role in police brutality in the United States. . . . One area that has been stubbornly resistant to change has been the treatment afforded racial minorities by the police."[12] But what does this really mean? The summary goes on to cite as "evidence" the fact that racial minorities allege police abuse far more often than whites and in larger proportion to their presence in the population. While this is certainly a good reason for inquiry, it does not serve as a basis for any reasoned conclusion whatsoever.

The *Washington Post* compiled a listing of all fatal police shootings for the year 2015.[13] They noted that unarmed black males made up less than 4 percent of fatal police shootings and then attempted to imply a racial bias by noting that, although black males make up only 6 percent of the population, they accounted for 40 percent of unarmed men shot by police. But a simple comparison of percentages does not constitute a study into the causes. The *Post* stated in another article that black Americans were 2.5 times as likely to be shot by police as white Americans. This is the worst sort of simplistic reasoning; it assumes that shootings should be evenly distributed across the entire population and implies that police prefer to shoot blacks. In the real world, very few things are randomly distributed across groups. Some groups are more prone to heart disease than others, and the same goes for high blood pressure, eye color, hair color, car crashes, and crime.

To illustrate the folly of simply comparing the percentage of population to the percentage of people shot by police, let us compare the number of something that *truly* is a random occurrence: being struck by lightning. Yet, between 1995 and 2000, 89 percent of people killed by lightning were white, while only 8 percent were black.[14] Yet, the *Washington Post* has never published a story decrying the irrefutable fact that whites are 11 times more likely to be killed by lightning than blacks or what "institutional" problems there are that result in such a "disparate impact" of lightning within the "white community." A researcher or an intelligent reporter would look deeper before claiming that lightning has a racial bias. Just a little casual analysis shows that many people killed by lightning are engaged in occupations more likely to be performed by whites and that many lightning strikes occur in the Midwest, where the black population is low.[15]

Another example: the U.S. population is 49 percent male and yet 97 percent of the people shot dead by police officers are men. To put this in the terms used by the *Washington Post*, men are 23 times more likely to be killed by police than women; yet absolutely no one accuses the police of being sexist because of this massive disparity in killing. Why not?

One more example: Americans aged 70 and over make up 9 percent of the population, yet they account for 0.7 percent of those killed by police, while citizens between 30 and 44 years of age are 20 percent of the population but account for 41 percent of people shot by police. Are the police biased in favor of the elderly and against those of younger age?

When you compare the numbers of any demographic in the entire population of Americans against the number of that group who get shot by police, you will almost always come up with numbers out of proportion to one another. When you use age, or gender, as the variable, you get ridiculous results that are not taken seriously; you were certainly thinking, "Of course the elderly are less likely to be shot by police" and "Obviously men are more likely to be shot than women"; but why?

To sum up, here is the "science" that indicates police bias: using the data on police fatal use of force from the *Washington Post* for the year 2016, police nationwide killed 963 people, 233 (24.2 percent) of whom were black—and black Americans make up 13.3 percent of the population; therefore, *ipso facto* the police are racist and deliberately targeting black people for death. Were the police *not* racist, say Black Lives Matter and other critics, and if the police were acting appropriately, blacks would account for roughly 13 percent of all police shootings. Using the identical reasoning, Table 5.1 compares the proportion of different population

Table 5.1   Comparison of Those Shot by Police by Race, Age, and Sex

Race	Percentage of Population	Percentage of Police Shooting Deaths	Difference	"Conclusion"
Black	13	24	11	Black genocide/racist police
White	62	48	–14	Bias in favor of whites
Hispanic	18	17	–1	No Hispanic bias
Age				
Under 10	13	0	–13	Bias in favor of children
30–45	20	41	21	Bias against middle-aged people
70 and over	9	0.7	–8.3	Bias in favor of the elderly
Sex				
Male	49	96	47	Male genocide
Female	51	4	–47	Female-controlled society

groups with the percentage of police shootings that would be "appropriate" for each group versus the actual number.

One does not need to be a professional researcher to recognize that Table 5.1 represents junk science. Comparing the percentages in the population of blacks, women, cab drivers, welders, Asians, blondes, or schoolteachers to their numbers shot by police follows the same logic and would yield similar specious results.

Police officers do not fan out evenly across the country and randomly shoot people; if they did, we would expect that, statistically, people of all races, ages, genders, religions, hair color, eye color, and occupations would be killed in proportion to their numbers in the overall population—but that's not how police shootings occur. The language used by the media is extremely misleading and is based on the pseudoscience shown in Table 5.1. The *Chicago Tribune* headline "More Whites Killed by Police, but Blacks 2.5 Times More Likely to Be Killed" suggests that police killings should be random events. People of any color who obey officers, don't commit violent crimes, and who don't attack police are not at all *likely* to be killed. Police shoot people when they physically attack or threaten the officer, brandish a weapon, or attack a third party. People who engage in criminal behavior—in particular violent behavior—are the ones *likely* to get shot by police. So, in order to determine the distribution of fatal police shootings, we must examine *that* population. The best way to examine the rate at which police shoot whites versus blacks is to look at the population of those groups that are arrested for violent crimes.

Using data from the FBI of individuals arrested for violent crimes and weapons possession by race[16] and comparing those numbers with the numbers of people killed by police by race,[17] we find that whites are *more* likely to be shot by police during the course of an arrest than are blacks or Hispanics.

For every 10,000 arrests of blacks, 13 result in death for the suspect. For every 10,000 arrests of white suspects, 17 result in death—meaning that, among Americans who get arrested for serious crimes, whites are actually 25 percent *more likely than blacks to be killed by the police*.[18] If we examine just the numbers of unarmed persons from this population killed by police, blacks are 2 percent more likely to be the victim—a statistically insignificant difference.

Using the *Washington Post*'s database on police fatal shootings for 2016 and examining only subjects killed by police who were not armed with a weapon reveals that police killed 48 unarmed individuals, of whom 28 were white and 17 were black.

Despite the lack of evidence, Black Lives Matter claims that police are "engaged in ethnic cleansing" of blacks and asserts that " 'feared for my life' language is the new execution motto of America's largest gang, the police," and "the police are killing people. Officer Friendly is akin to the myth of the American Dream—seductive, but a deadly illusion nonetheless."[19] The reality is that if you can fit the names of all the unarmed black men who have died by police actions over the span of two years on a single protest placard, it's not genocide.

Police across the country, on average, shoot less than 1,000 people every year, despite making 8.7 million arrests;[20] that's less than 1 shooting for every 8,700 arrests. Using a conservative estimate of 750,000 police officers nationwide, that's 1 officer in 750 killing a suspect. That is a vanishingly small number given the media portrayal of police as unaccountable, trigger-happy rogues, ravaging our neighborhoods, shooting first and asking questions later. Police nationwide kill fewer people in a year than the total murdered in just Chicago and Philadelphia in 2016.[21] In Chicago, where the police are under attack as racists, the police have killed fewer suspects in the past *six years*[22] than were gunned down in murders on the streets of Chicago in August 2016 alone—most of the victims were black citizens killed by other blacks.[23] African American males make up one half of all murder victims in the United States, and 93 percent of them are killed by other blacks.[24] Private citizens kill nearly a third as many people in self-defense as the police kill each year. Contrast the number of police shootings with the number of deaths caused by doctors in the United States. A study by Johns Hopkins University found that medical errors by doctors kill more than 250,000 Americans every year.[25]

This is not to say that police don't make mistakes or that sometimes officers shoot someone without any justification. In those instances, the officers must be dealt with severely and transparently. The shooting of Laquan McDonald by a Chicago police officer (discussed in Chapter 9) is a textbook example of how *not* to deal with a bad shooting and how to generate distrust among the public. By contrast, the April 2015 shooting of Walter Scott in North Charleston, South Carolina, resulted in the officer being quickly indicted on a charge of murder. The officer in that case shot the unarmed Scott in the back multiple times after he fled a traffic stop and the officer had attempted to use a Taser on Scott.

The real problem in police race relations lies elsewhere, in the general feeling of disenfranchisement in portions of the urban black community: failing schools, pervasive unemployment, crumbling neighborhoods, and rampant crime swirl in a growing downward vicious cycle in America's inner cities. When disaffected, frustrated individuals find themselves confronted by the police—especially when it seems unfair and unwarranted—they can explode. When that collective frustration is released in the wake of an event like the Michael Brown shooting in Ferguson or the Rodney King beating in Los Angeles, whole communities can explode. The police may play only a small role in the larger picture of urban misery, but they are the face of the law, of the system that disaffected people feel is unfairly rigged against them.

Despite the fact that much of the criticism leveled against them is unwarranted, police leaders must address the perception that officers treat African Americans unfairly, and when officers do use unnecessary force, they must be held to account. Police tactics that result in hundreds or thousands of arrests for petty or trumped-up offenses give all the reason frustrated people need to blame them for all the ills in a community. Police fanning out across a community with marching orders to come in with "numbers" result in bad and even illegal arrests. In 2012, New York City settled a lawsuit for $15 million because its police officers had arrested 22,800 people for "loitering;" a statute ruled unconstitutional decades earlier.[26] This sort of police activity among a poor population unable to pay fines breeds anger and contempt.

Who *Is* Killing Black Citizens?

The popular Web site and magazine *Mother Jones* published an article shortly after the Michael Brown shooting entitled, "Here's the Data That Shows Cops Kill Black People at a Higher Rate than White People."[27] The article states, "The Justice Department's Bureau of Justice Statistics reports that between 2003 and 2009 there were more than 2,900 'arrest-related deaths' involving law enforcement. Averaged over seven years, that's about 420 deaths a year. While BJS does not provide the annual number of arrest-related deaths by race or ethnicity, a rough calculation based on its data shows that black people were about four times as likely to die in custody or while being arrested than whites."

Referring to the publication cited by the article,[28] one may find the annual number of arrest-related deaths by race or ethnicity in the chart on page 4, titled, "Number of Reported Arrest-Related Deaths, by Demographic Characteristics, 2003–2009."

The article then provides an authoritative-looking graph entitled "Estimated Rate of Arrest-Related Deaths by Homicide 2003–2009." The graph shows that blacks die at a supposed rate of 3.66 per million compared to only 0.9 for whites. The authors then explain that they came to this "scientific conclusion" by dividing all arrest-related deaths by the U.S.

Census population for each race. So the journalists at *Mother Jones* took all arrest-related deaths, which includes suspects who die from suicide, from intoxication, by accident, or by natural causes, and divided it by the total population. Not only did they use the wrong data, but they compared it to the wrong population. The population in question is black and white people who are *under arrest*, not how many live in the entire country or from every age group from infants to the elderly.

According to Department of Justice statistics, black citizens committed 52 percent of the murders in the United States in the decades between 1980 and 2008,[29] despite the fact that black males make up only around 6 percent of the population. The overwhelming number of victims in those murders were other black people—93 percent of black homicide victims were killed by other blacks.[30] According to an analysis by Professor Richard Johnson of the University of Toledo, police nationwide kill an average of 120 black males annually. There are more black males killed by civilians in justifiable homicides (self-defense) than are killed by the police; 162 black men are legally killed annually by private citizens— 73 percent of them by another black person.[31] That means that, on average, black citizens kill almost exactly the same number of black men in self-defense (118) as are killed by the police (120).

Black citizens are being killed at a rate out of proportion to their number in the population, but they are being killed overwhelmingly by other black citizens, *not* by the police. The supposed "genocide" taking place in black communities, which Black Lives Matter blames on the police, is actually being carried out by other black citizens. Not only are blacks disproportionally victims of homicide at the hands of other blacks but innocent black folks suffer the brunt of the violence and rampant drug abuse that is attendant in many poor inner-city communities. In Baltimore's Eastern District black ghetto alone, 1 in every 160 males aged 15–34 is murdered; *fully 10 percent of all men are murdered before the age of 35.*[32] They are murdered not by the police but by other young black men. The police who exist to protect those innocents often find themselves hated and feared by the very community members they are sworn to protect.

A major part of the problem, which has been pointed out by black leaders such as Professor Walter Williams and attorney and media personality Larry Elder, among many others, is the breakdown of the family, which is particularly prevalent within the black community. Illegitimate births of black children have gone from 14 percent in 1940 to a staggering 75 percent today,[33] and as former president Obama said, "We know the statistics—that children who grow up without a father are five times more likely to live in poverty and commit crime . . . and twenty times more likely to end up in prison."[34]

Unemployment has consistently been demonstrated as a factor in predicting criminality. Today's unemployment rate among black youth (ages 16–19) is nearly 400 percent higher than the national rate.[35] These and many other social issues are, of course, a subject for other books, but there can be no doubt that the disappearance of the nuclear family and the rampant disorder in so many urban black communities have much to do with the increased rates of arrest and clashes with police among the young black men who were born into a social structure with such pathologies.

The police cannot fix social problems, but they must be educated about them, and they must consistently drive home the message to the good people of *all* communities that they are there to help and to protect the innocent from the lawless. Police need to remember and also to remind those in the neighborhoods they patrol that the police cannot carry out their mission without the support and cooperation of the community at large.

Profiling, Prejudice, and Policing

Police officers' brains function just like everyone else's, and they too create heuristic models to guide and protect themselves. They deal with the worst elements in society; and even when they deal with the best sort of people, those people are often at their worst—angry, frightened, terrified, injured, sick, mentally ill, or desperate. Cops quickly learn that certain age groups and types of dress, gestures, body language, eye movements, and behaviors indicate potential danger or that criminal activity is afoot. This is how policing is done.

While, as we have discussed, prejudice cannot be eliminated, it must be set aside by police officers when making critical decisions that involve inherent fairness and matters of honor and in the use of force. The term *racial profiling* has been in use for more than two decades and is essentially interchangeable with *prejudice* or *racism* in its application to the police. In common usage, the term refers to police officers basing their decisions to stop and question individuals based solely on their racial appearance, that is, a racist white cop who thinks all blacks are criminals and drives around looking for black people to pull over or hassle as they walk down the street. This of course is not only unacceptable behavior but terrible police work; cops who cannot use their knowledge and experience to identify *truly* suspicious individuals are going to waste nearly all of their time stopping and questioning citizens who have done nothing wrong and thus make very few good arrests. The real difficulty with this issue is the fact that *all police work involves profiling*. One does not need to be a trained or experienced police officer to grasp this fact.

Suppose you learn that your neighbor and many other people on your road in a very rural area had their mailboxes smashed overnight. If you were asked to figure out who did it out of all the tens of thousands of possible suspects, you would have to use a heuristic or create a *profile* of the perpetrator(s) to begin to narrow it down. Who would want to bash in random people's mailboxes? Who comes to mind? Bored, elderly people looking to spice things up with some late-night vandalism? Businessmen who got a little too drunk at happy hour and decided to drive down the road and play mailbox baseball with one of the golf clubs in the trunk of their BMW? Black kids from the housing project 12 miles away in town? Not likely. You probably would, without consciously thinking about it, rapidly create a profile of someone young, male, probably in his teens, white, with access to a car, and who owns a baseball bat. Could black businessmen or Asian old folks have perpetrated the deed? Of course, but in the absence of any reliable information, you would be a poor cop if you began your search for suspects at the retirement center rather than talking with local high school kids. Likewise, the FBI has a unit entirely dedicated to profiling serial killers based upon the types of victims they choose and the methods they employ to stalk and kill their victims. Since virtually all serial killers are white and male, this profiling unit never has generated any controversy.

Most of the research done on racial profiling has been seriously flawed or incomplete. Lazy researchers or those with a political agenda would like to believe that unfair treatment can be proven by doing nothing more than counting the numbers of black citizens and comparing this number to the number of police stops that involve blacks. This simplistic approach leaves out a host of other factors, including the objective number of blacks engaging in legitimately suspicious behavior and how many black citizens are in areas where the police are focused due to high levels of crime.

Researchers in the United Kingdom conducted a study that attempted to control for some of the variables to get a more realistic picture of any disparity in police stops based solely on race. In a report prepared for the British Home Office, researchers noted that previous studies based on nothing more than analysis of numbers of minorities versus stops showed a higher number of stops and searches for blacks compared to whites. They posited three potential explanations for such disparity:

- Officers had an ethnic bias with regard to whom they stop and search.
- Stops and searches were targeted in areas where there were large numbers of minorities.
- The population of people available for stops included a larger proportion of minority citizens.

The researchers in the study used CCTV cameras and observers on the ground to calculate the numbers of minority persons *available* to be stopped compared with their overall numbers in the community. The findings suggested that "quite clearly, measures of resident population give a poor indication of the population actually available to be stopped or searched. The available populations in the five sites [of the study] were quite different from the resident populations of the areas. Most significantly . . . young men and people from ethnic minority backgrounds tended to be over-represented in the available population."[36]

Researchers also concluded that comparing areas with high concentrations of searches to the crime rate in the area "suggested a high degree of consistency between the two." This seeming vindication for the police "suggest[s] that disproportionality is, to some extent, a product of structural factors beyond their control." The researchers wisely cautioned, however:

> Yet, if the police continue to stop and search those from minority ethnic backgrounds more often than their white counterparts, they can still expect this to impact negatively on level of confidence among these groups. That means that police forces must redouble their efforts to minimize the bad feelings that stops and searches cause, particularly among those from minority ethnic groups.[37]

American researchers at the University of Cincinnati and Pennsylvania State University examined 13 well-known studies of racial profiling and found that they failed to establish a proper base rate for expected numbers of stops and relied on simplistic number comparisons. These researchers criticized the lack of any coherent theoretical model for the collection and analysis of data and that racial profiling research "diverges from almost all other research on policing conducted in the past 30 years, which has focused on explaining police behavior. . . . Efforts to examine racial profiling have neglected the need to examine how and why officers make decisions."[38]

Another aggravating factor in relations with minority communities is the segregated nature of American cities. The areas where the poor and working poor live are usually divided into loosely defined black, white, or Hispanic areas. There are middle and working class neighborhoods, which are only slightly more integrated, and then there are the wealthy neighborhoods that tend to be fully integrated but mostly white. It is a reality that as people descend on the socioeconomic ladder, the more likely they are to come into contact with the police, either because they are statistically more prone to committing a crime or because of the general disorder in their neighborhood. If the cops drive around a black neighborhood and stop and frisk a bunch of young men with saggy pants and surly expressions, those on the receiving end will often assume it's because they are black. Because we live in such a segregated society, they don't see the police in a nearby poor white neighborhood doing the same thing to a group of similarly attired young Caucasian men. This is notwithstanding the legality or propriety of the officers' actions.

Poverty is greater predictor of run-ins with the police than is race or ethnicity. With the pseudoscience that abounds in discussions of police bias, there is always the proverbial "blacks make up 13 percent of the population, but account for a disproportionate number of. . . ." What is rarely mentioned is the higher violent-crime rate among African Americans and what is *never* mentioned is the higher poverty rate in that same population. Black Americans are more than 2.5 times as likely as a white person to be poor.[39]

Clearly, when it comes to racial disparities—or any other type of unfairness by police—it is perception that matters more than reality, and it is incumbent of police leadership to recognize and address this fact. Moreover, while there may be no hard evidence that police in general are racially biased, there is anecdotal evidence demonstrating that at least some officers are racially biased; and one racist police officer can cause a great deal of damage to community relationships. It takes only one or two cops who drive around and pull over every black man they see driving a nice car or roust a black citizen merely walking down the street to poison the attitudes of hundreds of people, the family, friends, and associates of the affected black man. Worse still, if the incident is captured on video, it may be seen by tens of thousands.

A Legacy of Distrust

While the police are far from solely responsible for the state of race relations in the country as a whole, their tactics can play a part—and can play a significant role in isolated jurisdictions. In the Deep South, Jim Crow laws codified the state governments' unofficial policy of keeping blacks segregated from whites, keeping black citizens subordinate to whites in all public settings, and preventing black participation in the legal system or government. As such, it fell to the police to enforce these laws and social norms.

While the consciousness of whites and blacks alike was turning toward such injustices, occasional cases would bring national attention to the lack of justice for blacks in the states of the old Confederacy. In 1931, nine teenage black boys were arrested in Scottsboro, Alabama, after a fight broke out between them and some white youths who were also riding the rails as hobos looking for work. The local police pressured two women who were riding on the train as passengers to claim that the black men raped them. Within 15 days, all 9 boys had been indicted and tried and 8 were sentenced to death, with the youngest (age 13) escaping the death penalty because one juror voted against the death penalty.[40] The incredible injustice of the boys' case drew wide attention to their plight.

Following the intervention of groups, including the NAACP and the Communist Party USA, the death sentences were stayed and a years-long odyssey of trials and prison began. Despite the obvious frame-up of the teens, they were convicted again and again by all-white juries, even after the U.S. Supreme Court overturned convictions for new trials. By 1937, the State of Alabama finally dropped charges against four of the boys, who had spent the past six years in prison, but the other five were sentenced to varying prison terms, eventually being paroled in the late 1940s and 1950s. The disgraceful saga of the Scottsboro Boys was the first case to bring widespread attention to the treatment of black citizens by police officials and the judicial system in the southern states.

The murder of a young man from Chicago in Money, Mississippi, in 1955 would become one of the seminal events in sparking the civil rights movement. Fourteen-year-old Emmitt Till was in Mississippi visiting relatives, when he had the misfortune of entering Bryant's Grocery Store and flirting with the white woman working the cash register. A few minutes later, when the woman exited the store, the brash young Emmitt made a "wolf-whistle" at her. Later that night, as punishment for paying sexual attention to a white female, the woman's husband and his half-brother kidnapped, savagely beat, and murdered Emmitt and then dumped his mutilated body into a river with a heavy industrial fan tied around his neck with barbed wire.[41] Despite the fact that the local sheriff had arranged for two key black witnesses to be held in jail on false charges in another town, the case against the two killers was open and shut. Nevertheless, the all-white jury waited only 68 minutes to return a not-guilty verdict; the sheriff had told them to wait some time "to make it look

good." The two murderers later sold the story of the crime to *Look* magazine for $3,500.[42] Emmitt Till's mother returned to Chicago with the body
of her son and insisted upon an open casket for his funeral, later saying,
"I wanted the world to see what they did to my baby."[43]

The U.S. Civil Rights Commission report in 1961 found that, while
police behavior in general had improved since the Wickersham era,
police brutality was still a problem in certain areas, especially the south.
The commission stated that the incidents of police violence fell into
four categories: enforcement of subordination or segregation; violence as
punishment; coerced confessions; casual violence as part of arrest. The
report chronicled numerous instances of police violence against blacks
in each category, as well as officers in the south standing idly by while
Klansmen and others carried out violence and even murder against
black citizens.[44]

Today, for so-called white Americans, including police, the perspective
of some African Americans is very difficult to grasp. With the exception
of a tiny minority of extreme racists, white people do not view themselves
as a group or "community." As a white male myself, I do not see other
whites on the street or the media and feel any kinship or shared experience or have reason to feel we have anything in common. Moreover, most
of "us" white people grew up after the civil rights movement in a society
where racism and bias are socially unacceptable.

The result is that nonblack Americans are often bewildered by claims
of widespread and "institutionalized" racism. They live their lives and
never witness obvious racism where they live and work and harbor no
racial bigotry themselves. They are offended by terms such as *white privilege*, especially when they can't afford to attend college or are barely able
to scrape by working at a low-wage job. The perspective is necessarily
different for black Americans who are not only in the minority but are set
apart by the pigment of their skin. While many blacks citizens have never
been a victim of overt racism and have also grown up since the civil rights
movement, the culture of the memory of discrimination and segregation
remains.

Some of the first organized police forces in the country were formed to
work exclusively as *slave patrols*, ensuring slaves on business for the master had proper documentation and being on the lookout for runaways.
From the post-Reconstruction era through the 1960s, police in the south
were charged with enforcing segregation laws and were in some places
were little more than an adjunct to the local Ku Klux Klan. While the
memories of Bull Connor, clubs, water cannons, church bombings, and
political murders from the civil rights movement are ancient history to

young whites, they seem somewhat less distant for their black compatriots.

What Can the Police Do?

Part of the problem for police is that, while they are supposed to be unbiased and treat all citizens fairly and equally, they nonetheless are the embodiment of the laws of the state and the state government. The government is almost by definition controlled and staffed by the powerful and privileged. It is the individuals or groups that are disenfranchised or prone to disorder that tend toward violent criminality. The result is that the police everywhere tend to spend the majority of their time dealing with individuals at the low end of the socioeconomic ladder. This is the case for a number of reasons.

Historically, low-status individuals and the poor are more prone to engage in the sort of behavior that draws police response: disorderly conduct, petty theft, assault, robbery, and open-air drug sale and use.[45] People in these circumstances are also more likely to lead chaotic lives,[46] necessitating police intervention to resolve conflicts in their personal lives or with their neighbors; middle and upper class people have "reputations" to maintain and would be embarrassed by the presence of police because they had a dispute with their spouse or neighbor, whereas in poor communities, a police response is a commonplace occurrence. So when poor people live in clusters based upon their race, the police will have much more contact with these communities, for example, poor black and Latino neighborhoods in urban areas. This same pattern holds true when there are virtually no minority individuals present; in all-white areas, the police still spend the majority of their time dealing with calls from poor whites, who are just as likely to engage in crime and call the police to referee disputes as are poor people of any other color. A far larger problem than police racial bias is the simple fact that poor communities are going to deal with the police most often, and when those communities are majority black or Latino, that interaction is going to have racial overtones where the officers are mainly white. There is little doubt that a nearly all-black sheriff's department would be viewed as racist by the criminal element in a poor, run-down trailer park inhabited entirely by white people. The problem is one of social class and income more than race; the disenfranchised—whether in that condition through their own fault or not—will always look for someone or something to blame and then direct their anger toward the perceived oppressor. In poor inner-city neighborhoods, of any color, it is police who get the blame; it is the police who arrest their family members who wind up in jail, and it is the police who work for the "system" that has seemingly left them behind. In poor rural areas, the police may be distrusted, but other scapegoats are found for the misery: big business, Jews, the wealthy, or the new world order conspiracy theories.

And so here we all are in America today; and the police are charged with protecting the liberties of all citizens, without fear or favor, and stand in that small, uncomfortable space where government meets the people. Police need to be aware of the nature and history of the communities they represent; they should be familiar with the demographics, languages, customs, and history of the people they serve. No matter how well intentioned, a white middle class officer hitting the streets as a rookie is going to find it nearly impossible to understand the mindset of a 14-year-old black or Hispanic gang member, especially when his or her only contact with these individuals is under confrontational or violent circumstances.

Police need to receive some minimal education in the characteristics and history of the communities they serve. They should be introduced to the culture and living conditions of varying ethnicities and socioeconomic groups before going out into the field; this is not so they can "feel sorry" for criminals because they may be poor or otherwise disadvantaged, as critics might contend, but rather so that they can better understand and communicate with people in general. Good police officers are fluent in intelligent discourse, basic legal language, and the vernacular of the street and can effectively converse with the diverse groups they work with on a daily basis.

As was recommended by the Kerner Commission and again most recently by Obama's Task Force on 21st Century Policing, community events should be attended and hosted by police agencies. These types of events allow the public and the police to see each other under circumstances other than times of confrontation, emergency, and tragedy; they allow the community to see police officers as people and fellow citizens and for the police to see neighborhood residents the same way, rather than as an amorphous group of people with nothing but endless problems and contempt for the law.

To encourage minorities to seek careers in policing, programs should be made available for young people to ride along with officers on patrol and to tour or work in police facilities. Such programs could also humanize the men and women in the police and hopefully create an interest in policing for young people before they are old enough to form negative opinions about police officers. This could help serve to improve the effectiveness of minority recruiting in the future.

Police leaders must seek out respected leaders in ethnic communities and begin to build—or rebuild—trust from the top down. The goals of the police are generally aligned with those of the community. People everywhere want to be free from violence and other forms of crime and to raise their children in safety and security. If the police can communicate the message that they are there to help improve the lives of residents and adjust their tactics, there may be ways to find common ground and gain the trust and cooperation of the citizenry.

What the Police Can't Do

There are many things police departments can and should do to improve race relations with the communities they serve. But, just as police need to learn about the perspectives of their fellow citizens, it is incumbent upon local community leaders and parents to teach respect—for police officers and *all* their fellow citizens. Police leaders can take steps to educate the public about the perspectives of the police officer on patrol, but the public has to listen and participate in order for there to be a dialogue and any progress made.

Police leaders cannot change the media narrative of the nation's police officers as agents of an anti-black genocide. Despite the vanishingly small chances of any black person being killed by a police officer, the *Washington Post* still ran a story with the headline "Unarmed and Black—A Year after Michael Brown's Fatal Shooting, Unarmed Black Men Are Seven Times More Likely Than Whites to Die by Police Gunfire."[47] *Vanity Fair* ran a story in July 2016 listing 16 studies or analyses that claim racial bias or disparities against blacks while listing only 2 that indicate no bias, despite the existence of numerous academic studies showing no police bias. They failed to mention a study released that same month by Harvard economics professor Roland G. Fryer, Jr., an African American, that clearly demonstrated no racial bias in police shootings.[48] Also left out was a Washington State University study showing that officers are in fact three times *less likely* to shoot unarmed blacks compared to whites.[49] Moreover, a close reading of the allegedly authoritative analyses in the story shows that a Black Lives Matter–affiliated group produced one of the reports, and some others were nothing more than comparisons of black population to vehicle stops—the same pseudo-analysis discussed earlier.

Police departments and police officers can control their training, rules, tactics, and demeanor, but they cannot change the laws, the nature of their local politicians, government policy, or the socioeconomic conditions that foster criminality. They cannot address the problem of

out-of-wedlock births or a society that breeds sociopaths who think nothing of spraying automatic gunfire in a crowded neighborhood. Since it is
impossible to prove a negative, police also cannot prove they aren't racist,
although I have yet to see a video of a police officer stepping in to stop his
fellow officers from using force by saying, "Stop! This guy is white!"

Police have little to no influence over morally bankrupt governments
that use the law as a means to increase their revenue on the backs of the
poor and the middle class. Local municipalities that criminalize all sorts
of behavior and impose obscene fines generate intense resentment toward
the police that are dispatched to enforce such laws. Arrest is not an appropriate way to increase government revenue, nor is it always the best way
to deal with disorder. The way to clean up a public park is not to issue a
summons to a young unemployed man who laid down on a park bench
because he had no place to sleep for the night. This accomplishes nothing
but imposing upon him a fine he can't pay and leads to his eventual incar-
ceration for failing to make payment. Such actions waste money, clog up
the judiciary, and create bitterness and anger. For the officer on the beat,
there is not much he or she can do when directives filter down from the
politicians, through administrators, and then supervisors, that ultimately
translate into demands for "numbers."

The police have no control over the rest of the justice system. They
cannot change the corrupt system of plea bargaining, where prosecutors
coerce the innocent into guilty pleas under threats of endless pretrial
detention or decades-long prison sentences for the crime of demanding
their day in court. Police leaders cannot control the judges who hand
down the sentences or the range and type of penalties that are available.
The police cannot change the nature of the so-called correctional system,
which does nothing to rehabilitate offenders but merely warehouses them
in bleak, violent, terrifying cesspools, where they learn nothing but bitterness and brutality.

The police cannot change the past—not the slavery of a century and a
half ago, not the era of KKK terrorism, nor lynchings, segregation, Jim
Crow, or Bull Connor's attack dogs and fire hoses. But they can educate
themselves about the past and the perspectives of their fellow citizens.
They can reach out and demonstrate that they understand and exhibit
friendly, firm, fair, professional behavior at all times, to inspire respect
and trust among those they have sworn to serve.

Police leaders cannot change the political and racial climate of the
nation. In order for Americans to begin to move past the issue of race,
we must begin to acknowledge the fraudulent nature of the very concept. We must also reject those who attempt to divide America into

competing groups. The multiculturalism movement, while generally well intentioned, has served to divide and embitter Americans. Constant attention to our differences—"diversity"—can only weaken the bonds of society. Our focus as a people should be on the values we share in *common*, our civic values of freedom and hard work and our shared tenets of family and personal responsibility. Ultimately, the problem of race relations in America is a political and societal issue far larger than our police institutions. However, given that our police are in the physical space where politics and government interface with individuals, they can begin to have a positive influence by making changes in the manner in which they conduct themselves and the way they handle those officers who demonstrate bias or engage in misconduct. *The police* do not exist as a monolithic group; they are comprised of thousands upon thousands of agencies spread across the breadth of the continent. There is no evidence to support the notion that "they" are racists. There is evidence to suggest that the tactics of some agencies have exacerbated racial tensions or have had a negative impact on poor communities. The police need to do a better job both in community outreach and in making sure their efforts to combat crime do not result in unintended negative consequences. Ethnic and community leaders, in turn, must do their part to acknowledge the role played by social problems in many communities and to make a good-faith effort to make common cause with police in the shared goal of making all neighborhoods a place where Americans can enjoy the blessings of liberty.

CHAPTER SIX

The Police as the Face of the Law

Your main job as a cop on the beat is not to make a lot of arrests, but to help prevent crime. The best way to do this is to start with the children. Make friends with them. Guide them towards law-abiding citizenship. Show them that the law is their friend not their enemy.
—August "Gus" Vollmer, Chief Berkeley, California Police, 1905–1931

As previously pointed out, the police occupy the space where the laws of the state intersect with the citizenry. While in free societies the police are staffed by ordinary citizens, in the aggregate they are the face of the state and its laws. If the state becomes overweening, invasive, capricious, unpredictable, and unfair, then its police will be so by default.

No matter how fair minded an individual officer might be, he or she is still expected to enforce the laws of the state. An officer arresting or ticketing someone in a polite, professional manner will many times still be resented if the underlying law is deemed unfair. When large segments of society feel disenfranchised and powerless, they begin to view the state, or, more vaguely, *the system*, as fundamentally unfair and therefore illegitimate. It then follows logically that they will view the state's enforcers—the police—in the same light.

While issues of race and class, state power, and legitimacy are tremendously complex and outside the scope of this book, they are nonetheless integral to any discussion about police-community relations. Police agencies can make every effort to be fair, compassionate, and professional, but if the community they serve views the entire underlying system the police support as corrupt and illegitimate, relations will inevitably break down.

No police force anywhere can maintain good relationships with its communities while enforcing the laws of a system the citizens view as unfair and corrupt.

The police are paid to keep the peace in their community and to enforce the laws of the state. With so many hundreds of laws—from state criminal laws, vehicle and traffic laws, and local ordinances—it is very likely that anyone could be in violation of some law on any given day. Like every other person who earns a paycheck, police officers are expected to do work. Police work is notoriously difficult to evaluate because of its varied nature and the fact that police do not create products and generally work alone. Police managers must therefore rely on other metrics to judge the officer's performance.

A good police officer is skilled at listening as well as verbal and written communication. He or she also should possess the traits of humility, courage, integrity, empathy, equanimity, self-confidence, good humor, perceptiveness, and curiosity. The problem for police administrators is how to measure these qualities. The short answer is, you can't. The only objective way to measure police performance is through things that can be quantified: arrests and tickets, or what is inaccurately referred to as *productivity*. Police, of course, do not produce anything—they perform a service, and sometimes that service involves arresting a violent criminal. As one would expect, frequently, such "customers" are not happy with the service they received.

Likewise, how are we to determine if the police force as a whole is doing a good job? How are we to objectively measure the performance of a police department? Numbers of arrests? Crime rate? Numbers of complaints against officers? Public opinion surveys? Police, despite efforts at being proactive, are generally a reactive agency; they come when called to settle disputes, solve a crime, or fix a problem that has already occurred. Because they are bound by the laws, are required to remain neutral, and frequently cannot solve crimes or secure a conviction, many people will be unsatisfied with the outcome of their interaction with the police.

If you call the police because your neighbor is blowing his leaves on your lawn just to make you angry, and the officer arrives and informs you that the laws of the state do not provide for making an arrest for such behavior and that you must sue your neighbor in civil court, you will likely be very dissatisfied. You might blame the officer for being lazy or ignorant or the police in general for being useless.

Unlike service workers at restaurants, hotels, or city sanitation, the police officer cannot simply serve the wishes of the customer. If a customer orders a medium-rare steak, asks for an extra pillow, or pays for trash pickup on a given day, the provider is expected to deliver as requested and in a timely manner. A police officer's customer, on the other hand, may be a drunken woman who wants her husband thrown out of their house for his infidelity. When the officer arrives, she discovers that the wife has slashed her husband's arm with a razor blade, and he has not broken any laws—notwithstanding his alleged infidelity. In this case, not only will the customer not receive the service requested but will wind up in handcuffs charged with a felony crime.

Despite the existence of so many statutes, the law simply cannot address all of the infinite combinations of circumstances that attend human interaction in our society. The laws are intended to provide a framework for free people to live in and limiting each person's liberty to the sphere where it does not infringe upon his or her neighbor's. The law and the government agencies that enforce it are generally geared toward significant or clearly defined offenses: murder, rape, theft, and the like. Some laws attempt to address public nuisances such as disorderly conduct or public intoxication, and while these can be somewhat subjective, they are usually a case of "you know it when you see it."

In our case of the guy blowing leaves onto his neighbor's lawn, trying to use the law to resolve the matter is like trying to use a sledgehammer to adjust a thermostat. Depending on your background and value system, you might think that such an action more than warrants a punch in the mouth—or maybe two. This would of course be a violation of law, resulting in the arrest of the initially aggrieved party—a seemingly very unfair outcome. Yet, if the complainant refrains from attacking his obnoxious neighbor and calls the police, he will be told there is nothing the police can do. This of course is where the police need to use their skills to resolve the matter outside of a legal framework. A good police officer will talk to both parties and try to discover any underlying disputes or grievances that have caused the conflict. The officer will try to make the leaf-blowing perpetrator stop antagonizing his neighbor while expressing empathy with whatever justification he thinks he has for his actions. The officer will also make sure the complainant understands what other legal avenues may be open to him, perhaps suggest erecting a fence or trying to work out the hurt feelings of a long-ago slight that began the neighbor feud. If successful, the officer will, at a minimum, have prevented the situation from escalating to an assault or worse. At best, the entire situation may have been attenuated to the point where relations will improve, making the lives of those involved and those of their immediate neighbors a little bit better. The time the officer spends to resolve the situation is time he can't spend writing summonses or tickets. Also of note is that his carefully conducted resolution of the problem, the elimination of further calls to 911, and the improved lives and neighborhood atmosphere he leaves behind will, in all likelihood, go completely unnoticed by his supervisors.

What Exactly *Are* the Police Supposed to Do?

The police are such a ubiquitous presence in society and in media and entertainment we tend to take them for granted and believe we know what their purpose is. However, it is a question that few people have ever addressed. Most people would agree that the police exist to come when called to investigate a reported crime, traffic accident, or some other hazard or nuisance. But the question gets tougher when you ask if the police are supposed to prevent or reduce crime. Most people may still agree but not know exactly how they should go about it, other than driving around and being otherwise visible.

Residents of a given community generally expect the police to pursue lawbreakers who burglarize their homes, steal their property, rob them in the street, and vandalize community property. However, if the police begin aggressive enforcement in an area where crime is prevalent, their tactics can easily be perceived as harassment—especially if the officers are not skilled in communication or are indiscriminate with people they single out for stops or questioning. If the police are supposed to prevent crime, they will not only need to be proactive but will need to involve themselves in nontraditional ways, by advising property owners and city agencies on the ways to make the spaces they control safer and less friendly to criminal operators.

Police would have to expand the use of so-called neighborhood watch programs and offer classes on how to protect oneself and property from criminals. Being proactive means gathering information on criminals and criminal activity in the area, pinpointing and targeting areas where crime is prevalent, and approaching and questioning those who appear suspicious. This entails gathering intelligence, talking with local residents, and targeting those who can reasonably be suspected of criminality. This all seems straightforward enough, but in communities where relations between the police and public are strained and mistrustful, such tactics can easily be perceived as intrusive at best and Gestapo-like at worst.

Police officers—especially those who work in high-crime areas—find themselves bewildered by the people they serve. The community demands "action" from the police to protect them and then condemns them as brutal, intrusive, and racist when they do act. The residents begin to feel that the community does not want to have police, and, in the face of repeated complaints, they begin to withdraw and take no action they aren't absolutely required to take, thus exacerbating the problem of crime and disorder. The community thinks the police don't care, and the police think they are hated and are in a no-win situation.

"Broken Systems"

In a speech at the University of North Carolina in December 2016, the head of the U.S. Justice Department's Civil Rights Division made a speech in which she painted the nation's police as engaged in systemic civil rights violations. While her characterization of police in general was mistaken and irresponsible, she acknowledged the important point that, while an incident involving the police may spark a violent protest, "we know that the true causes—the real reasons—for unrest run far deeper than any individual incident."[1] She spoke of "broken systems" involving not just the police but local government and courts that created resentment and outrage.

New York City instituted an aggressive sort of policing in the 1990s, which came to be known as *stop and frisk*. Combined with a zero-tolerance approach to minor offenses such as jaywalking and subway turnstile jumping, the police believed that these tactics were the reason for the drastic decline in the city's crime rate. Analysis of the crime rate in New York from 1990 to 2015, however, shows that crime was on a steep and steady decline before the NYPD began its more aggressive methods and was not affected by the policy.[2] Author Matt Taibbi described the actual effect of such a policy, when two African American men driving a Range Rover were stopped by the police in the Bronx.

Before they even had a chance to breathe, Michael and Anthony had their hands behind their backs, cuffed to the walls of the [police] van, headed for God knows where, for who knew what reason. Did the police say anything about why they'd picked you up? "You clearly don't know the New York City Police," says Anthony, "They don't be asking you anything." [As] the van screamed all over the Bronx . . . they worked out the method: an undercover policeman on the ground somewhere would stand on a street corner, wander over to a group of people, then walk off and whisper into his jacket, "These four." They later found out the undercover cop is called a "ghost." After an hour or so, the van was starting to fill up. The cops and their ghosts were scooping up dope fiends and tossing them into the back of the truck. Other times . . . the police in the backup crew snatched the wrong people—for instance, they grabbed a woman, when the ghost had been directing them toward a group of men. "They weren't even getting the right people," says Anthony. "They were just getting bodies." . . . When there were about four or five bodies in the van, he heard the ghost's voice come over the radio. "He's like, 'We need three more.' " Michael cocked his head and thought: *"They've got a quota?"*[3]

Taibbi later learned that the police, as an informal policy, were required to return with one person each.[4] This is what too often happens in police agencies; a policy is put forth—stop and frisk—and then first-line supervisors are left with the task of implementation. Lacking any method for measuring the success of their officers' efforts, they rely on the tried and true method of numbers, turning the policy into what officers everywhere cynically refer to as a "numbers game." Part of the problem is bad policies, partly a lack of direction from higher command staff, and partly a lack of creativity or trust in their officers on the part of first-line supervisors. If you don't trust your officers to work diligently and come back with only two people who truly deserved to be arrested, you tell them they *all* have to bring one back—leading to unlawful arrests and resentments that can last a lifetime. I'll always remember being brand new on the job and while getting suited up in the locker room with a 20-year veteran hearing him say, "Yeah, it's a nice sunny day—I'm gonna beat the balls of the public with tickets today; not because it's important or the right thing to do, but just to come in with a f[***]in' number."

I have a personal friend—let's call him Steve—who flew from New York to Los Angeles to attend a charity dinner, where he had the opportunity to meet a celebrity of whom he was a great fan. Deciding to go for a run—he's an extreme-sports enthusiast—he thought it would be cool to head up toward the famous "Hollywood" sign on a hillside not far from his hotel. As he cut off the sidewalk and up an unmarked trail in the direction of the sign, he was unaware that some YouTube celebrity and serial troublemaker was trespassing on the sign for a recorded stunt. Seeing the commotion of people and a police helicopter far above him on the hill, Steve thought it best to turn around and continue his run back on the sidewalk. When he reached the roadway, two police officers were there who accused him of being part of the stunt and arrested and handcuffed him despite the fact that he was on public land and had no connection whatsoever with the stunt up on the Hollywood sign. Steve was asked for identification, which he did not have since he was out for a run, and ultimately wound up spending hours chained to a metal bench in the police station until his identity and innocence could be established. He missed his $5,000 a plate dinner and his chance to meet his favorite star.

Steve's story is a perfect example of police incompetence. The police were not racist—they and Steve are white—nor were they harboring any ill intent. They simply were incapable of grasping the fact that an innocent person could be jogging within a half mile of an unlawful stunt taking place on one of the most famous landmarks in the world. Nor could they realize that someone who was involved would have more gear than skimpy running attire and sneakers—perhaps rope, video camera, radio, or cell phone? Nor did they realize the two most important facts: they had no lawful right to arrest him and the petty nature of his alleged offense—maybe trespass—was no justification for arrest or lengthy detention of a polite and cooperative citizen.

The story also highlights my contention that police are not racist, but some are incompetent and some use poor tactics at the direction of their supervisors. There can be no doubt that if Steve was black and in a bad neighborhood, many would claim he was treated so poorly because he was black. Yet, Steve is a white millionaire who was staying at an exclusive Beverly Hills hotel and was still unjustly detained and taken into custody, like Anthony and Michael—the black guys from the Bronx.

Unintended Consequences

The war on drugs has made criminals out of more than 50 million Americans,[5] who, prior to 1971, would have gone unnoticed or at worst been regarded as something of a bum. What's worse is that it has greatly damaged police-community relations—especially among the urban poor and blacks. The modern drug war began in 1971 with a proclamation from President Richard Nixon: "America's public enemy number one in the United States is drug abuse. In order to fight and defeat this enemy, it is necessary to wage a new, all-out offensive."[6] The president called on Congress to appropriate hundreds of millions of dollars for drug enforcement initiatives and, in 1973, issued an Executive Order creating the Drug Enforcement Administration (DEA).

While the federal agents and state and local police who fight the drug war do so in the belief that they are helping to make their communities safer and healthier, the origin may be somewhat more cynical. President

Nixon's domestic policy advisor, H. R. Haldeman, told a magazine reporter this about the war on drugs:

> The Nixon campaign in 1968, and the Nixon White House after that, had two enemies: the antiwar left and black people. You understand what I'm saying? We knew we couldn't make it illegal to be either against the war or black, but by getting the public to associate the hippies with marijuana and blacks with heroin, and then criminalizing both heavily, we could disrupt those communities. We could arrest their leaders, raid their homes, break up their meetings, and vilify them night after night on the evening news. Did we know we were lying about the drugs? Of course we did.[7]

While Haldeman's family has challenged the legitimacy of the quote (it was allegedly made in 1994 and Haldeman died in 1999), it fits with Nixon's style of politics. More than likely, the rising calls for government action over the spread of dangerous narcotics such as heroin simply and conveniently dovetailed with Nixon's list of enemies. Notwithstanding the initial motives, the drug war has morphed into a gigantic, nationwide effort that has put nearly two million Americans in prison, helped worsen social conditions in poor communities, and done nothing to end drug use.

While there are those who argue that the disproportionate impact the drug war has on the black community is due to implicit bias on the part of the police and criminal justice system and others who insist it's a problem of black culture, there can be no question as to its uneven impact. With the onset of the crack cocaine epidemic in the 1980s, the government, in its usual fashion, sought a criminal remedy to the problem. The federal and state governments began passing laws that criminalized the possession of crack far more heavily than cocaine. The obvious intent was to deter people from manufacturing, selling, or possessing the dangerous drug. The unforeseen consequence was, however, an explosion in arrests of blacks for crack cocaine offenses. Because crack is cheap to manufacture and is sold in small quantities, its creation permitted individuals an opportunity to make money in the cocaine business who theretofore had been too poor to buy their way into the market. So, in poor black neighborhoods, crack not only had a significant impact from a public health standpoint but also led to a disproportionate number of black citizens arrested and sentenced to long prison terms. Eventually, people in many black communities began to see white college students, doctors, and lawyers using powdered cocaine, while their fathers, sons, and brothers were sent to prison for decades for dealing in the crack form of the same substance.

Today, this is portrayed as a grand conspiracy by racist white politicians to reinstitute Jim Crow or criminalize being black. While Richard

Nixon may have seen the drug war as a convenient way to marginalize his political foes, black leaders and lawmakers were often in the vanguard of those pushing for tougher drug laws. During the 1970s, the pastor of Harlem's famous Mother AME Zion Church, Reverend George McMurray, called for life sentences for anyone selling heroin.[8] Congressman Charlie Rangel of New York City is someone who could never be accused of not having the interests of black Americans at heart. He has spent the past five decades in the U.S. Congress and was a founding member of the Congressional Black Caucus. As a newly minted congressman back in 1971, Rangel had an opportunity to meet with President Nixon in the Oval Office. In that meeting, just three months before Nixon announced the war on drugs, he urged the president to push forward with a campaign against drugs and harsh sentences for offenders. "We could bring a halt to this condition which is killing off American youth," Rangel told the president. He went on to suggest the use of the military and diplomatic measures to stop the flow of drugs into the country, calling heroin and cocaine use a "national crisis." Rangel urged quick action before more Americans began to believe that drugs should be legalized, saying, "It seems to me that more white America is saying, let's legalize drugs because we can't deal with the problem."[9]

President Clinton's 1994 Violent Crime Control and Law Enforcement Act, which has come under so much criticism lately from minority activists, was passed with the support of black congressional leaders, including Representative Kweisi Mfume, then chairman of Congressional Black Caucus.[10] Since the passage of the act, the federal prison population has more than doubled, from 95,000 to 215,000.[11] Fifty percent of inmates in federal prison are there for a drug offense.[12]

As discussed in the previous chapter, police-community relationship issues more often than not come down to police relations with the black community. The problems of black-white relations have haunted our republic since the day of its founding and sadly continue to do so today. Prejudice, ignorance, bigotry, and plain misunderstanding have too often poisoned relations between blacks and whites.

While corruption runs rampant in many state capitals, the criminal laws they pass are generally well intentioned and are meant to improve society, protect innocent people, and punish the guilty. However, as laws have proliferated in recent decades, attempting to address more and more societal ills, their effects have not always been what were intended. Primarily, these laws involve the possession and sale of illicit plants and narcotics—"drugs." Right or wrong, the drug war that began in the early 1970s has brought America's police into more intimate and invasive contact with the public than was ever envisioned by not only the Founders but even by the legislatures that passed the laws.

The police officer of today is, all too often, primarily a law enforcement officer. Police officers' mandates and their paths to promotion and plumb assignments are making arrests and writing tickets and summonses. Since there are only so many crimes committed against persons—rape, assault, theft—the key to making more arrests lies in enforcing drug laws or petty violations. The only way to do that successfully is to aggressively seek out contact with people who fit the profile of a drug user or drug dealer. Officers need to stop as many cars as possible for any trivial infraction and forcefully interrogate the occupants about their origin and destination and look for any tenuous justification for searching the car. The more pedestrians an officer stops and questions, the more likely he or she will find someone carrying small amounts of drugs or marijuana. Obviously, this circumstance creates thousands of additional confrontational contacts with police officers, which would not occur otherwise. Whereas the officer of the past would "hassle" you only if you were making too much noise or looked like you might be lurking around casing a store for a holdup, today you might be stopped because you look sickly, hyper, or just like somebody who might use drugs—which could be anyone. If you happen to be nothing more than an innocent person, you are going to be intensely resentful of being questioned about your activities when you've done absolutely nothing wrong. If you are carrying a baggie of marijuana to smoke with friends later on, you will feel that you were minding your own business and not bothering anyone and so were treated very unfairly and possibly illegally.

The hysteria of the drug war and the drumbeat of militaristic language has driven some officers and agencies to lunacy. The aggressive search for drugs in many cases leads officers to violate the rights of motorists, by making unlawful or pretextual stops or conducting illegal searches. The state of Texas was obliged to pass a bill specifically protecting its citizens from warrantless body cavity searches after numerous instances of officers probing the vaginas and anuses of hapless motorists became public. Two women had their private parts violated by a female trooper after they had been stopped for speeding and the male trooper who had made the initial stop found a small amount of marijuana in the car. He called a female trooper to the scene, who proceeded to sexually assault the two adult female passengers in search for more of the evil plant in their lady parts. This humiliation took place along the roadside and in view of one of the lady's 8-year-old niece and nephew who were riding in the car with them after a day at the beach.[13] This incident, along with numerous others, prompted the state House of Representatives to unanimously pass a bill to prevent such appalling police behavior.

On January 2, 2013, 64-year-old David Eckert was stopped for rolling through a stop sign in Deming, New Mexico. The officer said that while patting Eckert down he noticed his "posture to be erect and he kept his legs together." No clear reason was provided as to why Eckert was taken out of his car or frisked. After he was issued a citation, the officer told Eckert he was free to go and then immediately began questioning him. The officer then searched Eckert's car without consent. Finding nothing, a drug dog was brought in that allegedly alerted to the driver's seat. Based upon the "suspicious" manner in which Eckert was clenching his butt cheeks, the canine hit, and after another officer's false assertion that Eckert was "known" to hide drugs in his anus, the officers were able to get a search warrant for his person, "to include, but not limited to [his] anal cavity." The officers took Eckert into custody and transported him to a hospital to have his anus inspected. The doctor on duty refused to perform the search, stating that it was medically unethical. Undeterred, the officers took Eckert to a more obliging hospital, where he was subjected to an abdominal X-ray and a digital anal examination. When these turned up no evidence of drugs or any other foreign objects inside the hapless Eckert, a second doctor was summoned to probe his anus. Again coming up empty, he was given a series of three enemas to empty his bowels; the contents of his bowels were searched for contraband—again with negative results. Still determined to find evidence of an illegal substance, his tormentors proceeded, forcing Eckert to (inexplicably) undergo a chest X-ray and then a full-blown colonoscopy, which also found nothing of interest to the police.[14]

Months earlier, deputies from the same sheriff's office were involved in another incident that led to the anal penetration of another motorist. In October 2012, Timothy Young was detained by a deputy in a gas station parking lot for not using his turn signal. The deputy discovered the passenger drinking an alcoholic beverage and proceeded to search the car with additional deputies who had arrived to assist. Again, a K9 unit was brought in and allegedly hit on multiple places in the vehicle, although no contraband of any kind was found. After a two-and-a-half-hour search turned up nothing, the deputy turned to Young's body as the object of his search. He was asked repeatedly if he had heroin or cocaine, which he denied. He was asked multiple times, "Do you have it up your ass?" He was then coerced into stripping naked in the public parking lot in the belief that he would be released once no drugs were found. After this humiliation revealed no contraband, Young was taken to the hospital and subjected to two X-ray scans and a digital anal probe. Once Young was declared drug free, he was finally driven back to his truck and released some 7 hours later. Some weeks after the ordeal, Young received a bill for "services" from the hospital in the amount of more than $600.[15]

The idea that a citizen of a free republic could be repeatedly violated in what can only be described a sexual assault, in an effort to find whatever miniscule amount of contraband pharmaceuticals that would fit in his anus, should shock the conscience of every American. Not only were the police responsible for this atrocity, but it took place with the complicity of both the district attorney[16] and a judge, to say nothing of the ghoulish medical staff that carried out the repeated invasions of Eckert's anus and rectum. Eckert won a $1.6 million settlement in 2014 after filing a lawsuit for the violation of his Fourth Amendment rights. While this level of depravity is unusual, it does reflect the warped thinking engendered by the drug war.

The Supreme Court has been complicit in the diminution of the Fourth Amendment in furtherance of the drug prohibition laws. In the case of *United States v. Montoya de Hernandez*, the Court actually ruled that holding a woman incommunicado for 24 hours until she was forced to defecate in front of customs agents was not a violation of the Fourth Amendment because she was "suspected" of being a "drug mule" and carrying a small amount of drugs in a balloon inside her alimentary canal.[17] While this took place at the border where courts have traditionally given wider latitude to authorities, it should be noted that the courts have recognized an extended "border" as far as 100 miles inside the country, where border agents or police acting under their authority do not have to honor any Constitutional protections of citizens' rights.[18]

Justice William Brennan, in a full-throated dissent of the ruling in *Hernandez*, wrote, "Neither the law of the land nor the law of nature supports the notion that petty government officials can require people to excrete on command." He summed up the danger of the Court's ruling with a quote from former justice Felix Frankfurter, "[I]t is easy to make light of insistence on scrupulous regard for the safeguards of civil liberties when invoked on behalf of the unworthy. It is too easy. History bears testimony that by such disregard are the rights of liberty extinguished, heedlessly at first, then stealthily, and brazenly in the end."[19]

This book is not intended to be about the legalization of marijuana and narcotics; that is complex topic that needs to be dealt with by scholars, legislators, medical professionals, and police agencies, but it must be dealt with. Anytime the government of an ostensibly free society makes a personal activity subject to criminal penalties, it invites discord and delegitimization of the law. Such prohibitions also create black markets for the contraband with all the criminality and violence that come with them. Even the most repressive and totalitarian states have been unable to end the use of intoxicating drugs. With that being the case, how could a free society ever expect to do so? Drugs are rampant and easily obtainable inside our *prisons*; how do we ever expect to eliminate them in society? America's experiment with alcohol prohibition demonstrated the folly and danger of trying to prevent people from using a drug they desire.

The Eighteenth Amendment to the Constitution was intended to improve public health, reduce corruption, prevent a host of social ills, and reduce the prison population. During the 13 years of alcohol prohibition (1920–1933), consumption of alcohol among Americans actually increased,[20] and the dangers of drinking rose significantly because of the illicit nature of alcohol production. Worse, the high demand for illegal alcohol created tremendous opportunity for black market profits and served to enlarge and enrich organized crime in the United States, a scourge that would plague the nation for more than a half century.

Police officers are expected to enforce drug laws and are in fact rewarded for making drug arrests. The black market where drugs are traded brings with it violence and disorder—which creates a demand for police response. Basic economics teaches that if you make any commodity illegal, you will immediately create a host of new criminals and a black market for the product, with all the attendant violence that comes with it. There is in fact a significant body of evidence that indicates that our experiments in first alcohol and later drug prohibition are directly related to increases in the homicide rate.[21] One study of 30 major U.S. cities conducted during the early days of alcohol prohibition revealed a 24 percent increase in the crime rate between 1920 and 1921.[22]

By any measure, America's efforts at drug prohibition have been a total failure. Despite annual expenditure of more than $33 *billion* and more than 1.5 million arrests per year, drugs are cheaper and more available than ever—the price of cocaine alone has fallen by 78 percent since 1981.[23] America has more people in prison for drug crimes alone than the total combined prison populations of France, Germany, Italy, Spain, and the United Kingdom.[24] Drug use and the violence associated with the black market narcotics trade continue unabated after more than four decades the war of drugs began. August Vollmer recognized the irrationality of drug prohibition in its infancy, when he observed nearly a century ago that "stringent laws, spectacular police drives, vigorous prosecution and imprisonment of addicts and peddlers have proved not only useless and enormously expensive but they are also unjustifiably and unbelievably cruel in their application."[25]

Worse still, the drug war has served to further alienate and decimate the black community. While whites are actually more likely to sell drugs, blacks are more likely to be arrested for drug sales. Although some point to this fact as prima facie proof of racist police, it is, in truth, more due to the ways in which drug sales are conducted in the respective white and black communities. That is, black drug dealers are far more likely to conduct their transactions in public places, while whites are more likely to purchase drugs from acquaintances inside a residence. Clearly, conducting drug sales on a street corner is far more likely to lead to arrest than selling drugs in your living room.

Regardless of the reason, black communities are particularly hard hit by the war on drugs. This in turn makes them feel as though they are being unfairly targeted by police and by the criminal justice system in general. One does not need to be an expert in psychology to realize that if you live in a community where virtually everyone knows someone locked in jail for a nonviolent drug offense, you may begin to feel as though the system—and by extension its police—is inherently unfair.

Who Controls the Police?

There is a misconception that the police *are* the law. While it is true that police officers do have some significant discretion on how and when they enforce the laws, they do not write the laws, nor do they have much influence over which laws the city or state decides to place emphasis on. Police agency budgets and salary are controlled by the political entity that created them, and the federal government exerts its influence over state and local police through its system of grants. Congress provides more than $3 *billion* annually to police agencies to carry out its specific enforcement demands.[26]

A small village or city police department is, to a large extent, beholden to the city council and mayor in terms of its enforcement priorities. If the city council wants more money to spend, it will demand that the police step up their enforcement of the parking and traffic laws and of other local revenue-generating ordinances. Local governments will also exert pressure on police departments to aggressively pursue any perceived problem that garners the attention of the media and public. While this latter sort of influence is to be expected, the former causes the police to increase the numbers of negative contacts they have with citizens and will likely result in a lower opinion of the police generally.

The federal government exerts its desire for police to aggressively enforce seat-belt- and cell-phone-use laws by making its grants of cash dependent upon such enforcement. Washington, D.C.,'s politicians make billions of dollars available to state and local police to carry out their wishes in this regard.[27] Police agencies in turn either become dependent upon such monies or simply cannot refuse an infusion of cash to pay additional overtime and purchase much-needed equipment.

Police are supposed to be politically neutral, and police generally view themselves as apolitical arbiters of the law. However, the reality is that police are a part of government and therefore part of politics—whether they like it or not. They are the public personification of the laws passed by the state, and they are a department of the government's executive branch. Just as any governmental entity can push back against policies it views as detrimental or improper, so too can the police; but this power is a very limited one. Police are an armed force and, like the military, subject to civilian control. A police chief may argue his or her case or resign in protest, but in the end the police will have to carry out the lawful orders of the executive—whether that be a mayor or governor.[28] The drug war is the premier example of something the police can do virtually nothing about; police cannot change the laws or the priorities of governments.

State and federal legislatures create the laws, and the police make arrests, but it is the prosecutor's office that is the true arbiter of what is, and what is not, a chargeable offense. What constitutes a misdemeanor versus a felony assault varies from one county to the next on the whim of the state's attorney. One will say it requires a broken bone, while another will say it requires treatment at a hospital, while another may actually use the definitions provided by law. Prosecutors can and often do simply refuse to prosecute cases brought to them by the police. This can be a good thing when officers make bad or illegal arrests or a very bad thing when there is a real victim deserving of justice. While a police officer's decisions to arrest or not arrest are subject to scrutiny by supervisors, prosecutors, administrators, and internal affairs and mistakes can result in discipline or termination, prosecutors are answerable to no one. Prosecutors set "policies" that cops are required to follow with regard to certain types of arrests, and they decide which defendants will be permitted to plea bargain and which will have the book thrown at them. Prosecutors make sentencing recommendations that, more often than not, judges automatically rubber stamp. In a very real sense, it is the prosecutor who makes the law and decides the fate of those arrested by the police.

When the Law Is Unfair

As stated, the public views police as the face of the law, but it goes deeper than just the written statutes; they are viewed as the face of the entire societal power structure—*the system*. Even the most unsophisticated and uneducated people are quite adept at understanding the basic concept of fairness. While some people may have a warped sense of fairness, such as believing that the existence of wealthy people is the reason for their poverty, most can still recognize or sense when something is rotten.

In recent years, it has become increasingly apparent that the government does not punish corporate criminals the same way it punishes ordinary citizens. Individuals who were guilty of stealing millions of dollars and causing the loss of millions of people's life savings in the crash of 2008 were given a pass or their company was required to pay a token fine. At the same time, people nationwide were struggling to pay court fees for petty violations and traffic infractions, which were a much greater punishment—proportionally speaking—than was ever received by the corporate criminals. Here again, the Justice Department's report on the Ferguson situation is instructive, with its recounting of the woman who went to jail twice and spent months trying to pay off fines and penalties totaling nearly a thousand dollars for her parking ticket.

It is perfectly understandable that a person suffering this sort of injustice over something so petty as a parking ticket would tend to view the law as inherently unfair. Combine this with just a passing awareness of the free pass given to corporate criminals, who are mainly white, and the fact that, in her world, almost everyone she knows is black and many are dealing with similar situations, it would not be surprising if she began to view the entire system as being biased against black people.

A focus on race obscures the real issues. The Wall Street bankers and brokers who made billions destroying the lives of millions of American families walked away not because they were mostly white folks but because they were fabulously wealthy and politically and personally connected to the very people in the government who were supposed to regulate and prosecute them. The head of the Treasury Department in 2008 was Henry Paulson, the former CEO of the leviathan Wall Street brokerage of Goldman-Sachs. As such, he would have been personally or professionally acquainted with the criminals who perpetrated the scams that led to the economic collapse. Paulson had succeeded Jon Corzine as head of Goldman, who left to become a U.S. senator and later the governor of New Jersey. (Corzine later lost reelection, began his own investment firm, and went bankrupt—in the process "misplacing" $1.2 billion of his customers' money.)

In 2004, Paulson was part of the effort behind the repeal of SEC's Net Capital Rule, which required brokerage houses to maintain a minimum amount of assets on hand to prevent or limit their exposure to financial risk. This was a key factor in the 2008 financial collapse of so many Wall Street firms.[29] In 2006, he became treasury secretary under President George W. Bush, and in 2008, he engineered the transfer of more than $700 billion of your money[30] to his former Wall Street colleagues and other corporate cronies who had mismanaged their companies.

Goldman-Sachs executives have served at the highest levels of government for decades under both Democrat and Republican Administrations. A *CBS News* analysis found nearly four dozen former Goldman employees, lobbyists, or advisers who have worked at the very highest levels of the government.[31] Not only Goldman-Sachs executives get in on the action, but suffice it to say that the SEC and various government posts provide a convenient revolving door where the elite of the financial world essentially set their own rules—and they do so under Democrats and Republicans alike.

Wealthy people accused of crimes are able to hire expensive law firms to conduct their defense and are more likely to be released on bail and less likely to be convicted.[32] The problem is a difference in economic and social status more than one of race. In a majority black city like Ferguson, or black neighborhoods such as Cherry Hill in Baltimore, almost all of the poor residents are black and so, not surprisingly, they tend to see these disparities in racial terms. But for the ordinary rank-and-file officer on the beat, the Wall Street scandals and the unfair treatment of the lady in Ferguson with the parking ticket case that's dragged on for seven years are largely unknown and completely out of his or her control in any case. Such officers are trying to do their best, stay alive, and maybe get promoted one day to make a little more money for their family.

The challenge for police is how to bridge that gap in understanding. Police officers despise injustice as much or more than anyone else and often view themselves as agents of justice. Police leaders must work toward an understanding with their constituents that their officers are people like them, doing their best, and that larger issues of the overall justice and political system are beyond their control. Police leaders must also be vigilant in supervising their officers; it takes only one incompetent or overtly racist officer to spread a lot of poison through a community.

Take the case of Willie Jones, a black male and owner of Jones Landscaping in Nashville, Tennessee, who in February 1991 attempted to fly to Huston to obtain plants for his business. The ticket agent reported Jones to the DEA because Jones paid cash for his ticket and DEA agents detained him before he could board his flight. Jones permitted the agents to search his carry-on bag and found nothing. Although he declined the agents' request to search his person, Jones was searched anyway and the agents seized the $9,000 in cash he was carrying. The agents told Jones he intended to buy drugs with the money and that a K9 had detected cocaine residue on the money, though no dog was present. Jones was not arrested for any crime, but the agents took his money and would give him only a receipt that read "an undetermined amount of US currency." After a two-year-long court action, Judge Thomas Wiseman ordered the money returned to Jones, referring to the DEA's refusal to return Jones's money as "arbitrary, capricious, and an abuse of discretion."[33] The judge went on to describe the testimony of the agents involved variously as "misleading" and "unconvincing and inconsistent." The judge went on the chastise the agents for their officious, condescending attitudes, saying, "It is quite clear from the testimony that the officers' behavior at this point was casual and sarcastic, that they believed that the seizure of the currency was all but a *fait accompli*, and that they cared little for Mr. Jones's feelings of insecurity. Officer Perry's explanation is unconvincing."[34]

These types of abuses are not the norm, but they occur frequently enough to undermine respect for the law generally. And while Jones felt the issue was due to his race—which may or may not have been a factor in the calculus of the ticket agent and the DEA members involved—it is reasonable to assume that a white or black man in a suit and tie, who explained he was on business and who worked for a larger company than Jones Landscaping, would not have had his money quite so seized in such a cavalier fashion. In fact, the vast majority of Americans across racial and party lines oppose the entire concept of asset forfeiture, with fully 84 percent against the idea of seizing anyone's property without a criminal conviction.[35]

It is because of the absolute imperative that the law be seen as legitimate and that the justice system be respected that the famous English jurist Sir William Blackstone wrote in the 18th century, "Better that ten guilty persons escape, than that one innocent suffer."[36] This same maxim was woven into the fabric of American jurisprudence and was perhaps best expressed by future president John Adams, who famously defended the British soldiers accused of murder after the Boston Massacre. Adams said,

> It is more important that innocence should be protected, than it is that guilt be punished; for guilt and crimes are so frequent in this world, that all of them cannot be punished. . . . When innocence itself is brought to the bar and condemned, especially to die, the subject will exclaim, "it is immaterial to me whether I behave well or ill, for virtue itself is no security." And if such a sentiment as this were to take hold in the mind of the subject that would be the end of all security whatsoever.[37]

Adams was certainly correct in the moral and practical importance of defending innocence to a fault, for when people begin to feel as though obedience to the law is no protection from punishment, they will become far more likely to become lawless and view the power of the state as illegitimate. Police too must understand this imperative as they go about their daily duties.

Laws Meant to Be Broken

Respect for the law and its agents is also reduced when the government promulgates laws that the public understands full well are expected to be broken. There are a host of such laws and local ordinances, but the most commonly known such law is the speed limit. There is not a driver in America who believes that the posted speed limit represents the maximum speed you are permitted to drive. Everyone knows you can drive a little faster; the exact extent to which the police permit this excess is a source of mystery and urban legend. Some folks will tell you it's 5 miles per hour; others will say 10 or 15. Yet, we all know that, in the end, it is up to the whim of the officer behind the radar or laser.

The result is that the majority of people exceed the posted speed limit to some degree, and no one feels as though he or she is engaged in legal wrongdoing. Since virtually no one obeys the speed limit, when individuals receive a summons for speeding, many feel that the enforcement is arbitrary; as any cop can tell you, violators frequently give the explanation, "I was going with the flow of traffic." Drivers also instinctively know that driving 80 miles per hour on a deserted interstate highway is not inherently dangerous to themselves or anyone else and that a ticket issued for such an offense is merely for the purpose of police officers showing "productivity" to their supervisors. People view speed limits—correctly—primarily as a means for government to generate revenue, and this creates animosity between the police who are expected to write the tickets and the public that tries to avoid them. Placing a reasonable and absolute ceiling on the speed one can drive would take all the guesswork out of driving and enforcement of the speed limit. Police along the highway could then become a source of comfort rather than fear, as motorists would know that officers are there to protect and assist them and—as long as they stay below the real speed limit—they do not have to fear being ticketed.

In Ferguson, the police issued nearly 12,000 tickets in a city of 21,000.[38] That's roughly equivalent to a ticket for 71 percent of licensed drivers in the city. The city's municipal court in turn issued more than 9,000 arrest warrants for people who failed to pay the exorbitant fines handed out for these petty traffic infractions and code violations.[39] Nationally, somewhere on the order of 25 to 50 million traffic citations are issued annually, generating around $4 to $7 billion of revenue. Add in the cost to citizens of increased insurance premiums, safe driver programs, and attorney's fees, and the cost is $8 to $15 billion.[40] These expenses are troublesome for most individuals and families, but especially so for people living in or near poverty. In Los Angeles, the fine for making a rolling right turn at a red light is $446.[41]

The City of Baltimore also engaged in a policy of mass arrests for petty violations in its "zero tolerance" strategy,[42] similarly contributing to poisoned relationships with the public who were forced to pay fines or be imprisoned on arrest warrants after being unable to pay. Americans, especially in urban areas, live under a suffocating and confusing web of overlapping laws, ordinances, and regulations, which are especially burdensome for the disenfranchised and are virtually guaranteed to create resentment. This bitterness is made all the more worse when the police concentrate these types of strategies in minority and poor communities. The overall intention may be a good one—to reduce crime and fear in these neighborhoods, but they too often create a feeling of being under siege or unfairly targeted.

Police Strategies

The police departments in large urban areas all have particular districts or precincts that are ghettos, plagued with crime, violence, drugs, gang activity, illegitimacy, and all manner of social pathologies. These ghettos can be predominantly black or white and in many ways resemble war zones, with burned out and crumbling buildings, sounds of gunfire, and rampant, daily violence. In all of these ghetto neighborhoods filled with so many criminals, drug dealers, gang members, junkies, and homeless, there are good people stuck in a terrible situation, just trying to survive and raise a family.

The police leadership is called upon by the mayor, city council, and the media to "do something" about the soaring rates of murder and mayhem in the city and so must create a strategic plan for dealing with the menace. The problem is that drug abuse, homelessness, and many criminal behaviors are the result of pervasive social and economic problems that the police have no authority, training, or means to address. So the directive to do something morphs into a plan to target the proximate source of the violence—the black market for illegal drugs. Since there is no way to stop or even significantly disrupt this market, the officer on the street is left to carry out the department policy, which eventually boils down to making more arrests. Numbers on a page are the only way to concretely demonstrate that the individual officer and the department as a whole are "doing something."

For the officer on the street, he or she has to live every tour of duty in the world of the ghetto. The officers' lives are on the line every day, and they are literally surrounded by violent criminals with guns, many of whom would like nothing better than to kill them. Like prison guards and inmates, cops and ordinary bad guys have an unwritten code they live by to make each other's lives as predictable as possible. Police are vastly outnumbered by criminals and always at a disadvantage because bad guys don't wear uniforms and always get to take the first swing or fire the first shot. Just as police cannot fulfill their role without the cooperation of the rest of the citizenry, cops in the ghetto cannot function at all without a minimum of deference from the criminal element in the ghetto. Police officers will be obeyed only if they are either respected or feared. Some respect the police generally and will obey most police orders without question, whereas some respect police because they have had an interaction where they felt they were treated fairly and with respect. Many people, however, have no respect for any living being including themselves. These people will obey only out of fear, dread of arrest and imprisonment, or a fear of physical injury or death if they challenge or attack an officer.

Officers are told to make drug arrests and so endeavor to do that, but quickly realize that the "system" can't or won't keep most drug dealers and users in jail, and so they are just wasting their time with such arrests—as each arrest brings the chance of violent confrontation, contact with communicable diseases, or opportunities to make mistakes or become the subject of an internal affairs complaint. Some officers make many arrests and receive accolades and promotions, while others do their best to maintain peace and order, by shooing small-time dealers off their corner and dealing with other minor law violations with warnings, persuasion, and talks with parents or guardians. A perceptive officer quickly learns that the fix for the problems of the ghetto is not law enforcement and adapts to a peacekeeper role, using arrest sparingly when other policing methods fail or when a serious offense deserving of legal sanction takes place.

The push for action from the politicians leads to a push for arrests from the brass and then to numbers and unofficial quotas from first- and second-line supervisors. This takes the form of *zero tolerance* policing or *stop and frisk* strategies, made famous in New York City by police commissioner William Bratton in the 1990s. This policy, which pressed officers to aggressively stop large numbers of people and develop reasonable suspicion to frisk them, was heralded as a major reason for the precipitous drop in the city's violent-crime rate, along with an aggressive push to make arrests for all petty offenses in the hopes of finding wanted persons, weapons, or contraband drugs. The numbers, however, fail to definitively demonstrate any connection to the stop and frisk policy and a reduction in crime. During the period the strategy was employed, roughly 2002–2013, crime continued a steady decline that had begun 12 years earlier. The violent-crime rate has remained relatively unchanged[43] from the height of stop and frisk through 2015, when such police stops had declined by 97 percent[44] after a successful federal lawsuit curtailed the practice.

The legitimate stopping and frisking of individuals in high-crime areas and those who demonstrate clear, articulable reasonable cause to be stopped and subsequently frisked for weapons is not an unreasonable policy. If the police are to be proactive and try to make a difference in the crime rate, they need to aggressively seek out those who appear suspicious. Where it becomes a problem is in the implementation. What the leadership wants is smart, aggressive policing, and what they wind up with is a numbers game at the precinct level. Supervisors seek to implement the directive and motivate officers to begin stopping and frisking more people rather than simply driving by and exchanging dirty looks. They then are not provided with the proper refresher training on what constitutes reasonable suspicion to justify a stop and what further constitutes reasonable suspicion to frisk someone for a weapon.

Directives to engage in more aggressive policing need to come with simultaneous reminders and refreshers of the importance of remaining within the law. What happened in New York and other cities like Baltimore is essentially a situation where anyone at any time was subject to be publicly humiliated with an up-against-the-wall pat down anytime they appeared in public. Since the police logically concentrated their efforts in high-crime areas, the searches fell disproportionally upon racial minorities living in these areas. Officers were given simple cards with check boxes to indicate what sorts of suspicious behavior and other elements justified their stop. This eliminated the need for officers to *articulate* just what it was that gave them reasonable suspicion to stop the person. Checking boxes marked "high-crime area" and "furtive movements" does not adequately describe a legal basis for a stop under law. What sort of crime is the area noted for? What sort of furtive movement did the person make? Did it look like they were adjusting something heavy tucked in their waistband or repeatedly touching their pocket while looking rapidly around and appearing nervous?

Check box stops, pressures from supervisors, and no consequences for bad stops lead to a situation where officers feel justified in treating people any way they choose; and while some officers still maintain a professional demeanor, others do not. Regardless of an officer's attitude, someone stopped without cause repeatedly and subjected to the public humiliation of a pat down is likely to develop a strong resentment toward the police in general. Worse still, by every indication, the mass stopping and frisking of citizens was wildly unproductive:

- Between January 2004 and June 2012, the NYPD conducted over 4.4 million Terry stops.
- The number of stops per year rose sharply from 314,000 in 2004 to a high of 686,000 in 2011.
- Fifty-two percent of all stops were followed by a protective frisk for weapons. A weapon was found after 1.5 percent of these frisks. In other words, in 98.5 percent of the 2.3 million frisks, no weapon was found.
- Eight percent of all stops led to a search into the stopped person's clothing, ostensibly based on the officer feeling an object during the frisk that he suspected to be a weapon or immediately perceived to be contraband other than a weapon. In 9 percent of these searches, the felt object was in fact a weapon; 91 percent of the time, it was not. In 14 percent of these searches, the felt object was in fact contraband; 86 percent of the time it was not.
- Six percent of all stops resulted in an arrest, and 6 percent resulted in a summons. The remaining 88 percent of the 4.4 million stops resulted in no further law enforcement action.[45]

What was begun as an effort to aggressively target dangerous felons and take guns off the street morphed into something akin to a dragnet fishing operation: scooping up massive numbers of people in the hopes of finding a handful with active warrants or a little dope in their pocket. This is not the way to police a free society.

This form of policing, along with the so-called zero tolerance strategies, were intended to confront disorder head on but in places like Baltimore, Atlanta, and other cities morphed, in practice, to mass arrests for trivial violations of law and granted license to cops to stop, harass, and arrest virtually anyone at any time. Indeed the Justice Department's investigation into the Baltimore Police Department specifically identified zero tolerance and unlawful stops and searches as one of the major problems with the department and its relations with the minority community. "City and BPD leadership responded to the City's challenges by encouraging 'zero tolerance' street enforcement that prioritized officers making large numbers of stops, searches, and arrests—and often resorting to force—with minimal training and insufficient oversight from supervisors or through other accountability structures. These practices led to repeated violations of the constitutional and statutory rights, further eroding the community's trust in the police."[46]

Proactive policing can be done within the bounds of the law, and aggressive policing of minor violations may have some efficacy in limited, targeted areas with specific problems of disorder. Simply employing a blanket strategy of mass arrests for trivial causes across broad swaths of high-crime areas is a recipe for public dissatisfaction and distrust of the police and a serious erosion of police legitimacy. Here again, these failures are due to a breakdown in leadership and supervision. There is a consistent pattern of failed leadership in large urban agencies that have had seriously deteriorating relationships with their poor minority communities.

Police leaders and managers need to think creatively and act cooperatively with the communities they serve. Policies need to be implemented in consultation with community activists, political representatives, and religious leaders. It is not enough to create a broad plan, send it out to the field shotgun-style, with no additional training or guidance to either officers or supervisors, and then base the criteria of success on numbers of arrests. Officers need to be provided with the training and tools required and be given clear instruction on the purpose of their efforts and reminders to remain within the bounds of the law. It is easy for the police or anyone else for that matter to begin to view the world through a very narrow lens: the lens of their own viewpoint and personal experience. Police officers need to be able to empathize with others and see things from alternative points of view. This can serve to guide their behavior and the way they explain things to the people they come into contact with; and it is their leaders and supervisors who need to reinforce a commitment to this way of thinking. Still, it must be remembered that the reason we need police in the first place is because of the existence of irrational, antisocial, and psychopathic individuals who need to be dealt with and do not respond to displays of empathy or courtesy.

Police officers and their leaders need to remember always that they are the face of law and the government and that their actions directly affect the way people view their department, the entire justice system, and the legitimacy of our entire societal structure. A focus first on upholding rights, and mindfulness about their actions, would go a long toward improving relations.

CHAPTER SEVEN

Training the Police for Service Instead of Enforcement

Go about with the idea of helpfulness and friendliness that wins the confidence of the people. . . . Never hesitate to render assistance of any kind, and let nothing be too much trouble which you can do for the people you come in contact with. Always be a gentleman, courteous, kind, gentle, fair.
—Major George Fletcher Chandler, 1917

As we have established, the proper function of the police in a free society is to safeguard the rights of citizens so that they can exercise their fundamental rights as guaranteed in the federal and state constitutions. To this end, the principle job of the police officer is *order maintenance*, or more simply, keeping the peace. Police officers often respond to incidents where a violation of law has occurred but make no arrests, because the interests of fairness and expediency dictate another course of action. Despite this reality, police are generally not trained in *how* to exercise their discretion and instead have to learn from their peers or through trial and error.

Unlike a *law enforcement officer*, the job of a police officer is not to aggressively search for any and every violation of law but rather to keep the peace and use law enforcement as a means toward the end of protecting citizens and preserving their rights. This is where police training all too often fails both the officers and the public they serve. As stated in Chapter 1, young men and women entering a career in "law enforcement" find themselves spending the bulk of their time doing things other than enforcing the law and for which they have received little or no training. The academy training periods are too short to adequately prepare recruits for the array of problems they will be confronted with when they enter the field. As a result, training tends to focus on the mechanics of law enforcement, departmental procedures, and paperwork, to the detriment of education in problem solving and mediation.

Police officers are not soldiers engaged in a *war on crime*. They are guardians of the peace and of the rights of the people they serve. However, part of the job requires them take on the role of warrior when dealing with violent criminals. The job of a police officer is unique in nearly every respect. Superintendent Chandler was an early advocate of professionalizing police forces. In his first memo to his newly formed force he called *Troopers*, Chandler captured the essence of what it means to be a police officer:

> A physician aims to save life and cure disease; a lawyer helps people out of trouble; a clergyman tries to make people better; a soldier fights for his country in time of war. These are fine professions, all of them. They are professions of service.
>
> The service a State Trooper renders to his community is an auxiliary to all of these and his duty in a measure embraces the work of these four great professions.
>
> You who wear the uniform of the State Troopers must be ready to render first aid pending the arrival of the doctor; you must maintain the law which the lawyer expounds; you must instruct people to do right, and if the need arises, you must fight.

It is this unique blending of the doctor, lawyer, clergyman, and soldier that makes policing such a fascinating, demanding, and exciting career. However, constantly adapting to the shifting roles they must play can also create confusion, stress, and fatigue; that is why it's vitally important for officers to understand their role and *purpose* in the larger scheme of our justice system and society.

What Makes a Good Officer?

The unique nature of police work also requires a rare blend of personal characteristics and skills. The ideal police officer is as hard as iron, yet tender enough to comfort a frightened child. He must be able to command instant respect by his presence and personal appearance, yet be approachable to those in need or fear. He is required to be courteous to a traffic violator with a headlamp out, yet must approach the car with a plan to kill the driver if necessary. He must be psychologically prepared to go from talking to a confused senior citizen about missing items around the house to racing to the scene of an armed robbery in progress. The following is a list of personal traits and skills required in the model police officer:

Listening skills: Officers must be able to understand what a person is trying to communicate—not simply hearing his or her words. Police officers need to be able to effectively communicate with people of all levels of education, intelligence, and social status. Truly listening permits understanding of the other persons' situation, what their concerns are, and makes them feel more comfortable.

Verbal communication skills: Police must be comfortable speaking with people from all walks of life and able to adjust their speaking style to match that of their audience. They need the ability to clearly express ideas and intentions and do so in a way that is diplomatic and nonthreatening. Officers must be capable of understanding the street vernacular as well as speaking at least some phrases in a foreign language that may be in common use where they work.

Written communication skills: Police officers must submit written reports about every official action and investigation they take part in. These reports may later be seen by prosecutors, defense attorneys, judges, and even the media and public. The ability to communicate clearly, concisely, and intelligently with the written word is absolutely crucial to professional success as well as the reputation of their agency.

Perceptiveness: Officers must quickly and accurately read situations and observe details others tend to miss. They need to recognize inconsistencies, minute changes, and people, objects, or behaviors that seem out of place. These skills are required both for street survival and for success in criminal investigations and interrogations.

Self-discipline: This characteristic is required not only to complete the rigorous training but also for the day-to-day experience of policing. Officers must maintain their physical fitness, stay abreast of professional developments and community issues, and maintain self-control in the face of violent confrontations, chaotic situations, and emotionally traumatic situations.

Empathy: Police must have the ability to understand the feelings of others and to share and experience those same feelings. While they obviously cannot become deeply involved in every case on an emotional level, they still must be able to empathize with people who are frightened, angry, or sad or feel they are the victim of some great injustice; they need the ability to see situations from the viewpoint of others. Officers' options for helping people may be limited at times, but knowing that they empathize and are offering what assistance and comfort they can goes a long way toward good relations and obtaining the cooperation needed from the public.

Humility: While there are times when police officers are required to decisively exercise their authority over people and must always project a confident, professional image, maintaining a degree of humility is very important. First, the negative stereotype of cops is that they are swaggering bullies, drunk on power and deriving enjoyment from harassing people simply because they can. This is the worst type of police officer. Good cops have confidence in their abilities and know the limits and the purpose of their authority. It is precisely because of the authority they have that police officers must cultivate humility. This trait makes it much easier for officers to connect with others and allows them to recognize their fallibility and to readily admit mistakes.

Honesty/Integrity: As a police official, honesty is the only currency. Police officers who are not fully trustworthy are useless—both to their agency and prosecutors who must rely upon their truthful testimony. An officer must be unfailingly truthful, both for the integrity of the justice system and for his or her own professional future. Personal integrity off-duty is also important—especially in smaller communities where officers are widely known on an individual basis. Officers' personal habits and morals and interpersonal relationships impact how they are regarded in their professional capacity.

Physical fitness: Maintaining health, strength, and physical stamina is very important for several obvious and not-so-obvious reasons. Clearly, fitness is important for patrol officers who may have to fight for their lives or pursue suspects on foot. In fact, being physically fit may even protect an officer from being assaulted in the first place. Studies have demonstrated that offenders are much less likely to attempt an assault upon an officer who appears fit and confident.[1] Physical fitness is also the best protection against the negative health effects of the considerable job stress officers are exposed to.

Curiosity: A good police officer is a naturally curious person; he or she wonders what people they see on the street are doing or thinking. Good police officers wonder what's down a road or trail or behind a factory or shopping plaza. They are interested in how things work, what motivates people, and how people know and interact with each other; and they enjoy solving mysteries or puzzles.

Even temperament: A good officer is not quick to anger or to take things personally. Good officers have the normal range of emotions but are not easily driven to extremes of anger, frustration, or sadness. Police find themselves in the midst of all manner of highly charged emotional situations, and the ability to maintain emotional composure and professional demeanor is vital to proper performance of duty.

Sense of humor: Police culture values a highly developed sense of humor. Seeing humor in many circumstances allows officers to better deal with the stresses and frustrations of the job and to relate better with the public and coworkers.

Self-confidence: Police officers have to force people to comply with their commands and take charge in chaotic and deadly situations. While good training will help instill confidence in their abilities, officers must possess confidence in themselves and have a solid foundation of self-esteem in order to fill the role of authority figure.

Courage: Police officers must possess courage in order to do their job. Obviously, physical courage is required as their personal safety is in jeopardy every time they go on patrol or to conduct investigations and interviews. But they must also possess moral courage: the courage to do the right thing in the face of ridicule or criticism, the courage to persevere in their duty even when it seems unappreciated, and the courage to face disturbing scenes of violence, injury, and death.

The bad news is that there is not a population large enough to produce 700,000 people who possess all these traits and who want to be police officers. Add in the danger, the current climate of hatred toward police, generally low pay, and work on nights, weekends, and holidays and your candidate pool shrinks still further. If we require police officers to possess all these traits and deal with all the chaos, danger, and horror we prefer to not deal with and force them to live in a fishbowl, where their every action—on and off-duty—is subject to public scrutiny, we are going to have to train them much better and pay them a lot more money.

Current Police Training Standards

Today, every police officer is required to be trained to a set of standards created by each state's governing body for public safety. In many states, this is known as the police officer standards and training (POST) council, commission, board, and so forth. The creation of these bodies took place largely during the 1960s and 1970s era of professionalization. When the federal government published its famous report *The Challenge of Crime in a Free Society* in 1967, one of the recommendations for the police was the establishment of POST standards in every state. Seventeen states already had created laws mandating certain minimum training standards, and by 1981, all 50 states had followed suit.[2]

The standards vary significantly from state to state, with the length of academy training ranging from just four weeks to as long as six months.[3] For an idea of the necessary time to properly train as a professional police officer, consider the subject areas that need to be mastered:[4]

Operations

Report writing
Patrol operations/tactics
Criminal investigation
Interview/interrogation

Traffic accident investigations

Speed enforcement/radar theory and operation

Industrial/agricultural accident investigation

Use of computers and information systems

Emergency vehicle operation/high-speed driving

Radio operation/protocol

Station operations

Breath sampling instrument theory and operation

Computerized fingerprinting and booking procedures

Rules and regulations: personal/professional conduct, uniform, grooming standards

Weapons/Self-Defense

Firearms: pistol, rifle, shotgun

Active-shooter response

Pepper spray

Taser

Baton

Use of force—laws and regulations

Defensive tactics: ground fighting, weapon retention, pressure-point control, restraints, verbal command presence

Legal Education

Criminal law

Vehicle and traffic law

Criminal procedure law

Constitutional law

Mental hygiene law

Public officers law

Environmental/game/animal law

Juvenile law and procedures

Courtroom testimony

Professional/Special Topics

Ethics

Health/fitness

Stress management/employee assistance

First aid/CPR

Domestic violence

Terrorism

Gangs

Elder abuse

Hate crimes

Human trafficking

Clandestine drugs labs

Narcotics trafficking

Computer crimes

Crimes against children

Hate crimes

Mental illness

Victim response

Problem solving

Mediation

Public speaking

Community policing

Cultural diversity

Sexual harassment

Equal employment opportunity

Suicide prevention

Clearly, whether police training lasts four weeks or six months, no one can become an expert on this list of subjects in that period of time. Even allowing for a period of field training of up to 12 weeks, we are not giving our police officers enough time to become experts in all the things we expect them to know. And make no mistake—Americans collectively expect police officers to possess all the characteristics and skills listed here and to be experts in every topic.

Police academies tend to be intense, highly structured, and stressful crucibles that are intended to weed out those who cannot handle intense stress and (artificially induced) fear. Academics and hands-on skills training are similarly high pressure and conducted in as short a time frame as possible. This model certainly produces many thousands of fine officers, but it fails to create a fully developed professional, indoctrinated in a professional code of ethics and performance standards, who understands the role of police in society and the true nature of the job that awaits.

Stressful paramilitary training is valuable to condition cadets for dealing with chaotic and dangerous situations and to prepare them to deal with the day-to-day difficulties of the job, for example, long hours, cold, heat, inclement weather, boredom, and physical exertion. An intensely stressful environment is not, however, conducive to learning the law, the constitution, first aid, the role of police in society, or how best to make a death notification.

Academy staff and administrators everywhere struggle with the constraints of time versus the required curriculum as well as other topics they wish to cover. Every aspect of police training is important, and each instructor wishes for more time to train future officers. The result is the best training the staff can offer during what time and with what resources they have available. Clearly, the use of deadly force is one of the most significant topics covered in police training, yet a quarter never experience nonlethal live-fire training (actual use of weapons loaded with paint or chalk rounds in scenarios), and 36 percent never have any computerized-weapons training.[5] This means these officers will never have faced so much as a simulated shoot/don't shoot situation when they hit the street.

Why is police officer training so short? The short answer is cost. Even though policing has been "professionalized" to some degree, it still lacks some of the attributes of commonly recognized professions. One of these is the need for specialized higher education in the field. While many individual agencies require some college credits or an associate's degree for employment, only one state in the union requires all its police officers to have a college education of any kind: Minnesota requires all officers to possess an associate's degree or higher, although this can be waived with police training and experience obtained elsewhere.

A lawyer gets a law degree before applying for work at a law firm: likewise for engineers, architects, doctors, dentists, hotel managers, chefs, land surveyors, hairdressers, and psychiatrists. While many officers are college educated, the vast majority of American police agencies require no more education than a general high school equivalency diploma before being hired. The police agency then takes on the considerable cost of training the provisional officer, which depletes limited resources and also creates an unhealthy disincentive to fail academy cadets or probationary officers in the field. Given the difficulty of finding qualified candidates and the lengthy processing period, police agencies are disinclined to remove marginal cadets or newly minted officers who lack the aptitude to perform as a true professional. Once an officer reaches the field-training phase or beyond, he or she represents an investment of tens of thousands of dollars, funds that smaller or cash-strapped agencies can ill afford to throw away and start the process all over.

Police reformers face other difficulties when it comes to creating a more professional force. One problem is the small size of most police departments. Half of all police agencies employ fewer than 10 full-time officers.[6] This creates a very limited career path for a highly educated professional police officer, who is trained to understand human nature and the role of police in a democratic republic, greatly skilled and knowledgeable in the more than three dozen subject areas listed earlier, and at present making as few as $10 to $15 an hour. Can we as a society expect to attract educated and ambitious young people to spend tens of thousands of dollars for a college education to do such work? In a small agency, it could take decades for a promotional opportunity to present itself. Even if a young person had a strong desire to serve as a police officer, why would he accept such marginal pay and poor working conditions if he is motivated enough to obtain a college education and become knowledgeable in so many subject areas? Surely, such intelligent and hard-working people could find much more lucrative—and safe—employment elsewhere.

Even in larger agencies, the pay is not commensurate with the sort of superhuman, educated, warrior-philosopher that the modern police officer is expected to be. Take a young cadet joining the NYPD; her annual salary will be $45,744. Monthly rent for an *inexpensive* apartment in New York City will cost around $2,800, or $33,600 per year. After paying union dues, health insurance, pension contribution, and city, state, federal, Social Security, and Medicaid taxes, our young officer will be left with just over $500 per month for utilities, transportation, food, clothing, out-of-pocket medical expenses, and so forth—not nearly enough to live on. How many well-educated young people who have other opportunities in the private sector are going to do such a difficult and dangerous job for that salary?

Fully 50 percent of police officers make less than $53,000 per year, while fewer than 10 percent make over $73,000 annually.[7] These levels of pay reflect both the labor market—the salaries are just high enough to attract enough candidates to fill the positions—and the reality of severely limited budgets in local governments nationwide. There are different viewpoints on the job of policing that also affect the pay for officers. Those who see policing as a blue-collar union occupation that requires no post-secondary education and limited knowledge are more likely to view police salaries as already too high. People who see policing as a difficult, dangerous, and highly stressful profession, requiring intensive specialized training in a wide variety of skills, believe officers are severely under-compensated for their efforts. The reality is a blend of both viewpoints. The daily job of a police officer working in a low-crime area can be seem-ingly routine, even boring. This officer may go to only three or four calls daily involving minor traffic accidents or an occasional shoplifter. Never-theless, the potential for violence hangs over everything she does: any traffic stop or domestic dispute could result in a violent confrontation or death. This is why many veteran officers will say, "We don't get paid for we do; we get paid for what we might have to do."

Despite the relatively low pay and hardships, most police officers are competent and professional, if not always well led or highly effective. In order to train the next generation of police for service and not law enforce-ment, it is necessary to begin at the top. While people widely parrot the notion that problems and solutions begin at the head of an organization, it is not fully appreciated. Even in a large organization, the top leader truly sets the tone and atmosphere of the entire agency. The values, work ethic, and the expectations the top leaders place on their subordinates make themselves felt down through every level of supervision and the rank and file.

Training academies and colleges need to discourage the use of the term *law enforcement* and instead call the job what it is—policing. From this simple starting point, recruits can begin to understand the proper role they play in our communities. Even more importantly, aspiring officers have to actually be *taught* about what policing is, its purpose, and its place in the larger system of criminal justice. Very few training programs address anything like an overarching professional doctrine or philosophy. The training periods are short and tend to focus on the nuts and bolts of the job, so that new officers know how to make an arrest or write a sum-mons but not *why* they are doing it.

Even college-level training in "criminal justice" tends to teach only the most simplistic picture of the police role in the criminal justice system, that is, police make arrests, district attorneys prosecute, courts try cases, and prison or probation carries out sentences. Classes focus entirely on the concrete—definitions, laws, and agencies—with no larger discussion of why society created police, what their *purpose* is, and with what phi-losophy they should approach their chosen career.

On the surface, it may seem silly to some to talk about teaching phi-losophy to cops, yet everyone uses philosophy at some level. Everyone possesses a set of concepts that guide their lives and their reactions to what happens around them, even though they probably aren't even con-scious of the fact. Successful and happy people are those who consciously choose or create a philosophy to guide their actions. Put simply, police should be taught the basics of a professional philosophy: what do I know, how do I know it, and what should I do? The great American philosopher Ayn Rand described what happens when people allow their personal philosophy to develop without any purposeful direction and deliberation: "your subconscious accumulate[s] a junk heap of unwarranted conclusions, false generalizations, undefined contradictions, undigested slogans, undefined wishes, doubts, and fears, thrown together by chance, but integrated by your subconscious into a kind of mongrel philosophy."[8]

While we certainly cannot expect police officers nationwide to be schooled in the fine points of metaphysics and epistemology, they can be instructed on a basic philosophy and code of ethics for police. Police officers do not belong to a nationwide professional organization the way doctors and lawyers belong to the American Medical Association and the American Bar Association. The International Association of Chiefs of Police (IACP) is the closest approximation to such a body for police administrators. The IACP has taken the step of promulgating a code of ethics for the professional police officer:

> As a law enforcement officer, my fundamental duty is to serve the community; to safeguard lives and property; to protect the innocent against deception, the weak against oppression or intimidation and the peaceful against violence or disorder; and to respect the constitutional rights of all to liberty, equality and justice.
>
> I will keep my private life unsullied as an example to all and will behave in a manner that does not bring discredit to me or to my agency. I will maintain courageous calm in the face of danger, scorn or ridicule; develop self-restraint; and be constantly mindful of the welfare of others. Honest in thought and deed both in my personal and official life, I will be exemplary in obeying the law and the regulations of my department. Whatever I see or hear of a confidential nature or that is confided to me in my official capacity will be kept ever secret unless revelation is necessary in the performance of my duty.
>
> I will never act officiously or permit personal feelings, prejudices, political beliefs, aspirations, animosities or friendships to influence my decisions. With no compromise for crime and with relentless prosecution of criminals, I will enforce the law courteously and appropriately without fear or favor, malice or ill will, never employing unnecessary force or violence and never accepting gratuities.
>
> I recognize the badge of my office as a symbol of public faith, and I accept it as a public trust to be held so long as I am true to the ethics of police service. I will never engage in acts of corruption or bribery, nor will

I condone such acts by other police officers. I will cooperate with all legally authorized agencies and their representatives in the pursuit of justice.

I know that I alone am responsible for my own standard of professional performance and will take every reasonable opportunity to enhance and improve my level of knowledge and competence.

I will constantly strive to achieve these objectives and ideals, dedicating myself before God to my chosen profession . . . law enforcement.[9]

Today, every agency chooses its own code of ethics—or simply has none. While policing is, and should remain, a local function, the firm establishment of a professional society with basic universal principles should be established.

The service ideal and the concept of police as keepers of the peace rather than *crime fighters* should be stressed at every opportunity, in both criminal justice college programs and police academies. Police officers deal with the most violent and deadly people and situations our society produces and so must be fully trained and prepared for confrontations up to and including the use of deadly force. Nevertheless, they must also be prepared to deal with the demands and realities of order maintenance, which will occupy the bulk of their time. Having this training and understanding will make for not only better-prepared officers but happier ones as well. A police officer who believes he is going to be a gun-slinging crusader against the forces of evil and fighter in a war on crime is likely to be very dissatisfied with the realities of day-to-day policing.

Aspiring officers need to be educated not only about their role in society but about their specific role in the criminal justice system. Police are trained in criminal procedure and learn how cases are transmitted from the police to the prosecutor and then to the courts. They learn little about the perspectives of the prosecutor and judge and even less about the so-called correctional system of jail, probation, prison, and parole. Police officers who are going to arrest people who wind up in the courts and then prison ought to spend some time visiting and understanding the workings of a courtroom and daily life in a prison.

A police officer's job is to keep the peace and protect lives and property; arrest and prosecution is only one of the ways in which that mandate is upheld. Police officers have virtually no influence over what happens after the case is handed over to the prosecutor. When the *system* fails to deliver justice for a crime victim, the police are often blamed. If the case never goes to trial (as in most cases), the police are the only element of the system the victim and community sees. The police officer will have to see the victim again and be left to attempt to explain what happened to an innocent victim who has been denied justice, a pain prosecutors and judges rarely face.

A New Training Model

My career as a police officer began the same day as that of a friend of mine (who later became a school teacher). He applied to a local village police department and had an interview with the chief on a Tuesday. The chief offered him the job of patrolman, handed him a shoebox containing a .357 revolver and a box of 50 rounds of ammunition, and advised him to take it home and practice, with the admonition, "Remember, this isn't a toy." He left the department with a trash bag filled with gear, gun belt uniforms, badge, radio, and body armor, and reported for work on the midnight shift five days later—the same day I reported for the start of seven months in-residence training at the state police academy, followed by three months of supervised field training. For my friend to have remained on the force for more than a year, he would have been required to successfully complete an approved local police academy program. However, this example demonstrates the vast gulf that separates the training received among police agencies.

For police to transition to a service model and serve as worthy and competent guardians of their communities, police training must be adjusted to emphasize service over law enforcement. George Chandler's description of the police officer as part doctor, lawyer, clergyman, and soldier is an apt one—and one which recognizes that the warrior role is only one of the elements of policing. Training for what Chandler called *the policeman's art* requires instruction in elements of the other professions that policing mimics—the doctor, lawyer, and clergyman, or in today's parlance, the EMT, ombudsman, and counselor.

Today's police training is almost universally conducted in a paramilitary atmosphere, and the hierarchy in police agencies is denoted in military ranks. While this model is conducive to good order and discipline—a vital element in an effective police force—it is not the best environment for learning law or the finer points of human behavior and interpersonal communication. Recruits receive training that ranges from the barely adequate to the quite good, but as we have discussed, there is simply not enough time for excellence.

Police training is also provided without a solid basis in research as to its effectiveness.[10] A report by the National Academy of Sciences, which studied the influences of training and other factors on police behavior, stated, "Given the importance of these [scientific] tools to those striving to improve policing, the committee cannot overstate the importance of developing a comprehensive and scientifically rigorous program to learn what is and is not effective in the education and training of police officers."[11]

Police work is often a tough and dirty business: long hours, overnights, brutal weather, and repeated exposure to the shocking, violent, horrific, tragic, and chaotic. Because of this, officers need to learn to maintain focus under enormous stress. Since instructors cannot supply mangled bodies, bloodied children, suicidal adults, people crushed by grief, or knife-wielding maniacs, stress is artificially induced through shouted commands, harsh language, and extreme physical demands. They are generally required to pay strict attention to every detail in their personal appearance, movements, and language, which teaches skills vital to crime detection and officer safety; little things out of place, or a subtle movement or glance can indicate a crime or an impending attack. Maintaining attention to these details while under stress helps prepare cadets for the real world where minute details can make the difference between life and death for themselves or others. This sort of highly structured paramilitary training teaches poise, calm, courtesy, and professional bearing. These traits help clothe an officer in the appearance of confidence, competence, and respect for others—vital to the officer's job of assisting and reassuring others and in taking charge in emergencies or when confronting violent criminals.

While this harsh element of training is necessary, officers must learn to deal with other situations that are reasonably calm. As stated, although police deal with confrontation, violence, and death, most of their time is spent working out minor disagreements, traffic accidents, nonviolent crimes and a host of other problems most people don't even consider to be "real police work." Trainees must learn how to communicate effectively with the people they encounter. They must learn to recognize how others may view them and how to tailor their language to the person they are speaking to and the situation they are in. It takes very little to take a relatively calm situation and turn it into a volatile confrontation. Most people have little knowledge of military structure and courtesies; and while clear directions and forceful commands are useful when making an arrest or trying to evacuate a burning building, they are of little use when trying to interview the terrified mother of a missing child.

Nationwide, police officers should be indoctrinated with a service ethos, viewing themselves as guardians of the people and their liberties. They should be educated in their proper role as keepers of the peace and the vital role they play in permitting the citizens of their communities to

enjoy the freedom guaranteed to them in our country's founding documents. They should be conditioned to view themselves not as warriors,
crusaders, or even crime fighters but rather as *police officers.* The very term
law enforcement officer should be retired from the lexicon of the
profession.

Police training must be expanded to include verbal communication
skills and methods for de-escalation of volatile situations and individuals.
The police officer's authority—personal and professional—is central to
his or her job. The authority police officers hold by virtue of their badge of
office and that which they command by their personal presence is the
only way they can accomplish their mission. Officers must jealously guard
that authority and quickly respond to instances of flagrant defiance; once
an officer's authority is violated, the officer will lose respect and invite
further trespasses. Yet, officers receive precious little training about what
their authority really means—they are simply taught to "take charge" or
not to "take any shit" from the "scumbags."

New officers need to learn that, in most instances, offering an explanation for their actions does not undermine their authority. There is a prevalent mind-set among many police that explaining themselves is somehow
either beneath them or degrades their authority. This is rarely the case.
When dealing with a physically violent or demonstrably irrational individual, offering explanations in the face of such conduct could make an
officer look weak or indecisive, but absent violent or threatening resistance, a simple explanation of the law and the reason for an officer's
actions will lend great credibility and respect to the officer and his or her
agency. Officers who have not received the proper training will too often
reflexively overreact to the slightest challenge, such as a motorist asking
why she was stopped. A confident, skilled officer with a proper mind-set
is able to maintain control of both himself and the situation in the face of
challenges large and small—and is able to discern the difference.

Collectively, we expect our police to be professional in their dealings
with the public and not allow their personal feelings or biases to influence
their decisions. Yet, at the same time, we expect them to be compassionate, to "give us a break," and to understand our particular situation and
our feelings about the particular matter at hand. While police are professionals and deal oftentimes in matters of clearly defined laws, they more
often than not are alone and dealing with the most intimate matters of
life: personal problems, injury, loss, liberty, and honor. A police officer
may be professional and unbiased but what he or she does or does not do
in any given situation is intensely personal to the individual he or she is
dealing with. An officer may have written hundreds of traffic tickets, but

to the person the officer has stopped, this is a traumatic experience: there are flashing lights, perhaps a blast of siren, and a uniformed, armed government agent walking up to their window. The ticket will cost as much as a week's pay and maybe make car insurance unaffordable. The person may drive for a living and thus be in danger of losing his or her livelihood.

An officer who finds a pair of teenage lovers sharing a six-pack in a city park closed after dark is dealing with a routine situation of little consequence. For the teens, it is something quite different. They are confronted with a bright flashlight in their eyes, demands for identification, by men and women with guns, shiny badges, and creaking leather gear. The choices made by the officer will perhaps create horrific conflicts at home, trouble with school, or their future ability to attend the college of their choice—to say nothing of the potential for hefty court fines. They may have to dump out their beer and leave, or they might be arrested for trespass and illegal possession of alcohol.

A couple comes home from an evening out and, under the influence of alcohol, an argument breaks out about past infidelities and other intimate grievances. The shouting prompts a call to the police, who have been through dozens of such domestic quarrels. To the man and wife, however, they now have police officers standing in their living room asking about their names and their date of birth ("Why do you need that?"). One or both of the couple are airing all sorts of private dirty laundry and embarrassing intimate details about one another. The police are now required to compose a detailed report—on site—about what happened. Was there any violation of law? Does anyone want the other arrested? If neither party to the argument called the police, they may both be resentful and hostile about this intrusion into their personal lives. The husband will almost certainly feel that his masculinity is being threatened by the presence of the police issuing orders in his marital home. Both of them may ask questions of the officers such as "Do you think it's right that she's a mom and goes out and gets drunk with her mother every weekend?" or "Why don't you tell them about your little whore girlfriend from the diner?" These officers are in the midst of years of private hurts and the intimate relationship of a married couple they have never met. Their decisions and demeanor may have profound and lasting effects on their lives and how they view police officers in the future.

So, while police are professionals, they are much more than warriors or law enforcement officers; they are themselves individuals called upon to intervene in other individuals' lives under all sorts of circumstances—nearly all of them bad—and required to make decisions that impact people's lives in the most personal and significant ways. They need to understand human nature, what motivates and animates individuals, and the effects of trauma and intoxicants on behavior. They need to know how to referee a marital fight without seeming as though they believe they have the right to get involved. They need to understand how people in different situations and varying backgrounds feel when they are confronted by a police officer and how to tailor their speech and actions to maintain control and calm and achieve the best possible outcome.

After an initial period of intensive stress, cadets should move into a more relaxed academic atmosphere—maintaining discipline but emphasizing learning and assimilation into the police culture. Also vitally important is an increased emphasis on training for unarmed combat. Officers who are confident in their ability to defend themselves are far less likely to be fearful and consequently less likely to overreact or attempt to use verbal intimidation. The National Institute of Justice has pointed out that there is a lack of available research into the physical defense and control tactics training of our nation's police. Their study concluded that officers were generally dissatisfied with the training they received in this area.[12] As nearly every police officer has learned, people who are fearful can be dangerous and unpredictable, and it is no different for a police officer. Once an officer begins to become overwhelmed by fear, the physiological response of his or her body begins to preclude the rational thought process. This, by the way, is the reason for repetition in training: once engaged in a fight for your life, you can often remember only what your mind and muscles have learned from endless repetition, as your ability to think becomes severely impaired. Police who are confident in their ability to handle physical aggression are much more likely to remain calm, think clearly, and make better decisions.

Police academy training should include problem-solving skills. Since officers spend much of their time addressing these types of situations, police cadets should be equipped with the basic concepts of effective methods for resolving differences between individuals as well as identifying and solving various types of problems. There is in fact an entire field of study devoted to what is called *problem-oriented policing*, which aims to identify and address specific problems the police are expected to solve: approaching them as a three-sided triangle—the offender, the time and place, and the target or victim.[13] Instructing young officers that they are expected to be problem solvers will help prepare them for the actual role they will play once they are in the field.

Basic instruction in dispute resolution should also be a part of all academy training programs. New police officers will likely find themselves squarely in the middle of angry disputes from the very first day on patrol and yet generally receive little to no formal instruction on the basics of conflict resolution. While, as with many areas of policing, time constraints prohibit the levels of instruction to qualify as an expert, providing recruits with a rudimentary understanding of the fundamentals involved in mediating disagreements is essential. According to the Bureau of Justice Statistics, the average amount of time spent in police academies covering the topic of "communications" is just 15 hours. This is a broad category and very little of the time is likely devoted to mediation or crisis intervention. Social workers have years of college-level training in how to deal with child abuse, marital problems, incorrigible children, rebellious teens, runaways, delinquents, and individuals who lack basic life skills. Police officers deal with these issues every single day and yet receive little to no formal training in how to help or how to effectively communicate with individuals in these kinds of circumstances. Far too many recruits hit the streets prepared to arrest people for crimes, write tickets, and investigate traffic accidents but with no formal training on how to address the chronic problems that plague their patrol areas or settle the volatile disputes that they will be called upon to resolve nearly every day.

Ideally, police work should be a job for people who like people. When you ask most cops why they wanted to become an officer, they will tell you "because I wanted to help people." They are then disappointed to discover that their life of saving the innocent from the ravages of the criminal world is much different than they imagined. Many of the criminal complaints they receive come from other criminals who on that particular day find themselves in the role of victim. Most officers come from middle class backgrounds and don't have a good understanding of how the lower socioeconomic class lives and thus find themselves experiencing severe culture shock. Instead of riding to the rescue of good citizens in distress, they are standing in a filthy, smoke-filled apartment, reeking of body odor, cigarettes, and kitchen grease, refereeing a shouting match that began over who should possess the television remote. Aspiring police should understand the true nature of the work long before they go on their first patrol.

Police recruits need to be educated in the stresses that will accompany their work. Police agencies have come a long way in the past 30 years recognizing and dealing with stress-related problems but still have a long way to go. Not only should recruits learn the sources of stress and how to cope but also they should be able to rely on their agency to respond with compassion and assistance. Every agency should have its own or access to an employee assistance program and peer counselors to allow members to seek help for issues confidentially. Too many officers begin their careers without the information they should have about the stresses they will face and the effects they can have on themselves and their loved ones. Police stress, like stress in most occupations, comes from several sources. The most obvious for police is the threat of violence, danger, and the often confrontational and chaotic nature of their work. After becoming involved in a fatal shooting at a domestic dispute in June 2000, I wrote the following words that shed some light on some of the other sources of police stress.

As with most tragic incidents in life, it happened very quickly. One minute I was at the barracks mindlessly doing paperwork and 11 minutes later I was standing over the dead body of a man who had tried to shoot me.

It was five o'clock in the afternoon and my 12-hour shift was nearing the end. I wasn't even going to go to the reported domestic dispute I overheard other troopers being sent to, until I heard that the man had a shotgun. At the time, we did not carry shotguns in our cars, and I knew the responding troopers wouldn't have one. So I grabbed a shotgun from the armory and ran out the door.

The bad guy was drunk and angry that his pickup truck had not been repaired on schedule. So, he had struck his wife, who fled the residence, and fired at least one shot before I arrived. He used a classic ruse of holding the gun and his hands out to his sides, asking me not to shoot; then when he thought he was close enough, he quickly wheeled to his left and leveled his shotgun at me. I fired a single shot through his heart before he could pull the trigger. It was all handled very professionally. We made perfunctory attempts to administer first aid, mainly for the benefit of the onlookers. All of us knew he was already dead. I took notes quickly, in order not to forget any details, with a shaky hand but clear enough to be read later. My sergeant radioed the shots fired call and requested an ambulance. Another trooper secured and unloaded the suspect's shotgun.

Shortly, others began to arrive: another trooper who thought we were kidding when told of the shooting, a local deputy sheriff who had been interviewing the wife of the suspect, an investigator from my station, the county sheriff. Later in the evening, a small army of forensic specialists, investigators, and even the district attorney would descend on the quiet country road. Within half an hour, I was back at the barracks where I telephoned my wife to tell her I would be very late getting home—and why. This was the only moment I became emotional. I felt a sense of profound sadness at having to tell my wife that her husband had just killed a man and that someone had tried to kill me.

A few hours later, the troop commander and internal affairs investigators arrived. The process was relatively painless, although it took several hours. I gave a formal statement to the investigators, who had patiently explained the entire process to me earlier. The troop commander assured me that there was no question about the propriety of my actions and expressed his appreciation for a job well done. He asked if I was okay and offered whatever assistance I might need. My captain even telephoned from his vacation to ask if I was all right.

Before leaving, as was required, a counselor from the employee assistance program spoke with me about some of the emotions I might experience in the days to come. She was compassionate and pleasant and did not push any unwanted therapy or advice—she merely offered help if needed.

When I left the barracks at 11:30 P.M., four-and-a-half hours late from my 12-hour tour, I drove to a fellow trooper's home and met the other troopers from the shift along with some of the investigators from an adjoining station who had been called in to help. We drank some beer outside in the warm June night air and laughed at some of the funny events of the evening. Some talked about other shooting incidents they had been involved in or heard about. It was an unstated celebration of a feeling everyone felt but had not tried to name. (Troopers are not in the habit of talking about their feelings.) It was a celebration of being alive, of having triumphed over a bad guy who had tried to kill one of us.

Back in at 7:00 A.M. the next morning, I ate breakfast at the usual spot with my fellow troopers. It was like any other day, except all the newspapers the people were reading were emblazoned with the headline "Trooper Kills Man." Almost everyone had read or heard about the incident on television or radio. The people at the counter were reading my name and the story of what happened, but none of them knew that the person they were reading about was sitting among them. I was asked several times that day and for many days after if the trooper who had shot the man was doing all right. I told them he was fine.

The superintendent of state police telephoned from the state capital that morning to tell me that I had done a good job. He assured me that there would be no second guessing my actions and that I would be afforded any needed assistance. I spoke with the troop commander regularly, as he kept me informed of the progress of the investigation. I received no fewer than 14 cards and letters from ordinary citizens—complete strangers—expressing sympathy and gratitude. I received emails from academy classmates and from troopers I'd never met, congratulating me on a job well done and offering sympathy and support. An anti–domestic violence organization even issued a proclamation praising my actions. The only negative correspondence I received was from the man's mother, who sent me a hate letter along with rose petals from her son's casket floral arrangement; she said she hoped they reminded me of the blood that poured from her son's chest when I killed him.

As the first week or two passed, I began to become concerned that I felt no sadness or sympathy toward the man who had died. He had tried to shoot me and I shot him first. I could see no reason to feel guilty about going home to my wife and two little girls rather than the alternative: my death and the continued existence of a man who gets drunk at five o'clock in the afternoon, threatens his wife with a shotgun, and tries to kill policemen. I spoke to a clergyman who told me that I was right not to feel bad and to two academy classmates who had killed in the line of duty and who said their feelings had been very similar to my own. I quickly dismissed any worries about my mental health.

What is ironic and unfortunate is that shooting and killing a man on a sunny June afternoon would turn into the single most positive experience of my entire career. It was one of the few occasions that anyone ever told me that I had done a good job. It was the first time a commissioned officer had asked if I was okay or if I needed anything. I was praised and thanked by both my colleagues and civilians. I was a minor local celebrity, if in name only, for a few weeks. Myself and other area police were the beneficiaries of the increased respect and courtesy that police often receive for a month or so after a policeman kills or gets killed.

What only a police officer could understand fully is this: living through a shooting is not hard. What is hard, what tears apart your soul and eats like acid into the foundations of everything you have faith in, is what happens to you in the day-to-day experience of wallowing through the dregs of society. What is hard is waiting for the day that you will have to kill someone to save your life or the life of another, having to keep yourself honed razor sharp and ready to fight for your life at any moment for 12 hours at a time, yet treat the scum you often deal with with the utmost courtesy. What's hard is getting yourself ready to fight or kill five times a day, only to have nothing happen, then going home to think about what could have happened, and when the first—or next— time will come that someone tries to hurt or kill you. What's hard is being scared to death in a situation where you know your life is in jeopardy but, when described to another, sounds like baseless paranoia. What's hard is going alone to a trailer full of guns in the dark of night, because a violent drunk is arguing with the mother of his illegitimate children over cheese, then returning home to kiss your children in their beds while you contemplate whether such a mission is worth making them fatherless. What's hard is dealing with drunks, child molesters, drug addicts, thieves, rapists, and murderers and watching them escape justice almost without exception.

What's hard is dealing with all of this and then have people assume all you do is write traffic tickets. What's hard is to do and see all that you do and then have abuse heaped upon you by otherwise law-abiding citizens because you are required to write them tickets for not wearing their seatbelt; what's hard to do is to have to deal with the hopelessness, pointlessness, injustice, filth, and stark violence of the underworld and then listen to cute cop doughnut jokes when you try to take a break and buy a cup of coffee. Nothing is more corrosive to the soul than the anger engendered by the experience of being a police officer. Witnessing the violence, the battered and hopeless children, the savages who live among us and feed off the labor of others receiving welfare to subsidize their criminal careers, the brutish and purposeless existence of so many—this is what takes its toll on police and has taken its toll on me.

Still, I chose my career knowing the risks and the people I would deal with. But, what I could not know at the outset was the vastness of the problems in human society. I did not fully comprehend the violence and ignorance of the beasts that walk among us. I had no knowledge of the moral bankruptcy of the entire criminal justice system. I did not realize how utterly thankless doing my duty would be. I was not seeking to become a hero but did not know that even the most significant of efforts would not be recognized—that is, until I killed someone.

I do not regret becoming a trooper. It has been a grand adventure providing me a lifetime of experiences in just the first few years. I have been to riots and natural disasters across the state. I have had the privilege of meeting and working with some great people. Had I not chosen to become a trooper, I would have spent the rest of my life wondering what it's like and if I had what it takes to do the job. I would never have known all that I know about the world—and myself. I was seeking, like most others who enter law enforcement, the knowledge of what goes on behind the scenes, what happens in the mysterious world behind the crime scene tape, and what lies under the blankets in the street. I wanted to know and I wanted to help protect the innocent. But there are times now that I wish didn't know all those things, and though I have helped some innocent people, there are very few I can list by name.

I am now an administrator and almost entirely removed from the fieldwork of law enforcement. I no longer have to deal with the ugliness. The real answer long ago to the question "Is that trooper okay?" was no- not because he had to shoot someone but because of all the days that came before—what he had witnessed and the waiting for that moment to come.

Yes, police officers must be trained to fight and to kill when they have to, but young men and women embarking on a career in policing must also be prepared for the world they are about to enter. They need to know the stresses and how to cope. They need to be taught that simply by showing up to work and going about their daily duties they are making a difference, that the impact they hope to have on society and crime is probably not realistic, but that they can make small differences in individual people's lives by locking up a violent bully, comforting a lost child, or helping a frightened old lady make arrangements for her husband who just passed away at home. One of the four inscriptions at the National Law Enforcement Officers Memorial in Washington, D.C., are the words spoken by police survivor Vivien Eney Cross: "It is not how these officers died that make them heroes—it is how they lived."

In order for police officers to receive all the training they require, the process will require changes. First, the training period needs to be extended for most agencies. The average length of police training is 21 weeks, with some academies having it as short as four weeks.[14] Take another look at the subjects listed earlier in this chapter that require mastery for a professional police officer and then factor in the training in professional philosophy, ethics, problem solving, and mediation that is missing. Now contemplate the fact that the average number of training hours for police officers nationwide is a mere 850 hours.[15] Contrast that with the average number of training hours to qualify as a beautician, which is somewhere between 1,500 and 2,100 hours.[16] That means that, in the United States, we require our hairdressers to have more than *double* the amount of training as we do our police officers. While some police continue their training in the field under close supervision, only 37 percent of police training programs have any type of field-training component.[17] This means that we are presently sending people as young as 18 to 21 years old out onto the streets with as little as a month of training, alone, armed with a handgun and other weapons, to make life-and-death decisions, as well as to make arrests, determine fault at traffic accidents, intervene in volatile and dangerous situations, make the proper call in cases of child abuse and neglect, conduct criminal investigations, and interview crime victims, witnesses, and suspects. If we require someone to have no less than 10 months of full-time training to style hair, how on earth can we allow someone to shoulder the burden and wield the authority of a police officer with as little as a month of instruction? It is nothing short of irresponsible and does a disservice

not only to the public the officers are intended to serve but to the officers themselves.

Given the limited formal training most police officers receive, it is
remarkable that they do such good work in most cases. It is a testament to
the men and women who take on the responsibility to wear the uniform
that they take the time to educate themselves on the finer points of policing
and the laws to be able to carry out their duties. Indeed, continuous learning and development is the hallmark of a true professional, but our police
deserve better preparation before embarking on such a challenging task.

The reality of limited budgets dictates a pragmatic approach to reform-
ing police training. Certainly, a month of formal training will not prepare
anyone for performing adequately as a police officer. Six or seven months
of formal training followed by between two and four months of closely
supervised and structured field training should be the absolute minimum; there is simply too much to learn to adequately cover in less time.
Still, this only allows for officers to become proficient in the basic skills
and acquire the minimum knowledge they require to function, and it
does not allow enough time to cover other important topics in depth.

One option would be a requirement for applicants to complete some
form of pre-academy training to establish a foundation for instructors and
cadets to build upon once formal training begins. This training could
take the form of simple online classes in the history and purpose of the
police, the day-to-day activities of department members, the role of supervisors and administrators, professional philosophy, ethics, problem solving, and mediation. This sort of instruction could also continue as a
component of in-service training for serving field personnel and as a
means of beginning a change in culture immediately.

Police applicants could be required to complete some form of minimum
instruction from an educational institution before being admitted to the
academy. Requiring college degrees significantly shrinks the pool of eligible applicants, but they could be mandated to obtain some sort of certification from a private or community college in police fundamentals. This
would take the form of an abbreviated course in the police service, covering
not only the basics of the system but also those neglected topics discussed
here. Aspiring police officers must be taught to become just that—*police*,
not law enforcement officers. They need to understand their role is maintaining order and safety and that fighting crime and criminals is only one
of their myriad and unpredictable activities and responsibilities.

Police reformers must bear in mind the unavoidable reality that police
recruits are drawn from the population at large. That population has certain characteristics, and trying to find enough recruits with the requisite

skills, motivation, and character to be the type of police officer we want is becoming progressively more difficult. With the police under growing political as well as physical attack for much of the last decade, recruitment is down anywhere from 50 to 90 percent nationwide. Combine that drop with the fact that more than a hundred applicants may yield only one serious and qualified recruit and you have an impending crisis, for which there are no easy—or inexpensive—answers.

Police leaders have begun to realize that the time has come for a significant change in the way police officers are trained. Police trainers could go a long way by simply emphasizing at every stage of training that officers should treat people the way they would want another officer to treat a member of their family. Finding the means to properly train officers for the future of policing is a daunting challenge, but we must create training programs that produce officers who understand their role in society, are capable of communicating and de-escalating situations, and are confident in their defensive tactics abilities. Such changes will eventually bring us to the point of having a force of police officers prepared to protect and serve, instead of law enforcement officers ready to go to war.

CHAPTER EIGHT

Police Legitimacy and Public Relations

The only security of all is in a free press. The force of public opinion cannot be resisted when permitted freely to be expressed. The agitation it produces must be submitted to. It is necessary, to keep the waters pure.

—Thomas Jefferson in letter to Lafayette, 1823

The police in general have long suffered from a public relations problem. Because of perceived hostility from the press and the public, police culture has developed a very insular attitude and viewpoint. Of course, this attitude is not entirely unwarranted; reporters will often skew their stories toward sensationalism and attempt to promote false narratives that bring opprobrium on individual officers and whole departments. Nonetheless, police leaders must learn to embrace the concept of public relations; they are servants of the public and as such should do their best to communicate with residents in the communities they serve.

In a free society, police cannot perform their function without the support of the public they serve. Police officers are drawn from, and are a part of, the citizenry. In other countries, even democratic ones, the police are a part of the military or an arm of the executive power of the national government. In France, the national police, Gendarmerie Nationale, are under the control of the Ministry of Defense and perform military and judicial functions in addition to policing. Italy has its Carabinieri, a national police force that is a part of the military, in addition to local civil police authorities. Other Western democracies also have blurred lines between the police and military functions of the state.

The United States avoided creating a national law enforcement organization until an ambitious bureaucrat named J. Edgar Hoover used the chaos created by prohibition to transform the Justice Department's modest Bureau of Investigation into the Federal Bureau of Investigation in 1935. While this organization had some colorful successes in killing or capturing interstate gangsters, it also would become what many feared—the secret police force of the federal executive. The FBI has engaged in thousands of illegal wiretaps and surveillance of perceived enemies of presidential administrations and kept secret dossiers on political targets from Charles Lindberg to Martin Luther King to John Lennon.

In the United States, however, the FBI remains a civil institution and is generally limited to enforcing federal laws. They are not engaged in policing local communities or responding to calls for service. The United States in fact has a law specifically prohibiting the military from acting as a police force or using its powers inside American borders. The Posse Comitatus Act[1] was signed into law in 1878 and makes it a crime for anyone to utilize the federal military to enforce civil law. Although there are certain circumstances in which governors may use their state militias, or National Guard units, or presidents can use federal troops to enforce a federal directive, the police function in America has always been a strictly civil and almost entirely local prerogative.

The Founding Fathers were—rightfully—wary of any centralized power. This is why they created a *federal* republic, wherein the national government had only limited, defined powers, granted to it by the sovereign states in the union. While this arrangement has changed much since the Civil War, it is why America is made up of "states" and not provinces, prefectures, or districts; each state is supposed to be a sovereign entity unto itself, with its own government and laws. This is why policing has always remained a local function, just as governance has remained a local affair for most of our history. This has made for a unique, sometimes unwieldy, and sometimes wasteful system of policing. But regardless, a civil policing authority cannot carry out its mandate to enforce law and to protect the public without the cooperation of its constituent communities. Generally, police officers in the United States are too few and lack the tools to strictly enforce laws and maintain order without the general acquiescence of the people they serve. It is vital to the mission of the police and the maintenance of liberty that the people view the police as their protectors and servants and in turn give them respect and support.

Toward that end, many police agencies are beginning to embrace the use of social media such as Facebook and Twitter, although many do not utilize them to their full potential. A police agency of any appreciable size should have accounts on both of these platforms for communicating and interacting with the public. Full-time personnel should be employed by the agency to update social media regularly. Facebook allows an agency to put its best foot forward—for residents to see photographs and descriptions of the agency's officers engaging with the community, doing charity work, or making notable arrests. Facebook also provides an opportunity for people to share their specific neighborhood concerns with police, and allows the police to share information with the public to enhance safety or to request assistance in obtaining information or locating a criminal suspect.

Twitter provides a platform for a police agency to quickly disseminate notifications of traffic incidents, crimes in progress, or natural disasters. News media that subscribe to these platforms can get information they seek and pass it along immediately over television and radio. Being present on Facebook allows residents to feel more connected with their local police. Seeing the police department's posts in their newsfeed along with those of their family and friends can make people feel that the police are less of a mystery and see that police officers are people just like themselves, doing a difficult job.

The effectiveness of a department's use of social media depends to a great extent on the time and resources devoted to the endeavor and the strategy used. The technology can be used primarily to push forward information that improves a department's image and provide information during serious emergencies or to solicit input from the public about their concerns and crime tips, as well as create lasting networks among police and citizens.[2] Many departments have begun to utilize YouTube as well, both as a means of recruitment and for alerting the public about wanted persons or simply sharing interesting video of significant events. Police agencies need to understand that social media is the primary driver of public opinion during events such as a police shooting or protests and rioting. Public information officers need to be skilled users of social media platforms to be able to monitor them for information and to counter false reports and rumor that can quickly take on a life of their own if not quickly corrected. It is also vital to create and maintain a social media capacity *before* a major event occurs, since these capabilities cannot be simply created once an emergency develops. Use of these social media platforms allows the police to communicate directly and instantaneously with the public, something that was unimaginable just a decade ago. The widespread use of social media provides an opportunity for the police to be much more connected to the people they serve and doing so can greatly enhance their perceived legitimacy.

Police agencies in general must be more open with the press. The nature of criminal investigations often makes it difficult to strike a balance between what must be kept confidential and what can be released to the media. This often creates tensions between the police and reporters. Both sides must take into account the needs of the other. Reporters need as much information as they can get, and the police sometimes have to control the release of information so as not to compromise investigations in progress or issue conclusions before they have all the facts. If reporters feel that a police agency is cooperative in providing information to them, they will be less likely to be resentful when the police must demur and hold back on providing answers or comments.

Police can foster better relations with the news media by doing what they can to make access to information easy for reporters. Police leaders should recognize that the press, though they may seem to be a nuisance at times, performs a vital role in a free society. Without the press, there can be no liberty and no protection from tyranny. The press provides the information that is absolutely vital to the maintenance of self-government. Reporters, on a practical level, are people with a job to do and stories to write. Relations can be improved with basic empathy for their position and taking steps to make access to information faster and easier. Moreover, in cases of natural disasters, large-scale emergencies, or a need for public assistance in solving a crime, the media become indispensable for disseminating information on behalf of the police, making good relations vital. Police agencies should have staff available to answer press inquiries during business hours, or, for smaller agencies, a designated agency member to act as a PIO. This not only makes the acquisition of needed information easier for the press but also helps to create personal relationships that aid in understanding between police and reporters.

Police agencies should create online newsrooms that can be accessed by reporters. These private Web sites should contain brief write-ups of every newsworthy event the agency was involved with on a daily basis. This can be accomplished in a number of ways: either a dedicated staff can review police reports of the day and prepare synopses or a specified person in each precinct, district, or station can be made responsible for writing up the local newsworthy events and passing them along to a public information office or officer. This not only creates a great convenience for media but also can help streamline operations by preventing the need for reporters to telephone police supervisors in an attempt to get basic information about events such as fires, traffic accidents, and minor arrests.

The public information office—or a single officer for smaller agencies—can be responsible for maintaining and updating the newsroom as well as the agency's Facebook page and Twitter tweets. Daily updates, with photos of the agency's personnel in action and photographs of wanted persons, keep the department on people's minds and makes them feel more like the police are part of their community and not just some mysterious group of humorless people who write tickets. The cost of maintaining a newsroom Web site is minimal, and having dedicated personnel to handle the media should be at least partially offset by reducing calls from media outlets to field supervisors and administrators.

In addition to a robust public information program, both the police chief and mayor should maintain personal contact with influential community leaders and be able to contact them immediately in case of an incident, such as a police shooting or emerging disorder. In this way, the police may be able to get their version of events into the community quickly and from trusted sources.

Cooperation with the media can generate considerable goodwill that can be invaluable to police agencies during emergencies and times when the actions of the police come under scrutiny. During major disasters or long-term operations such as manhunts, it is wise to have arrangements for additional public information office resources. A recent trend is for agencies to share their personnel and other resources on an as-needed basis in the event of a major incident. Regional agreements can be set up to provide for immediate support to ensure that a single public information officer or office is not overwhelmed in the face of an unusual event. Some public information officers have begun local and regional information officer groups, which not only facilitate sharing of contact information and best practices but also provide a forum for discussing mutual support arrangements for unexpected or planned large-scale events. The National Information Officers Association provides training and guidance for public information officers and can serve to support and improve the operations of an agency's information program.

Educating the Public

A tremendous amount of the misunderstandings between the police and public are due to a lack of understanding about what the police do. Strangely, despite the ubiquity of police drama on television and the movies, there is very little understanding about what the police actually do, where their authority derives from, and what tactics they utilize and why. The law-abiding public, in my experience, views the police as fearless and invincible. The ordinary person is mildly intimidated by the paramilitary uniform, badge, duty belt, and openly carried pistol of the police officer. They tend to believe that the police officers' sidearm makes their word final and absolute and that their will is irresistible when backed by their weapons and training. The reality is somewhat different.

The law-abiding citizen may fear defying the police because of the potential physical and legal consequences, but the police have to deal with people who do not fear them and who pose a threat to their very lives. A seasoned criminal knows that a police officer may use his sidearm only under very strict laws and rules, and he knows how to defy an officer in ways that prevent him from using his weapons. The police have to deal with people who have no fear of fighting, people who think nothing of being punched or kicked or knocked to the ground and who think nothing of doing such things to other people. What folks tend to think of as "normal" people, who know they are going to be arrested one way or the other, are those who would simply put their hands behind their back and get handcuffed and driven to the station. The reality that there are people who would *prefer* to get into a fistfight or fight to the death is too difficult for some to wrap their minds around. Were the police able to convey these facts and circumstances to the public, it would greatly enhance understanding between the police and citizenry.

Society and popular culture provide confusing messages for our police officers. We watch Clint Eastwood, as Dirty Harry Callahan, put a .45 bullet in a slime ball's leg and then grind dirt in the wound to find out the location of a kidnapped girl and audiences cheer. Television viewers see Detective Danny Reagan on *Blue Bloods* name-call and punch out New York City's worst criminals on a weekly basis and love him for it. Yet, when a real-life police officer is caught on video doing similar things, the feeling and public reaction is often very different—especially when we don't know the full context like we do in a television drama. The truth of the matter is watching a police detective go about his daily business behaving the way police are supposed to behave would be very boring. A cop who never curses, never calls a bad guy a mean name, and generally follows the rules when pursuing a vicious predator would not make much of a cinematic hero.

Police officers have to relate to those with whom they are dealing, and that sometimes involves using foul language and vulgar vernacular street language to communicate with witnesses or suspects. Police officers and detectives are expected to behave professionally, but trying to find out from a drug dealer if he knows anything about a teenager murdered in his neighborhood would be very ineffective if he said, "Excuse me sir, may I speak with you for a moment? I am trying to acquire information regarding the murder that took place in front of the bodega here last Tuesday. If I could trouble you for a few minutes of your time, I would like to inquire as to whether you may have any information which might be germane to my investigation?" That officer would likely not be understood or taken very seriously. While the officer's approach and opening should be respectful, it may require the use of rough language or other inducements to get a potential witness to talk.

Police departments with adequate resources should operate *citizen police academies* (CPAs) to educate the community about the realities of police work. Just as officers should be schooled in the role of police as maintaining order, so the public should understand the purpose and role of their police. CPAs began to proliferate in the 1990s as part of various departments' community policing initiatives. These academies are educational only and do not train auxiliary police or people to serve in any other capacity. Generally, CPAs meet one evening per week for 1 or 2 hours over the course of 8–12 weeks, while some incorporate one or more weekend sessions as well, with many taught by volunteer officers, greatly saving on the costs. The curriculum varies widely but generally includes familiarization with police officers' duties and responsibilities, the situations they deal with, their training, equipment, and rank structure. The cost of operation of these programs also varies tremendously. Some, using volunteer officers, are virtually cost free, while others may cost thousands of dollars for officers on overtime teaching the courses. Some agencies charge a tuition fee to offset the costs.

A model curriculum should consist of familiarization with police training, criminal procedure, criminal law, Fourth and Sixth amendment rights (search and seizure, right to an attorney), use of force, firearms familiarization and safety, patrol operations, scheduling, police stress, and a review of different types of situations to include: accident investigations, death investigations, homicide, domestics, and traffic enforcement. When possible, attendees should have the opportunity to visit the police academy and firing range and participate in a ride-a-long with an officer on patrol.

The benefits of these types of programs are self-evident. They provide positive public relations by giving residents an opportunity to interact with and learn about their police officers in a relaxed setting and to participate in some elements of the job. Participants learn about the world of policing and understand the nature and difficulty of the work. They also learn through their interactions that police officers are ordinary citizens like themselves, who merely have taken on the role of protector and peacekeeper as a full-time job. One study of the impact of CPAs on attendees found that the training "improved their views on the fair mindedness of police from 58 to 90 percent, about the adequacy of police training from 62 to 92 percent, and about the presence of minority police officers in departments from 26 to 73 percent. . . . Their feelings that most citizens' complaints are unjustified doubled from 31 to 62 percent and, perhaps consequently, their views regarding the adequacy of internal investigations improved from 53 to 92 percent."[3]

Clearly, most of the clientele of CPAs could be expected to be at least somewhat pro-police. However, there is still value in improving relations and understanding further with members of the community, who can then pass along what they've learned to friends, family, and coworkers. If agencies are able to gain the attendance of those who may be somewhat negative or ambivalent toward the police, there is a great opportunity to change public attitudes toward the police. These sorts of initiatives would admittedly be difficult to implement in ghetto communities, where police are generally regarded with hatred or fear and where the apathy of the population precludes serious community engagement. Still, through concerted effort, agencies may be able to identify and recruit those typically silent members of the community who have been cowed by the criminal element and who view the police as uncaring, incompetent, or corrupt.

A variant of the programs are CPAs geared toward young people. This is perhaps an even more effective way of changing public attitudes toward the police, as it speaks to youths in many cases before they have had an opportunity to form firm opinions about the police. High school students attend and learn the same topics taught at the adult CPAs but perhaps with more hands-on participation such as lifting fingerprints and taking mug shots. One possibility that has not been explored is perhaps expanding such programs to allow for students to receive extra scholastic credit or college credits for attending. A police agency could operate a CPA right on school grounds for interested students as an elective or after-school activity. Agencies could offer a CPA program as a possible elective course for local community colleges to attract young adults who otherwise may not take the time to attend.

The biggest limitation of CPAs is the limited number of participants who are trained in any given class. In order to promote interaction with instructors, classes need to be relatively small, and this limits the number of per-year graduates. Cost is another factor that may check an agency's ability to consistently run an effective program. This can be offset by using officers who volunteer or by compensating instructors with nonmonetary rewards. State and federal grants also may be secured to pay for the cost of running a CPA. Even some corporations, including Target and Wal-Mart, among others, offer funding for these and other programs.

Some agencies seek to further capitalize on the goodwill created through their CPA program by creating alumni associations for graduates. These organizations keep past attendees connected to the department through newsletters, invitations to special events, or even participation in training exercises. The Metro-Dade Police Department has such an alumni program and has utilized graduates to serve in volunteer positions within the department and even as part of a simulated mob during a training exercise, where participants hurled tennis balls at officers.[4] For agencies interested in creating a CPA program, there is the National Citizens Police Academy Association, which provides resources, training, and assistance, including establishing the program as a charitable organization under IRS regulations.[5]

Most importantly, whether through CPAs or other means, police need to help educate the public about their peculiar perspective. A person walking through a park who matches the description of a man who tried to lure a child into the woods earlier in the day, and who is in fact innocent, may not understand an officer's curt tone or why he is being ordered to keep his hands out of his pockets. To the innocent man, the police officer may seem rude, and he may be very offended by the implication that he is either a child molester or someone who poses a threat to the officer's safety. The police can help by teaching their perspective to the public, that the hypothetical man matches the description of someone potentially dangerous and the officer needs to quickly ascertain the person's identity and move on to keep searching for the bad guy. Since people carry weapons in their pockets, the officer wants to be able to see the person's hands at all times until the officer knows the person is not a threat. The officer is not accusing anyone of anything but must proceed based on the possibility that the individual is guilty and dangerous for his or her own protection.

Running community members or media personalities through real-life scenarios or shoot-don't shoot simulations can go a long way toward enhancing understanding. I was a witness to my agency's first ever *media day* at the academy and listened angrily to reporters asking hostile questions that began with "what makes you think . . ." and "where do you get the right. . . ." One reporter asked, "What gives you cops the right to act as judge, jury, and executioner?" The question is of course absurd and was intended merely as an insult, since the police have no authority to act in any of those capacities. Later that day, I had the surreal experience of watching that same reporter shoot six holes in the first man on the screen in a shoot-don't shoot simulation. The man was angry and very animated but unarmed and made no overt threats. The reason the reporter gave for "killing" the man was "He wouldn't shut up."

For almost everyone, it is a very bizarre and stressful experience to be placed in a position where you are forced to compel another person to obey your commands. The real world is nothing like the movies; people will simply ignore an officer's commands, act like the officer isn't even there, or walk away passively. Alternatively, they might angrily challenge an officer's authority to stop them or ask for identification, spouting bits of legal gibberish they've cobbled together from urban legend and Internet chat rooms. This leaves the officer in the unenviable position of having to initiate a physical confrontation to forcibly detain or arrest a person. (This is also why police must know the law concerning stops inside and out.) Frequently, YouTube videos of police interactions begin once attention is drawn to the conflict, after the officer has politely asked for compliance and explained his reasoning. So a video begins with an angry or defiant person exclaiming, "I didn't do anything wrong!" and being immediately struck, sprayed, or Tasered by the officer, without any context documenting the minutes before the use of force. Just the knowledge that a police officer does not have the option of saying, effectively, "screw it" and walking away makes many confrontations seem much more understandable.

Humanizing the Badge

Police officers should take every opportunity to involve themselves in events and festivals that take place in their community. The more chances the public has to interact with a police officer in a relaxed social setting, the more police can be seen as human beings, and not dour automatons, the better relations will be. If officers can be seen as likable and friendly, they are more likely to be forgiven for their occasional mistakes or for times when necessity makes them seem short of patience.

Agencies must practice community policing. For too many departments, community policing is some sort of program; they assign a friendly officer to attend a bake sale, give a talk at a community group meeting, or show up with a display at the county fair. While these sorts of activities are useful, community policing must be a department-wide philosophy that involves all members and civilian employees. Everyone should be geared toward serving the community and being receptive to its needs, requests, and feedback. Line officers should be encouraged and incentivized to interact with people they encounter on patrol and to talk with local business owners and community leaders in their patrol areas. Officers should be encouraged to act as ombudsmen for their community, asking about any problems that the city might address, including potholes and trash-filled vacant lots. There should be a system in place for passing these concerns to a department member or civilian who contacts the proper city authority and tracks the response. A measure such as this would require enthusiastic support from the mayor or city manager to ensure concerns are addressed quickly. This is not only effective governance—as the police are always out and about in the community—but it allows police to be seen as helpful problem solvers who do more than just "hassle" people walking down the street. A community policing approach also requires agencies to de-emphasize numbers as a criteria for judging officer performance. In order for its members to have time to talk with residents and to address and follow up on problems, they must be given the time to do so. Moreover, ticket and summons writing only increases the frequency of negative contact between the police and the public. Officers should save their tickets for the few who truly deserve it and spend more time learning about the neighborhood and people they serve.

It is crucial that police leaders at every level develop close ties with community leaders and individuals across the spectrum of constituencies the agency serves. These lines of communication should be carefully maintained to foster understanding and goodwill as well as allowing the department to gauge the community's general attitudes and perceptions regarding crime and the performance of its officers. These networks provide critical avenues for disseminating accurate information quickly in the event of a police shooting or other controversial action that may occur. These lines of communication work both ways, permitting community leaders to quickly get answers to questions that may help defuse a volatile situation. Obviously, these relationships need to be established and strengthened over time and carefully maintained during periods of calm; they cannot be simply "activated" when an event occurs.

Partnering with local schools is another important step for departments to improve their image and to assist in intervening with at-risk youth. Police should not only be familiar with schools in their assigned areas of responsibility but make contact with the school's administrators. School officials should know that they can call on the police at any time for guidance and for officers to speak with students on topics such as drugs, driving under the influence, or policing in general. These sorts of partnerships can benefit both the school and department, as well as introduce kids to police officers at an early age, so they can understand that police forces are made up of human beings like themselves. Many schools nationwide have begun programs in partnership with the police to bring an officer into the school full time. These school resource officer (SRO) programs can provide a greatly enhanced sense of security for students, teachers, and parents, as well as an instantaneous police response to any serious incidents that occur on school grounds. These SROs can act as informal counselors and mentors to students, which also serves to build greater ties between police and the community.

Research into the effectiveness of SROs—sometimes referred to as school liaison officers—is still very limited. One study by the University of Tennessee found that at schools with an SRO, arrests for assaults and weapons possession decreased while arrests for disorderly conduct increased. One criticism or fear of SRO programs is the potential for criminalizing student behavior, that is, making behavior that was traditionally corrected by the school the subject of police intervention, resulting in misbehaving students being labeled as criminals rather than simply receiving detention or other administrative sanctions.[6] This possibility is something schools and police should actively work to avoid and create policies and procedures in advance to prevent a drift toward police action in areas better suited for school discipline. By doing so, they can ensure smooth functioning of the program and maintain the safety and community relations benefits of officer presence.

Finally, there is no better way to improve public relations than by officers getting out of their cars and chatting with people in their patrol areas, not to try to get them to inform on their neighbors or find out what's in their pockets but simply to discuss their interests or concerns. An officer can stop in a park and kick a soccer ball with some kids or shoot a couple baskets. Officers can stop at garage sales, lemonade stands, farmer's markets, schools, and local businesses. Police managers should encourage and reward officers who get to know their communities and who participate off duty in civic or charitable activities. Police officers sealed up in their cruisers, who are never seen except when making an arrest or writing a ticket, are far more likely to be viewed with apprehension or suspicion than are officers who are known to residents.

Procedural Justice

The concept of procedural justice is a new model for providing police services and measuring success. This concept is sometimes referred to as procedural fairness. The theory is that people in the justice system are influenced more by their perception of how fair the *process* is rather than their opinion of the *outcome*. This is not a new idea so much as treating the notion of fairness in the process as a policy and looking at the ways it improves the functioning and public opinion of the system. Citizens and police view the system and its processes differently. Police officers are trained to view everything through the lens of the law: what actions are permissible, what stops and searches are legal, what constitutes probable cause for arrest, and what elements constitute particular crimes. The average citizen views any given situation more broadly—in terms of simple fairness.

Being arrested physically or by receiving a summons or traffic ticket can be a confusing, frightening, and often utterly bewildering experience. There are issues of attorney's fees, court dates, language barriers, bail, finding the court, parking, navigating sometimes gigantic justice buildings, understanding each step in the process, and so on. The police are only the first step in the often confounding processes of the justice system, but there are steps the police can take to ensure people feel they are being treated fairly. Most people would be surprised at how frequently criminals will express gratitude or appreciation for being treated respectfully. During my years on the street, I was thanked many times—even by ex-convicts—for treating them with respect, despite the fact that I was arresting them for a serious crime and taking them to jail. This is the most vivid illustration of the way in which perceptions of fairness affect a defendant's opinion of the police.

In broad terms, procedural justice represents a shift in thinking away from a strictly deterrence method of achieving obedience to law and cooperation with authorities to one that incorporates a process-based method for police and courts to achieve voluntary compliance or acceptance. Professors Tom R. Tyler and Yuen J. Ho describe the goal as "facilitate[ing] cooperation, consent, and the voluntary acceptance of decisions through behavior that is linked to acting fairly and showing good faith."[7] Any police officer can tell you that they at times deal with people who are completely uncivilized and irrational. As a result, officers often tend to view new ideas of emphasizing fairness and humanizing the experience for people under arrest as absurd or muddle-headed thinking typical of academics. Clearly, some people don't care much about fairness or anything else, and some individuals understand no authority but superior physical force. But the vast majority of persons who receive traffic tickets, summonses for minor violations, or even those that commit misdemeanor or felony crimes do not react with irrationality and violence, and these people, although criminals in the eyes of police, can be treated with fairness and dignity.

Police can be the first step in this process simply by being polite whenever circumstances permit. Police can—and should—refer to both the store manager and the homeless person as "ma'am" or "sir." Officers in nonthreatening situations should phrase their directions in conversational form: "May I have a word with you?" "Please step over here." When police officers interview a crime victim, they should show empathy for the victim's loss, shock, fear, anger, or other emotions and should explain what they are doing and what the next steps in the process will be. Officers can ensure that victims are cared for, that a relative is notified, or that they get transportation home. Defendants who do not resist can also be treated with basic common courtesy, with those being released allowed to make calls for rides or other arrangements. Police should always take care to thank witnesses or other persons offering assistance and perhaps follow up with a departmental letter or certificate of appreciation for particularly conspicuous actions of assistance to the department.

Officers should be responsive to questions that are posed to them and avoid using legal jargon that may confuse victims, witnesses, or suspects. Officers should know how to utilize departmental or telephone-based translation services to ensure proper communication and explanation. Officers should be sensitive to those who express the feeling that they are being treated unfairly and clarify the law, their actions, and the limitations the police operate under—explaining that they will have additional opportunities to air their side of the story to the prosecutor before any trial or conviction.

Large police facilities should be user friendly for those visiting to make complaints, give witness statements, or pick up loved ones. Visitors should be able to easily find the proper entrance and speak to someone who will courteously answer their questions and see to it that they get an answer to their question or are seen by the appropriate officer or detective.

Again, police officers will often have to deal with individuals who do not respond to politeness, who are violent, drunk, stoned, or just plain rude and obnoxious. The police should not have to talk to and accommodate such people as they would someone who is behaving in a respectable manner. By the same token, they do not have to lower their language to the level of such people—there are ways to give forceful and effective commands and even put people in their place without resorting to profanity-laced screaming.

Prosecutors and the courts should employ these sorts of considerations as well. Just as there are far too many police officers who are dismissive of the concerns of people they come into contact with, there are too many prosecutors who do not take the time to talk with the people involved in their cases and who care more about clearing cases and getting convictions than they do about justice or the truth. If the police, prosecutors, and courts placed their focus more on the simple issue of fairness and justice, those who come in contact with the justice system would feel that their voices were heard and that they have been treated fairly by the system and the players within it, and consequently the legitimacy of the law and justice system would be enhanced.[8]

By becoming more cooperative with the media, engaging with the community, utilizing social media, focusing on fairness, and being open and forthright with the public when mistakes are made, police agencies can make significant progress in improving their public relations. Without the support of their constituents, police can never hope to accomplish their mission of protecting and serving their fellow citizens.

CHAPTER NINE

Handling Officers Who Abuse the Public Trust

He who fights with monsters should look to it that he himself does not become a monster. And if you gaze long into an abyss, the abyss also gazes into you.

—Friedrich Nietzche

The investigation and disposition of complaints about officers' behavior is one of the most persistent and important problems facing police agencies. While nearly every agency has some sort of process in place for handling citizen complaints, the procedures themselves vary widely, as does the extent to which they are followed. The investigation of accusations against officers goes to the very heart of police accountability, which in turn is the sine qua non of legitimacy. Yet, somehow this critical component of a police organization does not receive the proper attention it should and too often becomes the subject of management-union wrangling rather than adherence to some sort of professional standard for internal investigations.

On the night of October 20, 2014, Chicago police officer Jason Van Dyke shot Laquan McDonald to death on Pulaski Road in the Archer Heights area of the city. Around 10 P.M., officers had been dispatched to a report of a man with a knife, who had been stealing radios from semi-trucks in a parking lot and was now walking down the street. Responding officers located McDonald, who reportedly slashed the tire of a following police car. Now walking south down Pulaski Street wielding a knife, he refused repeated commands to stop and drop his weapon, continuing to walk in the southbound lane. Dash-cam video (no audio) shows McDonald walking and jogging down the street toward a stationary police cruiser, waving the knife wildly as the second patrol car follows from the rear. Officer Van

Dyke and his partner are seen to pull ahead of both police cars as a fourth approaches from the south. As the car containing Van Dyke and his partner comes to a stop, Officer Van Dyke exits the passenger side, drawing his sidearm and pointing it at McDonald. Van Dyke reportedly ordered McDonald repeatedly to drop his knife, which he ignored. The video clearly shows Officer Van Dyke to McDonald's left front as he exits his car. McDonald then begins to move obliquely to his right in what appears to be an attempt to keep walking south on Pulaski, past the officer. Five seconds after Officer Van Dyke exited his vehicle, he shoots McDonald, who spins nearly 360 degrees and falls limp on the pavement. It is impossible to see bullet impacts or determine the speed at which the rounds were fired, although at least one round can be seen kicking up dust on the pavement next to McDonald's prone body.[1]

The investigation at the scene would determine that Officer Van Dyke fired a total of 16 rounds at McDonald—emptying his entire magazine. The Chicago Police Department (CPD) reported that McDonald had "lunged at police, and one of the officers opened fire." The video was then hidden from the public for more than 13 months. After the CPD stonewalled a local reporter's Freedom of Information Act requests for the video for more than a year, the CPD was finally ordered by a judge to release the dash-cam video of the incident. The video clearly showed that the official account provided by the CPD was false and sparked a firestorm of protest from the community. This anger was exacerbated by the fact that Officer Van Dyke was white and McDonald was black. In November 2015, just a few days after the release of the video, Van Dyke was indicted for the murder of Laquan McDonald.

Before delving into the lessons that can be learned from this case, let me make one point perfectly clear: McDonald *was* the apparent victim of a murder, based upon the video and medical examiner reports. Once McDonald fell limply to the ground, there was no longer any reason to shoot at him, regardless of whether, in Van Dyke's words, "[he] appeared to be attempting to get up. . . ." The autopsy indicated that 9 of the 16 rounds struck McDonald at a downward angle.[2]

This case provides numerous lessons for the police and the public. First, the national media failed to properly cover the incident, characterizing the video as depicting the suspect "walking away from police" and referring to the shooting as completely unjustified. While Officer Van Dyke's actions in firing multiple rounds at McDonald as he lay on the ground is *clearly* unjustifiable, the first one or two shots were—at least legally—justified. McDonald was armed with a deadly weapon, was under the influence of PCP, ignored all police commands, and was acting wildly, waving a knife, and making guttural growling noises. While the video shows McDonald moving obliquely away from Officer Van Dyke and his partner, he nonetheless was close enough to be an imminent threat. An assailant armed with a knife can potentially kill an officer armed with a gun once he approaches within 20 feet; even if the officer is able to shoot the attacker, his momentum (and other factors including the effects of narcotics) will still allow the attacker to inflict a mortal wound.

McDonald was acting in a very erratic manner and moments earlier had tried to enter a Burger King and a Dunkin Donuts, where he would have posed a grave threat to innocent persons. Given those circumstances, McDonald's bizarre behavior, defiance of police, slashing a police vehicle's tire, and his continuing threat to anyone in his path, the use of deadly force was, at least arguably and legally justifiable.

Setting aside the subsequent hail of bullets fired by Van Dyke, the question at this stage is, While the use of deadly force could be justified, was it *necessary*? The Supreme Court made clear in its 1985 decision in *Tenneesee v. Garner* that deadly force is justifiable only when absolutely required to protect innocent lives. The Supreme Court also ruled that deadly force should not be used when a viable nonlethal option exists and further that, when feasible, some warning should be given before employing deadly force. Common sense police procedure before and since has been to resort to deadly physical force only when all other means either have been exhausted or are impracticable.

Officers had radioed for a unit equipped with a Taser to respond, apparently with a view to stopping McDonald with this less-than-lethal weapon. There were multiple officers on the scene, and officers could have continued to follow and attempt to contain McDonald until the arrival of a Taser. Yet, had the officers continued to simply follow a clearly dangerous and armed suspect, it would have created additional dangers to anyone in the path of McDonald. Surely, had McDonald suddenly bolted into another fast-food establishment and begun slashing customers to death, the police would have faced withering criticism for failing to act.

It seems apparent from looking at the video that Officer Van Dyke fully intended to directly engage the suspect from the outset; he exits his vehicle and immediately moves directly at McDonald without any cover. If they had decided that McDonald needed to be stopped immediately, Van Dyke and his partner should have taken up a position much farther down the street from McDonald and utilized their vehicle for cover—placing the large SUV between themselves and the suspect. A knife, regardless of the length of its blade, is an extremely deadly weapon—every bit as deadly as a pistol at close range.

Officer Van Dyke's actions in shooting McDonald repeatedly after he fell to the ground, not surprisingly, swept away any serious discussion of the event in its totality. Once the suspect no longer has the immediate ability to harm anyone, especially with multiple officers present, police are trained to be at the ready but to again attempt verbal commands or nonlethal force if feasible. While a knife is deadly, a wounded man on the ground poses a vastly reduced threat since, unlike someone armed with a gun, he must approach his intended target on foot.

The Aftermath

Every officer who was present at that shooting knew they had witnessed a murder. According to civilian witnesses, Van Dyke stopped shooting momentarily after McDonald fell to the pavement and then resumed firing another five or six rounds.[3] Notwithstanding the official report's claim that "McDonald appeared to be attempting to get up"[4] (a claim not supported by the video evidence), there could be no justification for continuing to fire bullets into his nearly motionless body.

Nearly as disturbing as the execution of McDonald was the behavior of some members of the CPD following the shooting. Van Dyke, his partner, and three other officers, who stated they saw the shooting, all mischaracterized or lied about what transpired in official reports;

Van Dyke:	"When McDonald got to within 10 to 15 feet of [me], McDonald looked toward [me]. McDonald raised the knife across his chest and over his shoulder, pointing the knife at [me]."
Officer Walsh:	"When McDonald got to within 12 to 15 feet of the officers he swung the knife toward the officers in an aggressive manner."
Officer Fontaine:	"McDonald ignored the verbal direction and instead, raised his right arm toward officer Van Dyke, as if attacking Van Dyke."
Officer Sebastian:	"Officers Joseph Walsh and Jason Van Dyke exited their vehicle and drew their handguns. McDonald turned toward the two officers and continued to wave the knife."[5]

Between May and August 2015, journalist Brandon Smith filed 15 separate Freedom of Information Act requests for the dash-cam video with the CPD—all of which were rejected. The video was eventually released after Smith sued and the Cook County Court ruled that the CPD must turn over the recording. Without Smith's resolve, and those he enlisted to assist him, it is likely the video may never have surfaced—and Officer Van Dyke would still be patrolling the streets of Chicago.

Clearly, the handling of this entire matter is deeply disturbing. Why would purported law enforcement professionals lie about what they witnessed? Why did follow-up investigators and superior officers not take immediate action when they viewed the video? The malfeasance on display runs from Officer Van Dyke right through the highest levels of the police department and even to Mayor Rahm Emanuel, who, even as the video was about to be released to the public, claimed not to have seen it.

In April 2015, seven months before the video was released, city attorneys met with Mayor Emanuel and they subsequently offered to pay McDonald's family $5 million for his wrongful death and pressured the family to agree to keep the video secret as part of the deal.[6] At the time, Emanuel was fighting for his political life in a runoff election against his party primary challenger, Chuy Garcia. There can be little doubt that the city attorneys viewed the video, which clearly depicted a crime, but they and the mayor did nothing to bring Van Dyke to justice—they simply wanted it all to go away.

One thing that becomes apparent as you move through the ranks of any organization and study problems that arise in police and other bureaucracies is that everything starts from the top: the fish rots from the head. Obviously, while a leader is responsible for everything taking place under his or her command, he or she can't possibly be everywhere and know everything. But over time, the leader's character, work ethic, and attitudes are passed like a virus—for better or worse—downward through the chain of command. This creates the atmosphere in which line officers and their superiors operate.

Personal and professional integrity should rank first and foremost among the qualities required to retain employment as a police officer. Police leaders and supervisors must demand it of themselves and their subordinates. It is honesty and integrity that allows a police organization to achieve and maintain legitimacy in the eyes of the public. It is little wonder that the officers in this case were so willing to lie, given the culture of corruption in the city. When their superiors, from sergeant right up to the mayor himself, have evidence that a police officer committed such an act of violence and their reaction is to first ignore it, then for the mayor to pay the family to keep quiet about the evidence, what sort of behavior would one expect from the rank and file?

Not until nearly two years after the shooting did the CPD begin to take any action against the officers who lied in an effort to cover up the crime. In August 2016, Superintendent Eddie Johnson announced that he was seeking the termination of seven officers involved in the shooting and its aftermath. There was no explanation offered as to why the department would wait so long to take action against officers who plainly lied about what they saw. Moreover, there is no explanation forthcoming as to why higher-ranking members who viewed the video and did nothing are not being fired for malfeasance. Every person who saw the video and read the report is culpable in the cover-up. It takes only a single incident like this to shatter public trust in both the police and the city government.

The subsequent federal investigation of the CPD by the Justice Department followed in the tradition of many others before it by failing to examine the role played by the police leadership and city government. The investigators made no detailed examination of the handling of the McDonald shooting or any effort to hold administrators and city officials accountable for their complicity.

Mixed Messages

Our entertainment media are saturated with images and stories about police officers and detectives. They are generally portrayed as heroic, if sometimes flawed characters. These officers also routinely engage in behaviors that, when they occur in real life, are met with shock and disgust by large swaths of the public. Watching our heroes on television and the movies, it would seem that our society wants its police to bend and sometimes break the rules when the interests of justice demand it. Heroic cops in the movies lie, beat up lowlife prisoners, plant evidence, and generally do whatever is required to get the job done. Of course, all the people they abuse clearly seem to deserve the treatment they get, and the officers' generally never really frame an innocent person, just plant evidence so as to be able to threaten them and thereby induce them to do the right thing by informing on a much worse criminal.

These television and cinema heroes commandeer cars, crash into civilians' cars during chases and just keep going, curse at people, and do all manner of things that in the real world often result in official complaints, investigations, and termination of employment. These are the stories we create, and the audience is okay with the misconduct, because they know the character is motivated by a desire to help others and protect the weak and the innocent. The fictional characters are well developed and audiences empathize with their dilemma of being caught between the law and the desire to see justice done. We know they have a flawless moral compass and envy them for their willingness to buck the system for the sake of what is right.

The reality of policing is vastly different from what many expect. Young men and women who grew up on this entertainment find themselves constrained by the law and departmental policies. They find considerably fewer gunfights and car explosions during a typical workweek and rarely find themselves in a situation where breaking the law seems like a good idea in order to serve some higher purpose. Yet, the image of the rogue, gun-slinging, warrior cop persists and can lead officers astray, especially when their training is lacking in adequate professional indoctrination and ethics instruction.

Our nation's police receive conflicting messages from both the general public and our popular culture as to how they are expected behave. The public at once demands that the police maintain order and "do something" about various criminal and other problems that arise. At the same time, they are expected to use restraint and behave courteously in their tactics. From the patrolman's viewpoint, the police department has a choice: prove the notion that they are a group of thugs by acting aggressively to stop violence or be accused of incompetence for not taking appropriate action. The mixed messages sent to our police is further illustrated by a Mike Royko column regarding the use of police force at a heavy-metal concert where fans were getting out of control:

> My disapproval [of police brutality] is strictly in principal—under those conditions I viscerally enjoy it. Chances are, those who are arrested for throwing things at the performers will be charged with disorderly conduct. . . . The punishment will be a small fine, or the charges might be dropped. That's really not adequate punishment. So a punch to the offender's chops by a policeman might not be within the strict framework of the law, but it does help balance the books.[7]

These comments from a noted crusader against police abuse of authority are particularly illustrative of the central problem of police use of force; we expect the police to occasionally rough up bad guys when the situation calls for it. Our popular television shows and motion pictures are filled with images of police portrayed as heroes, who routinely beat up the bad guys and use less-than-legal tactics to catch a criminal when the situation is serious enough to warrant them. In short, a significant but unstated part of the problem of police misconduct of all types is that as a society we tacitly expect and condone certain undefined forms of "improper" behavior on the part of our police officers in certain situations. Simultaneously, we are unwilling to loosen the formal controls on our police to permit them the latitude to employ extreme tactics when deemed necessary in the pursuit of law and order. Put another way, we expect our police to place themselves at risk not only in terms of facing dangerous criminals and other life-threatening situations but also to knowingly violate laws and procedures to get the job done. The implicit message is "please go ahead, just don't get caught." This only compounds the situation today's police officers find themselves in, living what Professor Michael K. Brown termed a *schizophrenic existence*.[8]

Disciplining the Police

The traditional process for dealing with police malfeasance involves the imposition of penalties—expressed as lost vacation days, suspension without pay, or loss of rank or special assignment. This allows for corrective measures to be taken for misconduct that does not rise to the level of termination of employment. The way a police department handles complaints of misconduct will, to a significant degree, determine its level of professionalism and its legitimacy in the eyes of the public. The internal investigative process is generally opaque; unless an officer is fired or arrested, complainants generally have no way of knowing whether their complaint was judged to be founded or whether the officer involved received any sort of punishment or admonishment.

The result is that many individuals who go to police supervisors with complaints come away feeling as though they have wasted their time. Many police officers who are eventually found to be guilty of gross misconduct or criminal activity, for example, Officer Van Dyke, turn out to have an outrageous number of past complaints made against them. In Van Dyke's case, he had 20 complaints filed against him for various forms of misconduct prior to shooting McDonald to death on Pulaski Avenue.

Now, while it's an old adage in police work that "if you don't have any complaints made against you, you aren't doing your job," it is also generally true that if an officer receives vastly more complaints than the average, or repeated complaints about the same sort of behavior, it's likely you have a problem cop on your hands. Of the 20 complaints against Van Dyke, 11 were for use of excessive force. Officer Van Dyke was disciplined in exactly *zero* of the 20 cases. In five of the cases, the outcome was listed as "not sustained," meaning there was not enough evidence to either substantiate the complaint or exonerate Van Dyke. He was "exonerated" in four of the cases, while five were listed as "unfounded." Six other cases have unknown classifications, but resulted in no discipline.[9]

Having said all this, good cops working in high-crime areas of Chicago or any major city are going to have complaints made against them. A lack of understanding of police responsibilities, miscommunication, and a belief that criminal charges or tickets will be dropped if a complaint is made against the officer frequently result in unfounded or completely false accusations against police.

In order for a police agency to have an effective program to ensure the integrity of the agency, they must have clear procedures in place for conducting thorough investigations of every complaint made. Supervisors who are found to cover up complaints made against officers need to face severe discipline, involving—at a minimum—loss of rank. Large agencies especially need to have a system in place for flagging officers who have repeated complaints of a similar nature made against them. Good officers who are proactive and work hard will likely have complaints against them for a variety of reasons: verbal abuse, illegal search, excessive force, and so forth. However, an officer who has complaints that indicate a specific pattern of behavior, such as repeated claims of verbal abuse and excessive force, should raise a red flag with administrators, especially if the complaints are not substantiated—meaning no clear evidence of guilt or innocence could be found.

Police departments of any appreciable size need to have in place what is often referred to as an *early warning system*, to alert command personnel of potential problem officers. Many complaints of simple rudeness or officious or condescending behavior are not only subjective but by their very nature are usually impossible to prove or disprove. Nonetheless, a police agency should have a means whereby officers with repeated unsubstantiated complaints of being obnoxious are flagged for greater scrutiny, counseling by superiors, or additional training.

Officer Van Dyke, with his 20 complaints from citizens, was one of only 265 CPD members with 20 or more complaints. The CPD has a little over 13,000 sworn members, meaning that such members constitute only 2 percent of the entire force. There is an additional 10 percent of the force with between 10 and 19 complaints, leaving 88 percent with between 0 and 9.[10] It should be obvious to professional police administrators that the top 2 percent of officers receiving complaints from the public need close supervision and more frequent evaluation.

Identifying the Problem

Police officers generally work with very minimal supervision. This is simply an unavoidable reality of the work officers perform: traveling around their assigned post, responding to calls for service in multiple locations, and so forth. With officers posted throughout a county or city, it would require practically every officer to have his or her own sergeant to ensure strict supervision.

Another major obstacle to properly evaluating an officer's work is the nature of police encounters. (The commonly used term is *police-citizen encounters*. Like *law enforcement officer*, it is a term that should be eliminated. Police officers *are* citizens and should not be set apart as a separate entity from the communities they serve.) The viewpoint of a police officer is most often very different from that of the individual he is dealing with. The individual knows whether or not he is guilty and whether or not he intends to run or attempt to kill the officer, while the police officer can only guess—and be prepared for the worst. This creates all sorts of opportunities for miscommunication and misinterpretation during these interactions. Combine this with the everyday prejudices that people bring to their daily interactions and you are frequently going to find two very different versions of events when trying to evaluate the conduct of an officer after the fact.

For example, if a police officer stops a vehicle that matches the description of a car used in an armed robbery, the officer must behave as if there is a very real possibility that the occupants are armed and dangerous and may attempt to flee or harm the officer. For the car's occupants, who are a father and son on their way home from a golf outing, the officer's command voice, un-holstered weapon, and invasive questions seem rude and totally unwarranted. Depending upon the particular officer's interpersonal skills, the seriousness of the robbery, the radio traffic in his ear, and his past exposure to violence and injury, he may offer a brief explanation or apology to the driver or quickly return to his patrol car to resume the search. A driver in this scenario who views police as officious, arrogant thugs will likely leave the situation having his opinions affirmed, regardless of whether the officer offers an explanation and cursory apology for the inconvenience. Likewise, the individual who holds the police in high esteem will excuse an officer's curt behavior because of the nature of the situation and the dangerous job the officer is performing.

The police officer is the embodiment of authority: he or she carries a visible sidearm and wears a badge of office and distinctive uniform. A host of factors determine how individuals perceive an officer's behavior, including their attitude toward authority in general, their beliefs about the legitimacy of *the system*, and their immediate frame of mind. Much work needs to be done to improve the understanding between police and their fellow citizens, and this is an area where the police can work to improve relations, as discussed in Chapter 7.

Accountability

For police agencies to ensure the integrity of their workforce, they must hold officers liable for their actions, have clear and meaningful punishments available to discipline those who break the rules, and have the fortitude to fire officers who violate the law or demonstrate a lack of aptitude for the job. This still presents police administrators with a host of difficulties, from proving "guilt" in a rudeness complaint to determining the officer's frame of mind (i.e., did the officer deliberately circumvent proper procedures or do they simply require some remedial training).

Presently, every police agency in the country has its own procedures and policies in place when it comes to handling complaints against officers, while many have no formal policy whatsoever. In most cases, complainants have no way of knowing what action, if any, was taken as a result of their complaint. A citizen may telephone the local sheriff to complain about a rude deputy who conducted an illegal search of his person and car and be told "I'll look into it" or "I'll have a talk with the deputy." This does not leave the aggrieved party with any sense that his complaint is being taken seriously or that the officer will suffer any consequences for his actions.

Police agencies, regardless of size, should have clear, written policies and procedures for handling complaints about their officers. This policy should make it clear that *all* complaints will be investigated, that any officer or employee of the department is authorized to receive complaints, and a well-defined procedure for passing the complaint to the investigating authority—the chief, sheriff, supervisor, or an internal affairs unit—should be in place. In addition, every complaint investigation should be recorded in writing and retained on file during the officer's tenure.

Rank-and-file personnel and first-line supervisors should be clearly prohibited from discouraging complaints or disregarding complaints they judge to be invalid on their face. While many false and invalid complaints are made against police officers, organizational integrity demands that every complaint be received and examined in some form. All complaints must be investigated, but procedures for investigating an officer charged with severe brutality may differ significantly from those for investigating a complaint that simply involves a citizen who is dissatisfied with the outcome of an investigation.

A citizen may complain about an officer because she failed to arrest the person who stole his 70-inch television. The complaint may turn out to involve no error by the officer, because a cursory review of the report indicates that the complainant's estranged wife, who still technically owns the home and all property within jointly with the complainant, took the television. In a case such as this, the complainant is upset that the law does not allow for justice be served to his satisfaction and is directing his anger at the officer. Nonetheless, if a simple explanation of the law does not satisfy the complainant, the complaint should be taken and submitted through the adjudication process.

A detailed form should be used to record the complaint and transmit the report up the chain of command, and a specific individual should be tasked with assigning a member to investigate. The investigating member should, in all cases, be of higher rank than the officer under investigation and (preferably) be somewhat removed from day-to-day contact with the officer. This means that a first-line supervisor should not be assigned to investigate complaints against the officers he or she supervises every day. In smaller departments, the chief, sheriff, or one of their top-level command staff should investigate complaints. In larger agencies, members assigned to a designated internal affairs unit can handle complaints.

Officers should be required to explain their actions either in a memorandum or in a formal statement, depending upon the severity and complexity of the accusations. There is no excuse for procedures that fail to require the officers to simply explain their actions. In the case of the CPD, investigators are prohibited from requiring officers to provide an account of their actions unless and until there is some sort of compelling evidence that they engaged in misconduct. As a result, there can be no way for internal investigators to determine if officers conducted themselves properly. This not only hinders uncovering serious problems but also prevents officers from receiving needed remedial instruction on developing probable cause and dealing with distressed individuals or other areas of potential weakness. Policing, like any other line of work, should involve a process of ongoing education and development. If, when their actions are challenged, officers do not have to offer any explanation for their actions, an agency's integrity is gravely threatened.

Except in cases of an anonymous complaint, every effort should be made to interview the complainant and take a written statement of his or her accusations. This can be done either at the police station or at the person's residence or other location if the complainant is uncomfortable coming to the station. In the event the complainant refuses to cooperate, this fact should be documented by the investigator, who nonetheless should complete the investigatory process to the extent possible.

Every police agency should have a system in place to track officer complaints, and an officer's record of past complaints should be reviewed as part of the adjudication procedure. This serves two functions: it allows administrators to impose harsher penalties on repeat offenders, and it permits identification of any negative patterns of behavior. For instance, most complaints of simple rudeness cannot be verified one way or the other, and rudeness is often subjective depending upon the perspective of the parties involved. Occasional complaints of rudeness are to be expected in a profession that involves giving orders and getting involved in confrontational situations. However, an officer who shows a pattern of repeated complaints of rudeness or other unprofessional conduct likely has a problem dealing with the public and should be identified as a candidate for remedial training.

In an environment where police are routinely subject to false and malicious complaints, they and their union representatives are wise to advocate for safeguards. Police officers, just like all citizens, deserve to be treated fairly in any investigation that could affect their employment. Nonetheless, police officers occupy a special position of public trust and should not be entitled to some of the excessive protections extended to other civil service workers, such as DMV clerks. The current contract between the CPD union and the City of Chicago offers an example of a protection no police officer should have. Section 6.1(M) of that contract actually prohibits officers from being charged with making a false report or statement about an event that was recorded until after the officer is allowed to review the recording and change his or her story.[11]

Keep Bad Cops Off the Job

Because of the existence of overly protective civil service regulations or permissive contractual agreements, it is often difficult to terminate the employment of problem officers. Because of this, police agencies will very frequently offer to allow an officer to resign in lieu of being brought up on formal charges and the risk of being fired. While this sort of practice might be fine in certain lines of work, it creates a serious problem for police. When an officer resigns, he or she can simply seek employment as a police officer elsewhere, and the previous agency will generally never disclose that the officer was forced to resign because of misconduct.

As a result, corrupt, violent, and incompetent officers can simply move to another jurisdiction or another state and apply at another police agency to begin all over again, abusing citizens' rights and tarnishing the reputation of another department and the policing profession generally. In the worst cases, a dangerous predator can continue his criminal behavior in the guise of a police officer because his previous employer lacked the fortitude or political support to officially terminate a malefactor. It is obvious that police officers who lack integrity or are prone to violence or other forms of criminality pose a more serious threat to society because of their position. An incompetent, rude clerk at the DMV, or a thief at the parks department, does not pose the same threat as police officers with the same characteristics. Even well-meaning officers who are ignorant of the laws, lazy, or cowardly can seriously endanger the public.

The case of Sean Sullivan, a small-town cop from Oregon, is illustrative. Sullivan was discovered kissing a 10-year-old girl on the mouth and sentenced to a jail term. Part of the sentence handed down was that he was barred from working as a police officer. Despite this, he had no difficulties being hired as the chief of police of Cedar Vale Kansas just three months later. Before long, he was arrested again for burglary and criminal conspiracy and was suspected of a relationship with another underage girl.[12]

Officer Timothy Loehmann of the Cleveland Police Department, who shot and killed 12-year-old Tamir Rice, who was playing with a toy gun in a city park in 2014, had been forced to resign from a smaller department due to incompetence before coming to work at the Cleveland Police Drepartment.[13]

Officer Eddie Boyd III of the St. Louis Police Department was forced to leave the agency after he was found culpable, in separate incidents, of having pistol-whipped a 12-year-old girl, striking another child in the face, and falsifying a police report. Boyd later went to work in St. Ann and then at the Ferguson, Missouri, Police Department, where he was sued in federal court for having arrested a woman because she asked for his name.[14]

Reason magazine described one of the more notorious incidents involving a gypsy cop:

> In the late 1980s, Chattanooga, Tennessee, Officer Stephen Lee Rollins—suspected of drug use and police brutality—made an agreement with then–Police Commissioner Tom Kennedy that he would work at least two states away if the commissioner promised to not reveal any damaging information about him. Rollins then went to work as a cop in West Palm Beach, Florida, where he and Officer Glen Thurlow (who had left another Florida department after beating a suspect badly enough to blind him in one eye) encountered hitchhiker Robert Jewett on the night of November 24, 1990.

Jewett died in custody, and Rollins and Thurlow were charged with second-degree murder.

According to testimony at the officers' trial, the victim suffered severe injuries including broken ribs, heart damage, a crushed throat, and blunt trauma to his testicles. West Palm Beach's medical examiner, Ronald Wright, testified that some of Jewett's injuries resembled torture.[15]

It comes as a shock to many that there is no official registry of police officers who have had their licenses revoked, been terminated, or been found guilty of serious misconduct in lawsuits, and so forth. The International Association of Directors of Law Enforcement Standards and Training (IADLEST) maintains its own database of police officers who have had their certifications revoked, but participation is entirely voluntary. This National Decertification Index presently holds the names of 21,590 former officers who have been stripped of their police powers in 40 different states.[16] Given the voluntary nature of the database and the fact that 10 states have submitted no names, it is safe to assume that many thousands of other known bad cops are not registered. Moreover, it is apparent that many departments have lax hiring standards and would be unlikely to check the IADLEST index.

In the United States, any worker in the securities field is required to be licensed by the Financial Industry Regulatory Authority (FINRA), and employers must update their employment status whenever there is a change. In the event a broker or agent is fired or resigns, the employer is required to report the separation to FINRA on a lengthy and detailed form. When reporting a terminated employee, the employer must answer questions including whether the firing was related to an internal investigation, a felony or misdemeanor conviction, disciplinary action, customer complaints, civil suits, or violation of securities or investment regulations.[17]

The Health Resources and Services Administration (HRSA), which maintains the National Practitioner Databank, tracks misconduct, malpractice, and license status of physicians and other health care providers. The HRSA even conducts compliance reviews to ensure that every state and territory is participating and reporting practitioners who have been disciplined or stripped of their license.[18]

Maintaining data on the professional status of these sorts of professionals is wise, given the damage they can do to the health and wealth of citizens. It is just as vital that police officers' status be tracked as well. It is well past time when an official database of police officers be created on the model of the FINRA or HRSA systems. The U.S. Justice Department should either create its own databank or fund the IADLEST index of decertified officers and require all states to mandate that their police agencies make detailed reports concerning officers terminated, forced to resign, or otherwise removed from their positions. If doctors and licensed securities agents are tracked for any indication of malfeasance, it follows that police officers should be subject to the same scrutiny. Such a system would go a long way toward ending the phenomenon of "gypsy cops" like Sean Sullivan, traveling around from department to department, committing crimes or just being corrupt or incompetent. The idea that a criminal can obtain employment as a police officer is appalling and there is no excuse. Far too many agencies, especially smaller agencies with limited resources, have very lax hiring standards and fail to conduct even a rudimentary due diligence investigation that would be carried out for any number of positions in the private sector. ·

Requiring police agencies to file reports when an officer's employment status changes would also alleviate another problem: the practice of police agencies not disclosing the reasons why an officer left his or her position. When an agency takes the easy way out to remove officers—by allowing them to resign in lieu of being brought up on formal charges and fired—they almost universally refuse to disclose to other agencies the reason why the officers left their position. This is due to fears of civil legal action taken by the disgraced officer. In the absence of a national database, states should amend their laws to protect police agencies from civil liability when they release or otherwise discuss the employment history of their members with another police agency. Regardless of changes in the law, police leaders should stand up and call upon their fellow agency heads to share information concerning officers who are moving from one jurisdiction to another. Shielding bad cops from the consequences of their actions and allowing them to resume their employment elsewhere is a betrayal of the professional standards and ethics to which most agencies profess.

Police agencies will hire these gypsy cops because it saves them the time and expense of having to recruit and train a new officer. Obviously, a solidly professional officer from another jurisdiction who just happens to be moving into your area can be a great find for a smaller agency that lacks adequate resources, but it is nothing short of irresponsible to simply hire an officer because it saves some time and money. Regardless, such action will not benefit the agency in the long run, as a problem officer will ultimately cost much more in wasted supervisory time and perhaps cost millions in a lawsuit.

Another problem is that while in every state individuals are required to be licensed to do such jobs as styling hair, installing plumbing, and in some places arranging flowers or trimming eyebrows, six states do not officially license police officers—New York, Massachusetts, New Jersey, Rhode Island, Hawaii, and California—and these states employ some 26 percent of police nationwide.[19] Since all states have minimum requirements for police officers, licensing is not absolutely necessary, but it does provide a record of those who have been stripped of their license for misconduct or incompetence, which potential employers could check if they were so inclined.

The only serious attempt to create an official national database for decertified police officers came with the introduction of a bill in Congress by Senator Bob Graham, entitled The Law Enforcement and Correctional Officers Employment Registration Act. This proposal failed to make it out of committee, as it was opposed by some police unions and was overly broad—planning to create a registry of all officers rather than just those who had been decertified.[20] Part of the federal government's agreement with the Ferguson, Missouri, Police Department requires that they check all new hires against the IADLEST databank.[21] One wonders why any agency would fail to take such a simple and cost-free measure.

Some police unions have strongly opposed such a registry for problem police officers, comparing it to "the witch hunts of Salem."[22] The International Association of Chiefs of Police has repeatedly stated its support of a national registry for decertified officers, but there seems to be little momentum for any sort of mandated reporting. Too many police unions behave like ordinary labor unions rather than as advocates for professionals. The International Brotherhood of Police Officers (IBPO), which called a decertification registry a "blacklist," refers to its members on its Web site as "workers." Labor unions too often tend to exist for their own aggrandizement and reflexively defend every member against discipline or termination regardless of their behavior. If police wish to be treated as true professionals, their union representatives will need to conduct themselves accordingly. No organization that represents skilled professionals would want a corrupt or utterly incompetent member in its ranks. An IBPO spokesman speaking out against a registry for decertified officers argued that since criminals are permitted to reenter the workforce after serving their time, police officers should not be barred for life from working in their chosen line of work because of a "mistake."[23] No union representing professionals—especially those charged with the gravest of public responsibilities—should advocate for its members to held to the same standards as convicted felons. A police union cannot argue on the one hand that its members are highly skilled professionals, deserving of commensurate pay and benefits while on the other hand demand that they be held to no higher standard than an ex-convict.

Police unions should behave as professional associations that work toward the continuous improvement and development of their members. They should of course advocate on behalf of their members for fair pay and proper working conditions, but they should not serve as a bulwark against the removal of individuals who betray the public trust and dishonor the profession and the other members of the union. An apt model would be the Air Line Pilots Association (ALPA). Serving as the pilot of a commercial aircraft is arguably a graver responsibility than that of a police officer: the lives of hundreds of people rest in the hands of the pilots every time they step aboard. The ALPA advocates vigorously for its members but also works to improve pilot skills, identify best practices in the industry, and works cooperatively with both airline corporations and the Federal Aviation Administration in an effort to continuously improve safety and the industry as a whole.

Decertification of police officers should be a separate process from simply being terminated for cause. The model should be similar to that of attorneys; a lawyer can be fired from a law firm for doing shoddy work, being chronically late or other shortcomings, and not be disbarred. He or she is free to seek employment elsewhere or work independently. Attorneys are removed from the bar only for gross misconduct that violates the core tenets of the profession. In this way, a police officer who is fired or resigns from a police agency would not be banned from the field unless the underlying conduct involved serious breaches of public trust, violation of criminal law, or some other offense demonstrating a clear lack of personal integrity or suitability. States should create a policy and criteria for decertification using a model similar to that created by the American Bar Association for evaluating claims of misconduct and making a determination for each officer accused.

Clearly, there is a role to be played by local and state governments in ensuring the integrity of our police forces. State governments set the standards for police officer training, and local governments provide the funding for their municipal and sheriff's departments. Politicians have a responsibility to ensure that the standards of their local police agencies are set high, that officers receive proper training, and that they receive adequate pay. Politicians do a disservice to their constituents when they defund a police agency to the point where it lacks the resources to adequately investigate the background of applicants or offer salaries that attract desirable candidates.

Police officers will make mistakes. In general, officers do not receive anything approaching adequate training for all the things they are expected to know and the chaotic and complex situations they are expected to handle. People make mistakes in all lines of labor and professions, and the police are no exception. Officers should be disciplined for simple breaches of rules or regulations and receive remedial training for errors involving skill or knowledge. When officers are found to have made errors that demonstrate a profound lack of honesty and integrity, serious consideration should be given to terminating their employment or commencement of decertification proceedings. Officers who lie under oath, plant evidence, or make false statements to cover up another officer's misconduct should not work in a police agency again. Integrity is the only currency a police officer has, both as an individual and as a member of the officer's agency.

Who Should Discipline the Police?

Police have traditionally conducted their own investigations into allegations of misconduct against their officers. Sometimes this arrangement works well and sometimes it fails. Various police departments around the country have experimented with different incarnations of a civilian review board that handles complaints made against officers. The board consists of individuals outside the police bureaucracy but sometimes may have representatives from the police, judiciary, and other entities to provide their experience and knowledge to the process. The reasoning behind the creation of such investigatory bodies is obvious: organizations in general have a tendency to excuse or minimize their mistakes because of our natural bias toward others like ourselves or those in similar circumstances. Many police agencies do a fine job of conducting their own internal investigations; individuals assigned to internal affairs understand the necessity of maintaining organizational integrity and that it not only benefits the public but every member of the department in the long run. Still, many feel that the police simply cannot be trusted to police themselves. A recent survey revealed that 79 percent of Americans supported the idea of outside agencies conducting investigations into police misconduct.[24]

Traditionally, police agencies have been extremely hostile to the concept of outside review of their actions. Because of the unique and isolating nature of the work, police culture tends toward the insular. Police officers and administrators take a dim view of someone who has never served as a cop passing judgment on actions they took in circumstances they believe outsiders can't comprehend. The Fraternal Order of Police (FOP), the largest police union in the country, flatly opposes all legislation that creates or funds civilian review boards.[25] The FOP even brought a failed lawsuit against Baltimore's City Civilian Review Board and the city's police department in a failed effort to block sharing of internal investigation findings with the board.[26] Despite the resistance from some police agencies and unions, outside review of complaints has come into being in many American cities; there are around 200 such civilian review bodies in existence in one form or another.[27]

An outside reviewing entity can take many forms and needs to have the right balance of authority, personnel, and training to do its job properly. The CPD, lately eviscerated by the Justice Department as engaged in patterns of illegal and abusive behavior, has a civilian oversight entity, known as the Independent Police Review Authority (IPRA). The existence of the IPRA apparently failed to prevent the department from descending into disrepute with its minority constituents and the Justice Department. The failure of the IPRA is due to its complex processes and rules, involving passing investigations back and forth between the authority and the CPD internal affairs unit and different levels of police command. Moreover, the police union contract mandates that complaints can only be investigated if the complainant makes a sworn statement. While this seems reasonable on its face, many people either are fearful of making a complaint or are unable to travel to the police station during the week. Also, individuals who may have charges pending will generally refuse to make any sworn statements on the advice of their attorney. While lack of cooperation should be considered, an investigation should still be conducted when a serious accusation of misconduct is made.

There are entire categories of citizen complaints that the IPRA simply does not investigate. They close all excessive-force complaints that involve handcuffing, takedowns during arrest, and displays of an officer's gun without any investigation whatsoever.[28] Worse still, this information is not tracked, meaning that an officer such as Jason Van Dyke, who killed Laquan McDonald, could have many more than the 20 recorded complaints against him. Incredibly, pursuant to the police union's collective bargaining agreement with the city, anonymous complaints also receive no investigation from internal affairs or the IPRA.[29] This precludes looking into misconduct reported by the most fearful individuals—including perhaps police officers who feel they can't openly accuse their colleagues for fear of retaliation.

The civilian review concept comes in many different forms. In addition to all-civilian panels, the civilian input model places a division of civilian investigators within the police department that investigates the more serious allegations, while the traditional internal affairs division investigates the remainder. The civilian monitor model generally involves the creation of an ombudsman's office, which takes complaints about any and all municipal services, including the police. Under this model, when the ombudsman receives a complaint, both that office and the police internal affairs conduct parallel investigations.[30] Studies conducted in several cities have found that some form of civilian review improves citizen satisfaction in the process, with the ombudsman model creating the most satisfaction for those whose complaints were founded and the civilian input model being best at ameliorating the dissatisfaction among those whose complaints were unfounded.[31] Most surprisingly, the studies revealed that civilian reviewers were found to be less likely to find officers culpable and more lenient in their punishments than was internal affairs.[32]

When a city considers the use of some form of civilian oversight, it should have a mechanism for input from someone with police experience. This would help to allay some of the fears of police officers and unions and provide valuable information for review board investigators. In addition, all members of the board and its investigatory staff should receive intensive training in applicable use of force law and case law, as well as department rules and regulations. The members should be familiarized with academy training, put through simulated shoot-don't training, and review and discuss case studies concerning use of force in a classroom setting before serving with such an entity. In this way, officers can be assured that those passing judgment on their actions have at least a rudimentary understanding of the rules of the game and the types of situations they find themselves in.

Another consideration when it comes to civilian review, as with all things concerning the police, is cost. Establishing a credible, trained, and efficient review board is expensive; they require office space, equipment, vehicles, salaries, and benefits. This is something each municipality has to grapple with and it is a problem that isn't going away.

Finally, there is the issue of organizational integrity; police managers must retain some rights and role in disciplining subordinates. If police supervisors have no control in discipline, a critical element of organizational integrity is lost. As former Los Angeles police chief Edward M. Davis put it, "The right to discipline carries with it the power to control the conduct, action, and attitudes of the employee of an organization. When the right to discipline is vested with management, management has the essential tool with which to attain the desired behavior from employees. . . . When employees are subject to disciplinary action outside the organization, a fundamental rule of organization has been breached and the employee becomes confused, diffident, and inefficient."[33]

One possible model to alleviate this concern and cut costs would be a review entity that is limited to conducting parallel investigations with internal affairs in only the most serious of cases and in all other cases conducts a review of the report completed by internal affairs, with the right to request clarification or make its own investigation where warranted. Regardless of the system that is put in place, the process must be transparent and completed with maximum efficiency. The convoluted system of Chicago's IPRA creates needless delay that is damaging to both to the morale of accused officers and public confidence in the system.

The integrity of any police agency and the profession as a whole depends upon a rigorous, fair, swift, and transparent system for recording, investigating, and adjudicating citizen complaints. Understanding that officers can make honest mistakes, police agencies should have procedures in place for remedial training and not simply rely on punitive measures as corrective action. Officers can receive additional training in tactics or civil liberties to better understand the bounds of their authority and how to properly deal with challenges to that authority. Officers lacking in personal skills can be trained in what some departments call *behavioral intervention*, or what cops refer to as *charm school*. Officers found guilty of gross misconduct, incompetence, dishonesty, or criminal behavior must be terminated, and this fact must be available to any police agency in the country where the officer might later apply. In some places, public confidence in the process may necessitate the creation of an outside entity to conduct or review cases of alleged police misconduct, but great care must be taken to ensure such a body can both serve its purpose and not undermine the authority of police administrators. Maintaining the integrity of our police organizations is the critical component in establishing and maintaining the legitimacy upon which their ability to function rests.

While it is possible for a police agency to effectively police itself, it requires real leadership and a tradition and culture of integrity in the ranks. This becomes more difficult for very large police departments and those with a long history of corruption or brutality. Where a legacy of distrust or police misconduct exists and creates barriers of trust between the community and the police, some variation of outside review of police actions discussed earlier must be put in place to restore public confidence.

Police leaders must recognize that police are human beings, and like everyone else, subject to human weaknesses and failings. To prevent corruption from beginning or spreading, it is necessary to put in place *systems* that both discourage misconduct and reward good behavior and honesty. There should be checks and balances in place whenever sensitive investigations are conducted or police will be handling money, drugs, or valuable property. Periodic checks should be made of reports to ensure that the paperwork submitted reflects the true nature of the complaint that was called in and that people listed as interviewed actually were spoken to. All complaints, anonymous or otherwise, should be investigated and be the subject of a report. Integrity tests should be randomly conducted, wherein individuals working for internal affairs present an officer with an opportunity to steal or accept a bribe. Finally, officers found to be guilty of serious misconduct or corruption must be dealt with swiftly and severely. In this way, agencies build an atmosphere of integrity, where misconduct is not tolerated and good conduct is rewarded. In any group of people, there are those who are good; they are good at their work and are motivated by a desire to do what is right. There are also a few bad actors who care for nothing other than themselves and will almost always do the wrong thing if given the chance. But the majority of people, cops included, tend to be followers; they will go whichever way the wind the blows and are not interested in sticking their necks out to do good or ill. If the culture of an agency condones corrupt behavior, the followers will go along. Some will decide to go over to the dark side, while others will just look the other way. By contrast, if the followers know there are serious consequences for misconduct and a very real chance of getting caught, they will gravitate toward the good officers and not be tempted to engage in corruption. As Detective Frank Serpico, the hero who exposed the endemic corruption in the NYPD, said in 1971, "Ten percent of the cops in New York City are absolutely corrupt, 10 percent are absolutely honest, and the other 80 percent—they wish they were honest."[34]

Police leaders must ensure the integrity of their agencies and of the profession as a whole. This requires an effective means of investigating misconduct and provisions for remedial training. Those in charge of a police agency owe a service not only to the general public they serve but to the honest and dedicated officers under their command, to safeguard the integrity of their organization, and in doing so fulfill their public obligations and honor the nobility and faithful service of their officers. It also requires no small degree of managerial fortitude to make the difficult decisions and to demand excellence from their officers. Only in this way can police commanders and the public be assured of having a force of men and women the entire community can take pride in.

CHAPTER TEN

The Police Force the Public Deserves

> In the final analysis, the people get the police they deserve.
> —Detective Frank Serpico

The problems facing the police in the 21st century are legion. Perhaps it will always be this way, as the police are in the business of responding to and dealing with virtually every problem human society generates. The ever-improving technologies capable of invading privacy, from facial recognition to drones and micro audio and video recording, will present the police and all three branches of government with challenges to properly safeguard Americans' rights and freedom. For the immediate future, a departure from law enforcement and a return to policing is the most pressing need.

If America wants to have better relationships between the police and the public at large, it will need to have fewer laws and much less aggressive enforcement of those laws that are designed simply for raising revenue. A police force that busies itself writing traffic summons, parking violations, and arrests for petty crimes is going to sow negative feelings in the community and imperil its legitimacy. In its investigation into the activities of the Ferguson, Missouri, Police Department, the U.S. Justice Department found that the police department's aggressive and nearly single-minded focus on making arrests for violations of the municipal code in order to generate revenue was a significant factor in the poisoning of relations between the community and the police.[1] The report also made clear that this policy was driven by the mayor and city council and perpetuated by the local municipal court.

The Justice Department report revealed that the government of the City of Ferguson figured annual increases in revenues from fines and fees into its budget, projecting that more than 23 percent of its total budget would come from these sources. The police chief and the court were pressured to increase the numbers of summonses and to maximize fines. The city even prepared a report crowing about its high fines and its prosecutor's office that was diligently recommending the highest fines possible for the most frequently occurring offenses.[2] Reading the report, it appears clear that the entire focus of the executive and judiciary in Ferguson was on generating revenue from violations of municipal codes. This atmosphere, combined with structural and leadership deficiencies in the department, led to increases in unlawful stops by officers looking for persons wanted for failure to pay fines and other abuses. This type of climate, in a majority black city with a nearly all-white police force, is what led to the explosion of unrest and violence following the shooting of a black suspect by a white officer in August 2014.

Training and Maintaining the Professional Officer

If America wants a different kind of police, the training standards for police need to be upgraded in every state. While the police officer standards and training standards created since the 1960s have done much to improve the quality of police officers generally, it is wholly inadequate for both the challenges and expectations of a modern police officer. Far too much academy training nationally is little more than an exercise in what officers call CYA, or "cover your ass." Cadets are sent to classes bearing the right titles, pass an exam, and can be marked "trained" in a given subject area. This sort of education is conducted not to prepare the officer for the real-world experience of policing or to improve his or her performance but to protect the agency from civil liability in case the officer screws up. For police training to be effective, it must be multifaceted and take place over a much longer period of time than the one or two months training some police officers receive.

Police trainees need to learn more than the mechanics of police work; they need to know the law, their purpose in society, a professional ethos, how to speak the language and vernacular of the people they will encounter, and how to mediate, problem solve, and deal with all the hopeless social problems they will encounter daily. They need to understand what a professional police officer is and how to fulfill that role in their own right, not merely bending to the trends of the day or succumbing to cynicism.

With the demands placed upon the modern police officer, more training is required beyond the academy level, with ongoing in-service training for officers in the field. Greatly expanded in-service training will not only serve to develop and enhance an officer's skills but can serve as a means to retrain officers schooled in the law enforcement model, who were never provided with a professional ethos or philosophy to guide their work. Maintaining a force of officers with positive attitudes, up-to-date knowledge, and razor-sharp skills requires that its members spend up to a third of their time in training and away from patrol duties.

Unfortunately, training is expensive and time consuming. While more police are not necessarily needed on America's streets, simple scheduling realities of manning round-the-clock shifts and answering the volume of calls requires a certain number of officers. Most agencies find it difficult to maintain adequate coverage just to rotate their personnel through even a single day of training. In order to send officers through regular refresher training in the field or at the academy would, in some agencies, require a larger force and better facilities—and that means money.

Not only does training take a significant amount of time, but for officers to avoid the burnout that accompanies their work, occasional breaks from the street are required. As far back as World War II, psychiatrists posited that between 80 and 90 days in a combat zone would result in the median soldier suffering a mental breakdown.[3] While police officers do not face the intensive horrors of wartime combat, they witness many of the gruesome scenes associated with war: death, misery, hopelessness, violence, fear, ghastly injuries, and the constant threat of violence and frequent volatile confrontations. This exposure adds up over the course of months and years and results in the same psychiatric injuries suffered by combat veterans. Thousands of police officers suffer from post-traumatic stress disorder and other forms of anxiety and depression as a result of their work.

Police officers experience suicidal thoughts at nearly double the rate of the general population[4] and are more likely to abuse alcohol due to the stress of their jobs.[5] The tremendous pressure of police work requires that aspiring officers be educated about these stresses and taught strategies for dealing with them. While many departments have finally acknowledged the existence of stress-related problems, creating employee assistance programs and the like, it is still something of a taboo subject in the police culture generally. Stressed, frightened, or alcohol-abusing officers are at best ineffective at their job and at worst a real danger to themselves and others.

The reality is that the money to accomplish these goals is simply not available in many parts of the country. In the absence of a new training model, it falls to political leaders to identify and hire police leaders who can do their best with what they have and inspire officers to excellence.

New Policing Models?

If Americans are not willing to pay for the costs associated with creating the force of superhuman, warrior-philosopher cops they demand, then they need to lower their expectations. If you want to pay a police officer with a high school equivalency diploma $15 per hour to patrol your neighborhood with a month of training under his belt, then don't expect much in the way of engagement, adherence to constitutional principles, innovation, or creative problem solving. If we decide as a society that policing is not a profession and is more akin to, say, serving in the military as infantry, perhaps new concepts should be tried.

It is true that policing in many small departments can become tedious and routine. Promotional opportunities are rare, and the paramilitary and bureaucratic nature of police organizations generally does not encourage or allow for personal growth. Perhaps policing should be something done as an avocation or for a short period of service, such as with the military. Prospective officers could prepare for police work with some preliminary training in college in addition to their regular major, then serve a term of three or four years' service with the police at a basic salary in exchange for tuition assistance. Only very few officers would stay beyond that term if they qualified as first-line supervisors and continue up the chain of command. Such a system would provide a stream of young and energetic officers, with those with the best leadership skills and aptitude staying on as sergeants and command staff. Such a system would have the added benefit of many more citizens having the experience of being a police officer and being able to share that perspective with their peers.

Hiring civilians to perform some of the functions of the police would be one possible solution to free up more police for patrol and allow greater flexibility to administer ongoing training. Nearly every police agency of any appreciable size in the country has hundreds of officers performing clerical and other tasks that could be performed by non-sworn personnel—usually for considerably less pay. There is no reason for a trained police officer with a uniform, badge, and gun to be filing papers, typing letters, or installing computer software. Specially trained civilians could be utilized to perform other tasks, including crime-scene processing, and in some places are already performing non-injury traffic accident investigations and taking reports of minor crimes.

Identify and Remove Bad Officers

All police officers make mistakes, and police supervisors and administrators need to have policies in place to address those errors with training, reprimands, and other disciplinary procedures. Officers who demonstrate a pattern of ineptitude or inaptitude or who are routinely the subject of complaints of rudeness or brutality must be separated from the police service. As discussed in Chapter 9, civil service law protections have grown too strong over the years and, combined with powerful police unions and a general reluctance to remove officers due to hiring difficulties and manpower shortages, there is a strong disincentive to remove bad cops. Police administrators must have the fortitude and respect for the service to fire officers who demonstrate that they are unfit for policing.

Just as recognizing good performance in policing can be difficult, so too can be identifying bad officers. However, the worst of the worst will tend to make themselves known through public complaints. All complaints must be thoroughly investigated and officers who have clear patterns indicating malfeasance or lack of aptitude must be fired. Just as importantly, there must be created a national database of officers who have been de-certified or fired for misconduct. There are far too many police officers who are fired—or more commonly forced to resign in lieu of termination—who simply move to another region of the country to work in another agency. Given the damage a single officer can do to the reputation of a department and to the police service more generally, this sort of practice needs to be ended.

Doctors, lawyers, and even securities brokers have some form of oversight and a registry where complaints, censure, and disciplinary proceedings can be recorded. At a minimum, the Justice Department or a police professional organization should create a searchable database for police agencies to register the names of officers terminated for cause. While making this information public would be very controversial, it should at least be available to police agencies when conducting background investigations on their applicants. Presently, the International Association of Directors of Law Enforcement Standards and Training maintains a registry of officers who have had their certificates or licenses to work as a police officer revoked. The registry contains over 20,000 records from 40 states,[6] but participation is entirely voluntary and its existence is not widely known. All states should be urged to pass legislation making reporting to and checking with such a registry mandatory when firing or hiring police officers.

All states should review their standards and either implement or tighten the rules concerning background investigations of prospective officers. No agency should be able to hire a trainee without conducting a thorough background check, including all previous employers, drug testing, conducting interviews at each location he or she has ever resided or attended school, conducting a military record review, checking adequate references, conducting interviews with past employers, making mental health system checks, checking the applicant's criminal and financial history, making a polygraph examination, and conducting interviews with all intimate associates.

Train a New Generation of Leaders

The police have long suffered from a lack of good leadership. The Wickersham Commission noted in 1931 that the lack of adequate leadership was the cause of much of the problems in policing, and that remains true to this day. The problem stems from the way in which police command staff and chiefs are selected. The career path for an officer rising through the ranks does not generally prepare him or her for the duties in the next job up the ladder. A patrolman or detective who is good at his job of catching the bad buys and dealing with the public is not necessarily suited for the job of a sergeant. The work in those positions does little to ready the officer for the administrative operation of a station, dealing with personnel matters, scheduling, dealing with complaints from the public, implementing orders from above, getting and measuring results, motivating officers, dealing with civilian employee issues, evaluating subordinates' work performance, or demonstrating leadership.

Likewise, the sergeant's position does not serve to equip its occupant for the transition to upper management, with its broader focus and greatly reduced emphasis on the technical matters. The higher one goes inside the organization, the more and more his or her attention is directed outside the agency: to politicians, constituent groups, interagency relationships, and the media. Being technically proficient as a patrol officer or sergeant is of little value when sitting down with the mayor, city council member, or community activist. Setting strategic goals, identifying problems within the community and department, ensuring accountability of supervisory personnel, equipment procurement, facilities operation, staffing, and budgeting require an entirely different skill set than does policing at the street level or first-line supervision.

The promotional process is generally not designed so as to select the most qualified candidates. Promotion is usually through passage of a civil service examination of some sort that tests the candidate's ability to memorize volumes of minutiae regarding rules and regulations and law and completion of standardized forms. This tests candidates' knowledge of policing but not of supervising. Being an expert at something, whether it's police work, medicine, engineering, or soldiering, does not by itself make a person suitable as a manager or leader. The talents required of a leader—especially in a large organization—are in many ways different from those needed to be a good patrolman or detective. Certainly, the experience of being a police officer is needed for a leader to be effective and to have the respect of the rank and file, but there should be a mechanism for training and mentoring subordinates for the next position in the hierarchy, rather than simply developing an examination that tests rote memorization. Agencies should experiment with both mentoring programs and exchange programs, where upper management personnel are detailed to other agencies to learn not only the next job up the ladder but also different approaches to problem solving.

Good leaders need to be individuals who question the status quo. They are not satisfied with something that simply "works." Leaders ask why things are being done a particular way and what purpose or goal the activity is trying to achieve. They do not simply accept procedures and rules with explanations of "That's how it's always been done." They constantly question *why* and seek to remove barriers to efficiency. Good leaders seek the input of field personnel for means of improving efficiency rather than simply imposing solutions from the top down. They understand that allowing others to participate in the decision-making process does not undermine their authority, but in fact enhances their influence and legitimacy. Good leaders understand their own strengths and limitations; they do not try to be an expert on everything and delegate tasks to others with specialized knowledge or skills. To be effective, leaders cannot be busy every moment with small tasks and try to do everything themselves. Leaders must be expert at delegating to trusted aides and determining which actions need their personal attention at a given point in time, as they cannot focus on every individual area of concern simultaneously. Delegating is a skill; it is much more than simply telling people what to do. Delegating properly means assigning the right tasks to the right people and structuring the work so that it is clearly understood, as well as ensuring that the person assigned has the tools and skills required to accomplish the goal. This not only creates successes but develops the skills of subordinates and improves morale.

Good leadership is also the key to combatting corruption. Truly bad officers are unusual but can influence others and set a negative tone within a department. A police leader sets an example not only through his or her personal conduct but also by demonstrating the courage required to combat corruption, discipline officers, and fire those officers who demonstrate a lack of integrity or aptitude. Guaranteeing supervisory accountability for subordinates and maintaining a rigorous and unbiased internal affairs division is a crucial bulwark against any creeping corruption within a department. Strong leadership lets officers and supervisors know that if they report corruption they will have the support of the department behind them.

Tomorrow's police leaders are the young officers and aspiring police of today. The current police leadership in America needs to look to the future and create new training models and hiring practices and promulgate a strong professional ethos that transcends agency divisions and regional differences. If policing is to be a true profession, there must be a guiding philosophy that undergirds and directs it. A new generation of leadership needs to be trained today. Future police officers need better training programs than the ineffective undergraduate criminal justice programs in today's colleges. Police officers need to be trained on how to be *police officers* and not law enforcement officers. They need to know why we created police and why we need police and understand that police officers are just fellow citizens who should, as Sir Robert Peele said, conduct themselves in a manner that "gives reality to the historic tradition that the police are the public and the public are the police; the police being only members of the public who are paid to give full-time attention to duties which are incumbent on every citizen in the interests of community welfare and existence."

Even though all officers may not rise to a leadership position, they should be taught practical leadership principles, so that they can inspire others and become leaders among their peers and in their communities. Those who will become the commanders and police chiefs of the future must learn from the beginning that the work of the police is order maintenance not law enforcement. They need to know precisely *how* to transmit a work ethic, concept, or operational plan through the ranks and ensure that it is properly implemented. They need to learn to deal with the difficulties involved in assessing the performance of officers and the importance of finding proper measures to assess the results of their policies. The future leadership cannot be afraid to admit mistakes or fail to be open to new ideas. Students need to learn leadership so that they can recognize bad leadership when they see it and learn not to be corrupted or become cynical because of it, in hopes that they can rise above it and one day impart good leadership to their organization.

Students of policing should learn how to mediate disputes, solve problems, make a connection with the community, and think creatively. They require a pedagogical study of the nuts and bolts of the justice system, laws, constitution, and principles of investigation, as well as reality-based teaching of how to write clearly, formulate legal arguments, articulate a professional philosophy, and explain the role of police in society. They need to have a clear understanding of why they wish to serve as an officer.

New colleges should be formed either independently or at existing universities to teach the art and science of policing. A traditional criminal justice degree at the junior college or undergraduate level does little to prepare a young person for a career as a police officer—it is usually better suited to someone pursuing a career in probation or social work who wants to understand something about the police and justice system. Such schools could offer certificate programs approved by state-level police standards boards to provide pre-academy training to those who do not wish to obtain bachelor's or higher degrees as well as undergraduate and graduate programs in police sciences and leadership. Colleges dedicated to the police profession can conduct and disseminate research into better policing and training methods and produce police leaders who understand leadership and how to identify problems, devise solutions, and measure results. In this way, we can produce professional police officers and trained leaders for the future and improve the police service until every agency can legitimately claim to be professional.

The Role of Unions

Police union leadership must place increased focus on the professional development of their members. Far too many police unions behave like trade unions rather than professional unions, with blind hostility toward upper management as well as unconditional advocacy for even the worst of their members. For example, the Fraternal Order of Police in Chicago continued to defend Officer Jason Van Dyke following the revelation of his murder of Laquan McDonald and even gave him a job at union headquarters.[7] Police unions should be strong advocates for their members but should disavow those who disgrace the union and the profession of policing. Additionally, unions should devote more resources to providing training for their members and promoting professional best practices among other organizations and police agencies. Leaders of unions should cultivate cooperative relationships with police management for good of the agency and the public they and their officers serve. Far too many public sector unions forget they are servants of the public and not the other way around.

Prepare for Future Technologies

As technology in general continues to advance at a seemingly exponential pace, police leaders should remain abreast of developments on the horizon and evaluate new technologies in the light of upholding the rights of citizens, rather than merely in the efficacy or expediency of new devices to solve crimes. Police are always keen to find new and innovative ways to solve crimes or track down criminal suspects. This not only brings swifter justice but can protect the public from particularly dangerous fugitives. However, the police should not necessarily use all technology, and some tactics should be very tightly controlled to ensure protection of rights.

Surely, most crime could be eliminated and violators quickly apprehended if we lived in George Orwell's world in the novel *1984*, where every citizen is under surveillance around the clock with ubiquitous cameras and tele-screens. This is not how Americans wish to live, however. Neither do they want hovering police drones overhead, nor do they want their conversations or call data recorded by the government, or their movements tracked through their cell phones and license plate readers. Yet, some of these things are happening today. Some local police agencies have possession of cell tower simulators that mimic a real tower and scoop up all the phone data and even communication from phones in range. There are at present no applicable laws for their use, and the agencies that use them are required by the FBI to keep knowledge of their possession secret from the public.[8] These types of devices were developed for use by the CIA and Special Forces for tracking terror suspects abroad and not for local cops to use to catch a marijuana dealer. Intrusive devices such as these should be tightly controlled and utilized only in the most extreme circumstances where there is an immediate threat to public safety. More technologies are on the way courtesy of the U.S. military and its generosity to local police agencies. The military has developed the active denial system, which sends a directed beam of high-intensity energy that causes severe burning sensations on the skin of its targets. Such devices could easily be used break up lawful protests and deny people their right to free speech and assembly. Drones are in use by some police agencies as well as the FBI, and the Pentagon's DARPA program has more gems on deck, including miniaturized killer drones, autonomous fighting robots, and ever more effective eavesdropping and surveillance devices. Police leaders need to get ahead of these innovations and evaluate their value or danger to the public they are sworn to defend.

The Police We Deserve

Ultimately, the police are nothing more than the public face of the government we elect and the laws they pass in our name. Just as government reform requires public engagement, so too does reform of our police. Citizens must first realize that the police *are* the government; they are part and parcel of the executive branch of government, and the people they vote into local or state councils and legislatures enact the laws and ordinances the police enforce. Moreover, these politicians control the money that fuels police agencies and often dictates what those agencies focus their efforts upon.

The people of a free country must be informed and engaged if they expect to maintain their freedom. As Thomas Jefferson said, "If a nation expects to be ignorant and free in a state of civilization, it expects what never was and never will be."[9] Communities must demand that outrageous laws and ordinances be repealed; and they must engage with their police and political leaders. The police, in turn, must act as ombudsmen, becoming a liaison between the community and the politicians. Police leaders must push back against politicians like the ones exposed in Ferguson, who see the police as nothing more than a means of extracting ever-increasing amounts of revenue from their constituents.

The people need to realize that it is the governments they elect that set the tenor for their enforcement agents—the police. If governmental powers continue to grow and our Constitutional protections continue to shrink, the police will become ever more intrusive and overbearing. A restrained government will have restrained police forces. In a society where every social and personal problem is regarded as a legitimate area for government action and the bureaucratic state becomes more authoritarian and high handed every year, the citizenry should not be surprised when their police officers begin to act the same way. Just as the swaggering building inspector justifies his bullying and interference in people's liberty with the shield of "public safety," so too will the police, who are led to believe that public safety requires the eradication of marijuana leaves from people's underpants. It is a maxim that police will reflect the attitudes and morals of the times, and given the attitude of our government toward the people's liberties, the police are actually behaving quite well—for now.

That is why it is so vital for police to shed the title and attitude of law enforcement officer and recognize that they are an integral part of the communities they serve, fellow citizens who have accepted the role of guardian of their neighbors' liberty and safety. This in turn needs to be conveyed to the community as a whole through outreach and transparency. It is up to the police leaders of today and tomorrow to keep faith with their communities and with the thousands of young men and women drawn to the police service out of a desire to assist and protect their fellow citizens. Police need solid, enlightened, and innovative leadership to provide better training and guidance and to prevent police from becoming tools for revenue generation or further suppression of the rights of citizens.

Without greater engagement by the general public in both politics and police issues, there can be little progress. People can watch a YouTube video of a questionable police shooting and damn all police or a see a protest on television news and curse the haters, but until the public is moved to engage constructively within their own communities with the police and their political leaders, more misunderstanding and conflict will be in store. The police need to make an effort to educate the public about their role, tactics, challenges, and limitations, but the public must want to understand for there to be any value in educational efforts of the police.

Americans must also move beyond simplistic and artificial distinctions and explanations based upon skin color. We must collectively reject those who profit from fomenting discord and throw accusations of racism in the most unintelligent and irresponsible ways for their own financial gain and personal aggrandizement. Where actual racial bias or racist conduct is exposed, it should be dealt with severely and forthrightly, but to reflexively blame racism for every injustice and social problem forecloses any possibility of a proper discussion, prevents identification of true causes, and guarantees no workable solution will be found. Americans must focus on the many things we share in *common*: our common humanity and our shared values of family, freedom, and community. Police make up only a tiny fraction of the population but can do their part to stress our similarities even as they make a greater effort to understand the differences.

In the end, Americans will get the police force they deserve. Through their choices of political leaders, their interaction with their local police and police leadership, and their support of one another, they will have the type of community and police force they deserve. The problem in the United States today—and this problem is not limited to ghetto or economically poor areas—is that there is very little *community* in our communities. For eight decades, Americans have increasingly come to rely upon the government to fix all the ills of society, often to the detriment of our social fabric. Children are to be taught, civilized, babysat, and entertained by one government agency or another. Even their sustenance is to come from government checks and food stamps. In an earlier time, Americans cared for the poor in their own communities through charity and volunteerism; today, people lock their doors and peer out at their neighbors, whom they don't even know. The city or town is expected to clean up litter and graffiti, kids misbehaving are to be dealt with by calling 911, and the police and courts are supposed to get people off drugs. A free society cannot turn to the state and its police to remedy all its problems and expect to remain free from the abuses that arise from such a dangerous grant of authority.

The good folks of poor urban communities need to band together to resist crime and disorder. They need to watch out for their neighbor's children and see that they are fed and cared for. They need to work together to clean up vacant lots, cover graffiti, and help those addicted to drugs. They also need to work cooperatively with their police—and their police need to reach out to them and remain true to that tradition, which is that the police *are* the citizenry and the citizenry *are* the police. Dysfunctional and cash-strapped local governments and their inadequately trained and equipped police cannot repair the social fabric of the nation; that is up to all of us, individually and collectively. Self-government requires just what it says, that we govern ourselves first as individuals and then in our homes and neighborhoods. No police agency in a free society can impose social harmony and domestic tranquility on a town, city, or nation that refuses to govern itself. As Frank Serpico said, "It is up to every individual to be and do the best they can in some small way, with the opportunity apportioned them, to create the kind of society we wish to live in for ourselves and our families."[10] Police officers need to return to policing and their fellow citizens must better attend to governing themselves for us all to have the sort of communities and police forces we aspire to.

Notes

Preface

1. This account is based upon the U.S. Department of Justice report on the Michael Brown shooting incident: *Department of Justice Report Regarding the Criminal Investigation into the Shooting Death of Michael Brown by Ferguson, Missouri Police Officer Darren Wilson*. Washington, D.C.: U.S. Department of Justice, 2015. Print.

2. "2010 Census Summary File 1, Ferguson, Missouri." *American Factfinder.* n.d. U.S. Census Bureau. Accessed November 29, 2016. https://factfinder.census .gov/faces/tableservices/jsf/pages/productview.xhtml?src=bkmk.

3. Department of Justice. *Investigation of the Ferguson Police Department.* Washington, D.C.: U.S. Department of Justice, Civil Rights Division, 2015.

4. Jacob Siegel. "The Monsters Who Screamed for Dead Cops." *Daily Beast.* December 23, 2014. Accessed November 29, 2016. http://www.thedailybeast .com/the-monsters-who-screamed-for-dead-cops.

5. Amanda Prestigiacomo. "5 Things You Need to Know about Black Lives Matter." *Daily Wire.* July 11, 2016. Accessed November 29, 2016. http://www .dailywire.com/news/7353/5-things-you-need-know-about-black-lives-matter-amanda-prestigiacomo.

6. Cleve R. Wootson, Jr. "Yesterday's Ku Klux Klan Members Are Today's Police Officers, Councilwoman Says." *The Washington Post.* October 11, 2016. Accessed November 29, 2016. https://www.washingtonpost.com/news/local/ wp/2016/10/11/yesterdays-ku-klux-klan-members-are-todays-police-officers-councilwoman-says/?utm_term=.d7d0a500f88e.

7. "Platform—The Movement for Black Lives." *The Movement for Black Lives.* August 1, 2016. Accessed November 30, 2016. https://policy.m4bl.org/platform/.

8. "Views of Race Relations Are More Negative Now Than They Have Been for Much of the 2000s." Pew Research Center's Social & Demographic Trends Project. June 21, 2016. Accessed November 30, 2016. http://www.pewsocialtrends .org/2016/06/27/2-views-of-race-relations/.

Chapter 1: The Paradox of Policing a Free Society

1. Thomas Jefferson. *The Jeffersonian Cyclopedia: A Comprehensive Collection of the Views of Thomas Jefferson Classified and Arranged in Alphabetical Order under Nine Thousand Titles Relating to Government, Politics, Law, Education, Political Economy, Finance, Science, Art, Literature, Religious Freedom, Morals, Etc.* Edited by John P. Foley. New York: Funk & Wagnalls, 1900.

2. While this quote reflects Orwell's opinions, it is not directly attributable to him. For a discussion of its origins, see Garson O'Toole. Quote Investigator. March 28, 2014. Accessed December 19, 2015. http://quoteinvestigator.com/2011/11/07/rough-men/.

3. *Serpico.* Dir. Sidney Lumet. Perf. Al Pacino, John Randolph. Paramount Pictures Release, 1973. Film.

4. "History." *Federal Law Enforcement Training Accreditation.* FLETA. n.d. Accessed September 20, 2016. https://www.fleta.gov/history.

5. Robert R. Friedman. "University Perspective: The Policing Profession in 2050." *American Police Chief Magazine*, International Association of Chiefs of Police. August 2006. Accessed May 20, 2016. http://www.policechiefmagazine.org/magazine/index.cfm?fuseaction=display_arch&article_id=958&issue_id=82006.

6. Linda S. Frost. "Part 1." In *An Introduction to Policing*, edited by John S. Dempsey, 8th ed. Sydney, Australia: Cengage Learning, 2015, 7.

7. Jonathan Allen. "New York to Pay $15 Million in Wrongful Loitering Arrests." Reuters. February 8, 2012. Accessed February 1, 2017. http://www.reuters.com/article/us-newyork-unconstitutional-idUSTRE81804920120209.

8. Christine Eith and Matthew R. Durose. *Bureau of Justice Statistics/Contacts between Police and the Public, 2008.* October 2011. Accessed December 5, 2016. https://www.bjs.gov/content/pub/pdf/cpp08.pdf. Report.

9. Hannah Fingerhut. "Beyond Distrust: How Americans View Their Government." Pew Research Center for the People and the Press. November 23, 2015. Accessed February 17, 2017. http://www.people-press.org/2015/11/23/beyond-distrust-how-americans-view-their-government/.

10. Jeremy Ashkenas and Haeyoun Park. "The Race Gap in America's Police Departments." *The New York Times.* September 2, 2014. Accessed May 20, 2016. http://www.nytimes.com/interactive/2014/09/03/us/the-race-gap-in-americas-police-departments.html?_r=0.

11. Brian A. Reaves. "Census of State and Local Law Enforcement Agencies, 2008." Bureau of Justice Statistics. July 2011. Accessed November 13, 2016. http://www.bjs.gov/content/pub/pdf/csllea08.pdf.

12. Jodi M. Brown and Patrick A. Langan. "Policing and Homicide, 1976–98: Justifiable Homicide by Police, Police Officers Murdered by Felons." Bureau of Justice Statistics. March 2001. Accessed May 14, 2016. http://www.bjs.gov/content/pub/ascii/ph98.txt. Twelve percent of murdered officers were killed with their own weapon in the 22 years between 1976 and 1998.

13. "Law Enforcement Officers Killed United States, 1961–2012." *Sourcebook of Criminal Justice Statistics.* 2013. Accessed March 1, 2017. http://www.albany.edu/sourcebook/.

14. *Summary of Law Enforcement Officers Killed and Assaulted—2015.* FBI. 2016. Accessed February 23, 2017. https://ucr.fbi.gov/leoka/2015/officers-feloniously-killed/leoka-felonious-summaries-2015.pdf. Report.

15. Ibid.

16. Ibid.

17. Ibid.

18. John S. Dempsey and Linda S. Forst. "Chapter 1." In *An Introduction to Policing.* 7th ed. Clifton Park, NY: Delmar Cengage Learning, 2014. 7. Print.

19. George Fletcher Chandler and Albert B. Moore. "Chapter 1." In *The Policeman's Art: As Taught in the New York State School for Police.* New York: Funk & Wagnalls, 1923. 22. Print.

20. "Major Current Responsibilities of Police." Aba.com. 1980. Accessed February 27, 2017. http://www.americanbar.org/publications/criminal_justice_section_archive/crimjust_standards_urbanpolice.html#1-1.1.

21. Kim Hjelmgaard. "Ambush-Style Killings of Police up 167% This Year." *USA Today.* November 3, 2016. Accessed March 1, 2017. http://www.usatoday.com/story/news/nation/2016/11/02/ambush-style-killings-police-up-300/93155124/.

Chapter 2: The Evolution of the Modern Police Force

1. Robert W. Brown. "London in the 19th Century." April 16, 2004. Accessed January 8, 2016. http://www2.uncp.edu/home/rwb/london_19c.html.

2. Elaine A. Reynolds. *Before the Bobbies: The Night Watch and Police Reform in Metropolitan London, 1720–1830.* Stanford, CA: Stanford University Press, 1998.

3. Ibid.

4. Susan A. Lentz. "The Invention of Peel's Principles: A Study of Policing 'Textbook' History." *Journal of Criminal Justice* 35, no. 1 (2007): 69–79. Accessed December 5, 2016. http://ac.els-cdn.com.webster.sunybroome.edu:2048/S0047235206001449/1-s2.0-S0047235206001449-main.pdf?_tid=f13db7a4-bb08–11e6-aeb6–00000aab0f26&acdnat=1480955956_b1f26ebe0f88cb4105869abbb3cfd6ff.

5. Clive Emsley. "A Typology of Nineteenth-Century Police." *Crime, Histoire & Sociétés* 3, no. 1 (1999): 29–44.

6. Linda S. Frost. "Part 1." In *An Introduction to Policing,* by John S. Dempsey, 8th ed. Sydney, Australia: Cengage Learning, 2015, 7.

7. Ibid.

8. Robert C. Kennedy. "The Big Chief's Fairy Godmother." *The New York Times.* 2001. Accessed February 20, 2017. http://www.nytimes.com/learning/general/onthisday/harp/0906.html.

9. Christopher P. Wilson. *Cop Knowledge: Police Power and Cultural Narrative in Twentieth-Century America.* Chicago: University of Chicago Press, 2000.

10. Ibid.; Stanley Cohen. *The Execution of Officer Becker: The Murder of a Gambler, the Trial of a Cop, and the Birth of Organized Crime.* New York: Carroll & Graf, 2007.

11. George L. Kelling and Mark H. Moore. *Perspectives on Policing.* Office of Justice Programs, U.S. Department of Justice. National Criminal Justice Reference Service. Accessed November 27, 2016. https://www.ncjrs.gov/pdffiles1/nij/114213.pdf.

12. Randolph Boehm. *Records of the Wickersham Commission on Law Observance and Enforcement.* Bethesda, MD: University Publications of America, 1996. Accessed December 2, 2016. http://www.lexisnexis.com/documents/academic/upa_cis/1965_WickershamCommPt1.pdf

13. *Report of the National Commission on Law Observance and Enforcement.* Vol. 14. Washington, D.C.: U.S. Government Printing Office, 1931. Report.

14. Nicholas DeB Katzenbach. *The Challenge of Crime in a Free Society: A Report by the President's Commission on Law Enforcement and Administration of Justice.* Washington, D.C.: U.S. Government Printing Office, 1967.

15. *Report of the National Advisory Committee on Civil Disorders—Summary of Report.* New York: Bantam Books, 1968. Report.

16. Jesse Kindig. "Selma, Alabama, (Bloody Sunday, March 7, 1965) | The Black Past: Remembered and Reclaimed." Black Past.org. March 7, 1965. Accessed December 5, 2016. http://www.blackpast.org/aah/bloody-sunday-selma-alabama-march-7–1965.http://www.blackpast.org/aah/bloody-sunday-selma-alabama-march-7-1965.

17. Don Whitehead. *Attack on Terror: The FBI against the Ku Klux Klan in Mississippi.* New York: Funk & Wagnalls, 1970.

18. Tony Ortega. "What Frank Serpico Started: The Knapp Commission Report." *Village Voice.* April 18, 2011. Accessed December 7, 2016. http://www.villagevoice.com/news/what-frank-serpico-started-the-knapp-commission-report-6663567.

19. Ibid.

20. Interestingly, the bombing was perpetrated against Don King, then a numbers runner in Cleveland, who would go on to become the most famous and wealthy boxing promoter of all time.

21. Thomas C. Clark. "Mapp v. Ohio." Legal Information Institute. 2010. Accessed December 14, 2016. https://www.law.cornell.edu/supremecourt/text/367/643.

22. Ken Armstrong. "Dollree Mapp, 1923–2014: The Rosa Parks of the Fourth Amendment." The Marshall Project. December 8, 2014. Accessed November 2, 2016. https://www.themarshallproject.org/2014/12/08/dollree-mapp-1923-2014-the-rosa-parks-of-the-fourth-amendment#.7JfQUFKnR.

23. Taken from the Supreme Court Syllabus: "Terry v. Ohio." Legal Information Institute, Cornell University. Accessed March 1, 2017. https://www.law.cornell.edu/supremecourt/text/392/1.

24. "People v Debour." New York State Unified Court System. 2009. Accessed December 14, 2016. http://www.courts.state.ny.us/reporter/archives/p_debour.htm.

25. Earl Warren. "Miranda v. Arizona." Legal Information Institute. Accessed December 14, 2016. https://www.law.cornell.edu/supremecourt/text/384/436.

26. "Ernesto Miranda." NNDB. 2016. Accessed September 19, 2016. http://www.nndb.com/people/596/000125221/.

27. Alex McBride. "Supreme Court History." PBS. Accessed September 19, 2016. http://www.pbs.org/wnet/supremecourt/rights/landmark_miranda.html.

28. "Gideon v. Wainwright." Legal Information Institute, Cornell University. Accessed March 1, 2017. https://www.law.cornell.edu/supremecourt/text/372/335.

29. "Lyndon B. Johnson: Special Message to the Congress on Crime and Law Enforcement, March 9, 1966." The American Presidency Project. Accessed December 2, 2016. http://www.presidency.ucsb.edu/ws/?pid=27478.

30. U.S. Department of Justice. "The War on Crime: The End of the Beginning." Justice.gov. Accessed December 2, 2016. https://www.justice.gov/sites/default/files/ag/legacy/2011/08/23/09-09-1971.pdf. News release.

Chapter 3: From Neighborhood Patrolman to Law Enforcement Officer

1. *Report of the National Advisory Committee on Civil Disorders—Summary of Report*. New York: Bantam Books, 1968. Report, p. 18.

2. Steven Pinker. *The Better Angels of Our Nature: Why Violence Has Declined*. New York: Penguin Books, 2012.

3. "Estimated Violent Crime Rate." Uniform Crime Reporting Statistics. Accessed December 17, 2016. https://www.ucrdatatool.gov/Search/Crime/State/RunCrimeTrendsInOneVar.cfm.

4. "Officer Deaths by Year." National Law Enforcement Officers Memorial Fund. Accessed December 17, 2016. http://www.nleomf.org/facts/officer-fatalities-data/year.html.

5. Francisco Alvarado. "1981: Miami's Deadliest Summer." *Miami New Times*. May 25, 2016. Accessed December 17, 2016. http://www.miaminewtimes.com/news/1981-miamis-deadliest-summer-6565290.

6. "Federal Bureau of Investigation—Shooting Incident 4/11/86 Miami, FL." Vault.FBI.gov. Accessed December 17, 2016. https://vault.fbi.gov/FBI%20Miami%20Shooting%204-11-86%20/Miami%20Shooting%204-11-86%20Part%207%20of%2011%20.

7. Ibid.

8. Ibid.

9. "History of the DEA." DEA.gov. Accessed February 25, 2017. https://www.dea.gov/about/history.shtml.

10. John Marzulli and Alison Gendar. "20 Yrs. Ago: Cop Shooting Led to War Gangs." *New York Daily News*. February 24, 2008. Accessed December 17, 2016. http://www.nydailynews.com/news/crime/20-yrs-shot-nypd-began-crushing-drug-gangs-article-1.307155.

11. "Rudy Giuliani." History.com. 2014. Accessed December 17, 2016. http://www.history.com/topics/rudy-giuliani.

12. Andrew Glass. "Reagan Declares 'War on Drugs,' October 14, 1982." POLITICO. October 14, 2010. Accessed December 18, 2016. http://www.politico.com/story/2010/10/reagan-declares-war-on-drugs-october-14–1982–043552.

13. Ibid.

14. See 10 U.S.C., Chapter 18.

15. "10 U.S.C., Chapter 18—Military Support for Civilian Law Enforcement Agencies." LII/Legal Information Institute. Accessed December 18, 2016. https://www.law.cornell.edu/uscode/text/10/subtitle-A/part-I/chapter-18.

16. Joel Brinkley. "U.S. Panel Urges Testing Workers for Use of Drugs." *The New York Times*. March 3, 1986. Accessed December 18, 2016. http://www.nytimes.com/1986/03/04/us/us-panel-urges-testing-workers-for-use-of-drugs.html.

17. "Thirty Years of America's Drug War: A Chronology." PBS—Frontline. Accessed December 18, 2016. http://www.pbs.org/wgbh/pages/frontline/shows/drugs/cron/.

18. Jerry Seper. "Brutal DEA Agent Murder Reminder of Agency Priority." *The Washington Times*. March 5, 2010. Accessed December 18, 2016. http://www.washingtontimes.com/news/2010/mar/05/dea-has-25-year-burning-reminder/.

19. "H.R. 2461 (101st): National Defense Authorization Act for Fiscal Years 1990 and 1991." GovTrack.us. Accessed December 18, 2016. https://www.govtrack.us/congress/bills/101/hr2461/text.

20. "The Excessive Militarization of American Policing." ACLU.org. April 17, 2015. Accessed December 18, 2016. https://www.aclu.org/files/field_document/ACLU%20-%20%20Militarization%20of%20Policing.pdf.

21. Law Enforcement Equipment Working Group. "Recommendations Pursuant to Executive Order 13688." WhiteHouse.gov. May 2015. Accessed December 18, 2016. https://www.whitehouse.gov/sites/default/files/docs/le_equipment_wg_final_report_final.pdf.

22. Andrew Soergel. "War on Terror Could Be Costliest Yet." *US News* and World Report. September 9, 2016. Accessed February 25, 2017. https://www.usnews.com/news/articles/2016-09-09/war-on-terror-could-be-costliest-yet.

23. Recent testing revealed a 95 percent failure rate for TSA screeners. E. Bradner and R. Marsh. "Acting TSA Director Reassigned after Screeners Failed Tests to Detect Explosives, Weapons." June 2, 2015. Accessed June 12, 2017. http://www.cnn.com/2015/06/01/politics/tsa-failed-undercover-airport-screening-tests/index.html.

24. Andrew Becker and G. W. Schulz. "Local Cops Ready for War with Homeland Security-Funded Military Weapons." *Daily Beast*. December 21, 2011. Accessed December 19, 2016. http://www.thedailybeast.com/articles/2011/12/20/local-cops-ready-for-war-with-homeland-security-funded-military-weapons.html.

25. Ibid.

26. "Bossier Parish Crime Remains Low While Population Steadily Rises." Bossier Sheriff: Public—Crime Statistics. Accessed December 19, 2016. http://www.bossiersheriff.com/crime-statistics/.

27. Jillian Rayfield. "The Right to BearCats: Local Police Gun for Armored Tanks." TPM. March 7, 2012. Accessed December 19, 2016. http://talkingpoints memo.com/muckraker/the-right-to-bearcats-local-police-gun-for-armored-tanks.

28. "Keene, New Hampshire." Keene, New Hampshire. NH 03431. Accessed December 19, 2016. http://www.city-data.com/city/Keene-New-Hampshire .html. Profile.

29. Stephen Dawkins. "Hoover Police to Purchase Armored Vehicle." *280 Reporter.* August 16, 2016. Accessed December 19, 2016. http://www.shelby-countyreporter.com/2016/08/16/hoover-police-to-purchase-armored-vehicle/.

30. Radley Balko. "A Decade after 9/11, Police Departments Are Increasingly Militarized." *The Huffington Post.* September 12, 2011. Accessed December 19, 2016. http://www.huffingtonpost.com/2011/09/12/police-militarization-9–11-september-11_n_955508.html.

31. Rhonda Cook. "Military Equipment Flowing to Local Law Enforcement Raises Questions." *Atlanta Journal Constitution.* January 27, 2013. Accessed December 19, 2016. http://www.ajc.com/news/military-equipment-flowing-local-law-enforcement-raises-questions/6KuK57UWg3mxGwqCh5Ab6O/.

32. Emily Ekins. "54% of Americans Say Police Using Military Weapons." Cato Institute. December 14, 2016. Accessed December 21, 2016. https://www .cato.org/blog/54-americans-say-police-using-military-weapons-goes-too-far.

33. Gene Healy. *Deployed in the U.S.A.: The Creeping Militarization of the Home Front.* Washington, D.C.: Cato Institute, 2003.

34. Jonah Green. "NYPD Could Take Down Plane in an 'Extreme Situation': Ray Kelly." *The Huffington Post.* November 26, 2011. Accessed December 26, 2016. http://www.huffingtonpost.com/2011/09/26/nypd-could-take-down-plan_ n_980883.html. Video.

35. Craig Horowitz. "The NYPD's War on Terror." NYMag.com. 2011. Accessed December 26, 2016. http://nymag.com/nymetro/news/features/n_ 8286/.

36. "'I Have My Own Army in the NYPD—The Seventh Largest Army in the World': Bloomberg's Bizarre Boast about City's Police Force." *Daily Mail Online.* December 1, 2011. Accessed December 28, 2016. http://www.dailymail.co.uk/ news/article-2068428/Bloomberg-I-army-NYPD-State-Department-New-York-City.html.

37. Ibid.

38. "State and Major Urban Area Fusion Centers." Department of Homeland Security. Accessed December 26, 2016. https://www.dhs.gov/state-and-major-urban-area-fusion-centers.

39. *The Modern Militia Movement.* Jefferson City: Missouri Information Analysis Center, 2009. February 20, 2009. Accessed January 2, 2017. http://consti tution.org/abus/le/miac-strategic-report.pdf. Report.

40. Ibid.

41. "Fusion Center Encourages Improper Investigations of Lobbying Groups and Anti-War Activists." ACLU.org. February 25, 2009. Accessed January 2, 2017.https://www.aclu.org/news/fusion-center-encourages-improper-investigations-lobbying-groups-and-anti-war-activists?redirect=cpredirect%2F38835.

42. Ibid.

43. "The Oklahoma Question." Oklahoma Information Fusion Center. Accessed December 26, 2016. https://www.ok.gov/okfusion/About_The_OIFC/The_Oklahoma_Question/index.html.

44. "Idaho Criminal Intelligence Center." Idaho Criminal Intelligence Center. Accessed December 26, 2016. https://www.isp.idaho.gov/icic/; Bryan Costigan. "STATEMENT FOR THE RECORD." Senate Committee on Homeland Security and Governmental Affairs. March 2015. Accessed December 26, 2016. https://www.google.com/url?sa=t&rct=j&q=&esrc=s&source=web&cd=10&ved=0ahUK Ewjb39PXwpLRAhWBWCYKHbswDYcQFghVMAk&url=https%3A%2F%2F www.hsgac.senate.gov%2Fdownload%2F%3Fid%3D05729f27-be22–48a1–95de-880e07cadc86&usg=AFQjCNEnYQto7I7LQIq_1XL_WwhskM93sA&sig2=-k8p VT_7NP55X3Q4OGqNrw.

45. "2016 Chicago Murders—Explore Data." DNAinfo Chicago. December 2016. Accessed December 26, 2016. https://www.dnainfo.com/chicago/2016-chicago-murders/explore-data.

46. "The Terrorism Statistics Every American Needs to Hear." Global Research. May 19, 2014. Accessed December 26, 2016. http://www.globalresearch.ca/the-terrorism-statistics-every-american-needs-to-hear/5382818.

47. Annie Sweeney and Hal Dardick. "Chicago: Front Line in War on Terror." *Tribune Digital*. November 11, 2010. Accessed December 26, 2016. http://articles.chicagotribune.com/2010–11–11/news/ct-met-terrorism-chicago-police-1114–20101111_1_david-coleman-headley-chicago-cops-mumbai.

48. Greg Botelho. "Texas Shooting: Officer with Pistol Stops Rifle-Wielding Attackers." CNN. May 5, 2015. Accessed December 26, 2016. http://www.cnn.com/2015/05/05/us/texas-police-shooting-hero/.

49. Radley Balko. *Overkill: The Rise of Paramilitary Police Raids in America.* Washington, D.C.: Cato Institute, 2006. Accessed December 27, 2016. https://object.cato.org/sites/cato.org/files/pubs/pdf/balko_whitepaper_2006.pdf.

50. Radley Balko. *Rise of the Warrior Cop: The Militarization of America's Police Forces.* New York: PublicAffairs, 2013.

51. *The Cato Handbook for Policy Makers.* 8th ed. Washington, D.C.: Cato Institute, 2017.

52. Steven Elbow. "Hooked on SWAT." Madison.com. August 18, 2001. Accessed February 25, 2017. http://host.madison.com/ct/news/local/writers/steven_elbow/hooked-on-swat/article_f1bc13e6-b29b-5ab0-a7cf-ba46b1b3860c.html.

53. Ibid.

54. Radley Balko. *Overkill: The Rise of Paramilitary Police Raids in America*. Washington, D.C.: Cato Institute, 2006. Accessed December 27, 2016. https://object.cato.org/sites/cato.org/files/pubs/pdf/balko_whitepaper_2006.pdf.

55. Associated Press. "Ruby Ridge: 20 Years Later, Randy Weaver's Daughter Lives in Peace." PennLive.com. August 20, 2012. Accessed December 28, 2016. http://www.pennlive.com/midstate/index.ssf/2012/08/ruby_ridge_20_years_later.html.

56. Susan Jones. "After Two Raids, DOJ Decides No Criminal Charges against Gibson Guitar Company." CNS News. August 7, 2012. Accessed December 27, 2016. http://www.cnsnews.com/news/article/after-two-raids-doj-decides-no-criminal-charges-against-gibson-guitar-company.

57. Jan Morgan. *Rampant Injustice*. YouTube. October 31, 2012. Accessed December 28, 2016. https://youtu.be/bFALonjLay0.

58. Radley Balko. *Overkill: The Rise of Paramilitary Police Raids in America*. Washington, D.C.: Cato Institute, 2006. Accessed December 27, 2016. https://object.cato.org/sites/cato.org/files/pubs/pdf/balko_whitepaper_2006.pdf.

59. Ibid.

60. *Benjamin Burris v. Garnett Riley, et al*. United States District Court for Western Virginia. November 18, 2015. Accessed June 11, 2017. http://rutherford.org/files_images/general/11-19-2015_Burruss-_complaint.pdf.

61. Radley Balko. *Rise of the Warrior Cop: The Militarization of America's Police Forces*. New York: PublicAffairs, 2013.

62. Ibid.

63. Steven Elbow. "Hooked on SWAT." Madison.com. August 18, 2001. Accessed February 25, 2017. http://host.madison.com/ct/news/local/writers/steven_elbow/hooked-on-swat/article_f1bc13e6-b29b-5ab0-a7cf-ba46b1b3860c.html.

64. *Hollywood Florida Police Attack Man for Refusing to Give His Name*. YouTube. December 27, 2016. Accessed January 4, 2017. https://www.youtube.com/watch?v=XUsuTsdSxL4.

65. Ibid.

66. *Department of Justice Report Regarding the Criminal Investigation into the Shooting Death of Michael Brown by Ferguson, Missouri Police Officer Darren Wilson*. Washington, D.C.: U.S. Department of Justice, 2015. Report.

67. "The Government War on Kid-Run Concession Stands." Freedom Center of Missouri. Accessed January 21, 2017. http://www.mofreedom.org/2011/07/the-government-war-on-kid-run-concession-stands/.

68. Bernie DeGroat. "Road Chat: Talking to Passengers Can Be as Dangerous as Using a Cell Phone." *Michigan News*. February 21, 2006. Accessed January 21, 2017. http://ns.umich.edu/new/releases/116-road-chat-talking-to-passengers-can-be-as-dangerous-as-using-a-cell-phone.

69. *Do Not Resist*. Dir. Craig Atkinson. Vanish Films, 2016. Documentary.

70. Ibid.

71. George Fletcher Chandler. Major. *Bulletin #1.* 1 November 1917. Memorandum. New York State Police Headquarters, Albany, NY.

Chapter 4: The Consequences of Eroding Respect

1. "Head of the Civil Rights Division Vanita Gupta Delivers Remarks at University of North Carolina Center for Civil Rights Conference." Justice.gov. December 2, 2016. Accessed December 5, 2016. https://www.justice.gov/opa/speech/head-civil-rights-division-vanita-gupta-delivers-remarks-university-north-carolina-center.

2. Harvey A. Silverglate. *Three Felonies a Day: How the Feds Target the Innocent.* New York: Encounter Books, 2011.

3. This account was first published in my 2015 book: Todd Douglas. *A Republic, If You Can Keep It: A Chronicle of the American Counterrevolution.* Oklahoma City: Tate Pub & Enterprises Llc., 2015.

4. "Cops Called on 13-Year-Olds for Selling Cupcakes." NBCNews.com. November 15, 2010. Accessed March 1, 2017. http://www.nbcnews.com/id/40194328/ns/us_news-life/t/cops-called—year-olds-selling-cupcakes/#.WLcXOxiZPVo.

5. Ibid.

6. *Report of the Independent Commission on the Los Angeles Police Department.* Los Angeles, 1991. Washington, D.C.: National Criminal Justice Resource Service.

7. The full video is available at https://vault.fbi.gov/rodney-king/video/rodney-king-video.

8. David Margolick. "Beating Case Unfolds, as Does Debate on Lawyer." *The New York Times.* March 16, 1991. Accessed December 14, 2016. http://www.nytimes.com/1991/03/17/us/beating-case-unfolds-as-does-debate-on-lawyer.html.

9. Melissa Pamer. "Los Angeles 1992 Riots: By the Numbers." NBC Southern California. April 20, 2012. Accessed December 14, 2016. http://www.nbclos angeles.com/news/local/Los-Angeles-1992-Riots-By-the-Numbers-148340405.html.

10. Ibid.

11. *Report of the Independent Commission on the Los Angeles Police Department.* Los Angeles, 1991.

12. This number was calculated using the total numbers of complaints received by all officers with three officers with four or more complaints as compared to the total number of complaints and the number of personnel in the LAPD in 1991.

13. *Report of the Independent Commission on the Los Angeles Police Department.* Los Angeles, 1991.

14. Ibid.

15. Ibid.

16. *Investigation of the Ferguson Police Department.* Washington, D.C.: U.S. Department of Justice, Civil Rights Division, 2015. Report.

17. Joseph Shapiro. "As Court Fees Rise, the Poor Are Paying the Price." *NPR.* Corporation for Public Broadcasting. May 19, 2014. Accessed February 13, 2017.

18. Ibid.

19. Ibid.

20. "Profiles of Those Forced to 'Pay Or Stay.' " NPR. May 19, 2014. Accessed February 13, 2017. http://www.npr.org/2014/05/19/310710716/profiles-of-those-forced-to-pay-or-stay.

21. Joseph Shapiro. "Measures Aimed at Keeping People out of Jail Punish the Poor." NPR. May 24, 2014. Accessed February 13, 2017. http://www.npr .org/2014/05/24/314866421/measures-aimed-at-keeping-people-out-of-jail-punish-the-poor.

22. "Clerks of Court Generally Are Meeting the System's Collections Performance Standards." Office of Program Policy Analysis & Government Accountability. 2007. Accessed February 12, 2017. http://www.oppaga.state.fl.us/reports/pdf/0721rpt.pdf. Report.

23. Matt Taibbi. *The Divide: American Injustice in the Age of the Wealth Gap.* New York: Spiegel & Grau Trade Paperbacks, 2014.

24. Many details of this story were taken from an article by Jennifer Gonnerman of *The New Yorker*: Jennifer Gonnerman. "Before the Law." *The New Yorker.* June 8, 2015. Accessed February 14, 2017. http://www.newyorker.com/magazine/2014/10/06/before-the-law.

25. Laura Sullivan. "Inmates Who Can't Make Bail Face Stark Options." NPR. January 22, 2010. Accessed February 14, 2017. http://www.npr.org/templates/story/story.php?storyId=122725819.

26. "Statute of Westminster 1275." Project Gutenberg, World Library Foundation. Accessed February 14, 2017. http://www.gutenberg.us/articles/eng/statute_of_westminster_1275.

27. Samuel Wiseman. "Discrimination, Coercion, and the Bail Reform Act of 1984: The Loss of the Core Constitutional Protections of the Excessive Bail Clause." *Fordham Urban Law Journal* (2009): 122–56. Accessed February 14, 2017. http://ir.lawnet.fordham.edu/cgi/viewcontent.cgi?article=2298&context=ulj.

28. *United States v. Salerno,* 481 U.S. 739 (May 26, 1987).

29. Nick Pinto. "The Bail Trap." *The New York Times.* August 13, 2015. Accessed February 14, 2017. https://www.nytimes.com/2015/08/16/magazine/the-bail-trap.html?_r=0.

30. Ibid.

31. Matthew R. Durose, et al. *Recidivism of Prisoners Released in 30 States in 2005: Patterns from 2005 to 2010.* NCJ 244205. April 2014. Accessed February 14, 2017. https://www.bjs.gov/content/pub/pdf/rprts05p0510.pdf.

Chapter 5: The Police and Racial Conflict in America

1. Audrey Smedley. "Race—The Power of an Illusion." *Anthropology Newsletter*, 1997. Accessed December 10, 2016. http://www.pbs.org/race/000_About/002_04-background-02–09.htm.

2. Catherine A. Cottrell and Steven L. Neuberg. "Different Emotional Reactions to Different Groups: A Sociofunctional Threat-Based Approach to 'Prejudice.'" *Journal of Personality and Social Psychology* 88, no. 5 (2005): 770–789. Accessed October 22, 2016. http://psychology-dev.clas.asu.edu/sites/default/files/Different%20Emotional%20Reactions%20to%20Different%20Groups-%20A%20Sociofunctional%20Threat-Based%20Approach%20to%20_Prejudice_.pdf.

3. Isabelle Khoo. "Morgan Freeman Calls Black History Month 'Ridiculous.'" *The Huffington Post*. February 10, 2017. Accessed February 26, 2017. http://www.huffingtonpost.ca/2017/02/10/morgan-freeman-black-history-month_n_14642958.html.

4. This account is based upon a *New York Times* report: Al Baker, J. David Goodman, and Benjamin Mueller. "Beyond the Chokehold: The Path to Eric Garner's Death." *The New York Times*. June 13, 2015. Accessed December 11, 2016. http://www.nytimes.com/2015/06/14/nyregion/eric-garner-police-chokehold-staten-island.html?_r=0.

5. Eric Garner Video—Unedited Version. YouTube. July 12, 2015. Accessed February 2, 2017. https://www.youtube.com/watch?v=JpGxagKOkv8.

6. Barry Paddock, Rocco Parascandola, and Corky Siemaszko. "Eric Garner's Death Ruled a Homicide: NYC Medical Examiner." *NY Daily News*. August 1, 2014. Accessed December 11, 2016. http://www.nydailynews.com/new-york/nyc-crime/eric-garner-death-ruled-homicide-medical-examiner-article-1.1888808.

7. Larry Celona, Kirstan Conley, and Bruce Golding. "Police Fury at Mayor's Racial Smear." *New York Post*. December 4, 2014. Accessed December 11, 2016. http://nypost.com/2014/12/04/police-union-prez-rips-de-blasio-over-eric-garner/.

8. "The DOJ Report Doesn't Say How Freddie Gray Died, but It Does Explain Why." Baltimoresun.com, Baltimore Sun Media Group. August 11, 2016. Accessed January 25, 2017.

9. "Freddie Gray's Death in Police Custody—What We Know." BBC News. May 23, 2016. Accessed January 25, 2017. http://www.bbc.com/news/world-us-canada-32400497.

10. Ryan M. McDermott. "Marilyn Mosby Never Should Have Charged Officers in Freddie Gray Death, Lawyers Say." *The Washington Times*. July 27, 2016. Accessed January 25, 2017. http://www.washingtontimes.com/news/2016/jul/27/marilyn-mosby-never-should-have-charged-officers-i/.

11. Michael Daly. "Baltimore Mayor Gave Permission to Riot." *Daily Beast*. April 28, 2015. Accessed January 25, 2017. http://www.thedailybeast.com/articles/2015/04/28/baltimore-mayor-s-tone-deaf-handling-of-city-s-riot-crisis.html.

12. Allyson Collins and Cynthia Brown. *Shielded from Justice: Police Brutality and Accountability in the United States*. New York: Human Rights Watch, 1998.

13. Kimberly Kindy, Marc Fisher, Julia Tate, and Jennifer Jenkins. "A Year of Reckoning: Police Fatally Shoot Nearly 1,000." *The Washington Post*. December 24, 2015. Accessed December 10, 2016. http://www.washingtonpost.com/sf/investi gative/2015/12/26/a-year-of-reckoning-police-fatally-shoot-nearly-1000/.

14. Nelson Adekoya and Kurt B. Nolte. "Struck-by-Lightning Deaths in the United States." *Journal of Environmental Health* 67, no. 9 (May 2005): 45–50. Accessed December 10, 2016. http://www.bls.gov/iif/oshwc/cfoi/jeh5_05_45–50.pdf.

15. Ibid.

16. Table 43—Arrests, "Crime in the United States—2014." FBI. September 19, 2015. Accessed December 10, 2016. https://ucr.fbi.gov/crime-in-the-u.s/2014/crime-in-the-u.s.-2014/tables/table-43.

17. "2015 Washington Post Database of Police Shootings." *The Washington Post*. Accessed December 10, 2016. https://www.washingtonpost.com/graphics/national/police-shootings/.

18. These numbers were obtained using crime data from 2014—the most recent available—and police shooting data from 2015.

19. David Rutz. "Black Lives Matter Leader Stands by Controversial Tweets." *Washington Free Beacon*. July 11, 2016. Accessed December 10, 2016. http://free beacon.com/issues/black-lives-matter-leader-stands-controversial-tweets/.

20. Table 43—Arrests, "Crime in the United States—2014." FBI. September 19, 2015. Accessed December 10, 2016. https://ucr.fbi.gov/crime-in-the-u.s/2014/crime-in-the-u.s.-2014/tables/table-43.

21. Chicago recorded 746 murders, Philadelphia recorded 271, totaling 1,017.

22. Jennifer Smith Richards, Angela Caputo, Todd Lighty, and Jason Meisner. "92 Deaths, 2,623 Bullets: Tracking Every Chicago Police Shooting over 6 Years." *Chicago Tribune*. September 17, 2016. Accessed February 18, 2017. http://www.chicagotribune.com/news/watchdog/ct-chicago-police-shooting-database-met-20160826-story.html.

23. "Chicago Homicides." *Chicago Tribune*. Accessed February 18, 2017. http://crime.chicagotribune.com/chicago/homicides.

24. Erika Harrell. *Black Victims of Violent Crime*. NCJ 214258. Washington, D.C.: U.S. Department of Justice Office of Justice Programs, 2007. Accessed February 18, 2017. https://www.bjs.gov/content/pub/pdf/bvvc.pdf.

25. Vanessa McMains. "Johns Hopkins Study Suggests Medical Errors Are Third-Leading Cause of Death in U.S." *The Hub*. May 3, 2016. Accessed February 15, 2017. https://hub.jhu.edu/2016/05/03/medical-errors-third-leading-cause-of-death/.

26. Jonathan Allen. "New York to Pay $15 Million in Wrongful Loitering Arrests." Reuters. February 8, 2012. Accessed February 01, 2017. http://www.reuters.com/article/us-newyork-unconstitutional-idUSTRE81804920120209.

27. Jaeah Lee. "Here's the Data That Shows Cops Kill Black People at a Higher Rate Than White People." Mother Jones. September 10, 2014. Accessed January 26, 2017. http://www.motherjones.com/politics/2014/08/police-shootings-ferguson-race-data.

28. Andrea M. Burch. *Arrest-Related Deaths, 2003–2009—Statistical Tables.* NCJ 235385. November 2011. Accessed January 26, 2017. https://www.bjs.gov/content/pub/pdf/ard0309st.pdf.

29. Alexia Cooper and Erica L. Smith. *Homicide Trends in the United States, 1980–2008.* NCJ 236018. Washington, D.C.: U.S. Department of Justice, Office of Justice Programs, Bureau of Justice Statistics, 2011.

30. Ibid.

31. "Crime in the United States." Ucr.fbi.gov. May 18, 2014. Accessed February 19, 2017. https://ucr.fbi.gov/crime-in-the-u.s/2013/crime-in-the-u.s.-2013/cius-home.

32. Peter Moskos. *Cop in the Hood: My Year Policing Baltimore's Eastern District.* Princeton, NJ: Princeton University Press, 2009.

33. Walter E. Williams. "The True Black Tragedy: Illegitimacy Rate of Nearly 75%." CNS News. May 19, 2015. Accessed January 30, 2017. http://www.cnsnews.com/commentary/walter-e-williams/true-black-tragedy-illegitimacy-rate-nearly-75.

34. "Obama's Father's Day Remarks." *The New York Times.* June 15, 2008. Accessed January 30, 2017. http://www.nytimes.com/2008/06/15/us/politics/15text-obama.html.

35. Ali Meyer. "Unemployment among Black Youth 393% Higher Than National Rate." CNS News. November 9, 2013. Accessed February 4, 2017. http://www.cnsnews.com/news/article/ali-meyer/unemployment-among-black-youth-393-higher-national-rate.

36. Joel Miller. *Profiling Populations Available for Stops and Searches.* London: Home Office, Policing and Reducing Crime Unit, Research, Development and Statistics Directorate, 2000.

37. Ibid.

38. Robin Shepard Engel, Jennifer M. Calnon, and Thomas J. Bernard. "Theory and Racial Profiling: Shortcomings and Future Directions in Research." *Justice Quarterly* 19, no. 2 (2002): 249–73.

39. The percentage of whites and blacks living below the poverty line is 9.9 and 25.8 percent, respectively. Suzanne Macartney. *Poverty Rates for Selected Detailed Race and Hispanic Groups by State and Place: 2007–2011.* ACSBR/11–17. Washington, D.C.: U.S. Census Bureau, 2013. February 2013. Accessed February 18, 2017. https://www.census.gov/prod/2013pubs/acsbr11–17.pdf.

40. "Scottsboro Timeline." PBS—American Experience. Accessed December 4, 2016. http://www.pbs.org/wgbh/amex/scottsboro/timeline/index.html.

41. Douglas O. Linder. "Emmett Till Murder Trial: Selected Testimony." UMKC.edu. 2014. Accessed December 4, 2016. http://law2.umkc.edu/faculty/projects/ftrials/till/tillaccount.html.

42. Ibid.

43. Big Tex. "The Face of Emmett Till (Updated)." *Daily Kos.* May 14, 2009. Accessed December 4, 2016. http://www.dailykos.com/story/2009/5/14/731205/-.

44. *1961 Commission on Civil Rights Report.* Washington, D.C.: U.S. Government Printing Office, 1961.

45. John R. Lott, Jr. "A Transaction-Costs Explanation for Why the Poor Are More Likely to Commit Crime." *The Journal of Legal Studies* 19, no. 1 (1990): 243–45. Accessed December 8, 2016. http://www.jstor.org.webster.sunybroome .edu:2048/stable/pdf/724420.pdf.

46. G. W. Evans, C. Gonnella, L. A. Marcynyszyn, L. Gentile, and N. Salpe-kar. "The Role of Chaos in Poverty and Children's Socioemotional Adjustment." *Psychological Science* 16, no. 7 (2005): 560–65. Accessed December 8, 2016. https://pdfs.semanticscholar.org/1ed7/fe9d504d7100d787dd3b79baa464c 83b02c9.pdf.

47. Sandhya Somashekhar, Wesley Lowery, Keith L. Alexander, Kimberly Kindy, and Julie Tate. "Unarmed and Black—A Year after Michael Brown's Fatal Shooting, Unarmed Black Men Are Seven Times More Likely Than Whites to Die by Police Gunfire." *The Washington Post*. August 8, 2015. Accessed December 11, 2016. http://www.washingtonpost.com/sf/national/2015/08/08/ black-and-unarmed/.

48. Roland G. Fryer, Jr. "An Empirical Analysis of Racial Differences in Police Use of Force." Cambridge, MA: National Bureau of Economic Research. July 2016. Accessed January 25, 2017. http://www.nber.org/papers/w22399 .pdf.

49. Valerie Richardson. "Police More Reluctant to Shoot Blacks Than Whites, Study Finds." *The Washington Times*. May 2, 2016. Accessed January 25, 2017. http://m.washingtontimes.com/news/2016/may/2/police-more-reluctant-shoot-blacks-whites-study-fi/.

Chapter 6: The Police as the Face of the Law

1. "Head of the Civil Rights Division Vanita Gupta Delivers Remarks at University of North Carolina Center for Civil Rights Conference." Justice.gov. December 2, 2016. Accessed December 5, 2016. https://www.justice.gov/opa/speech/ head-civil-rights-division-vanita-gupta-delivers-remarks-university-north-caro lina-center.

2. Philip Bump. "The Facts about Stop-and-Frisk in New York City." *The Washington Post*. September 26, 2016. Accessed December 12, 2016. https:// www.washingtonpost.com/news/the-fix/wp/2016/09/21/it-looks-like-rudy-giuliani-convinced-donald-trump-that-stop-and-frisk-actually-works/?utm_ term=.9905b9c174bd.

3. Matt Taibbi. *The Divide: American Injustice in the Age of the Wealth Gap*. New York: Spiegel & Grau Trade Paperbacks, 2014.

4. Ibid.

5. According to a government survey, more than 50 million Americans report using illicit narcotics, marijuana, or illegal prescription drugs in the previous three months. "Substance Abuse and Mental Health Services Administration Survey on Drug Use and Health." NIDA.gov. June 2015. Accessed February 26, 2017. https://www.drugabuse.gov/publications/drugfacts/nationwide-trends.

6. "Richard Nixon: Remarks about an Intensified Program for Drug Abuse Prevention and Control." The American Presidency Project. 1973. Accessed November 6, 2016. http://www.presidency.ucsb.edu/ws/?pid=3047.

7. Dan Baum. "Legalize It All." *Harper's Magazine.* April 2016. Accessed November 7, 2016. http://harpers.org/archive/2016/04/legalize-it-all/.

8. Arun Venugopal. "Black Leaders Once Championed the Strict Drug Laws They Now Seek to Dismantle." WNYC. August 15, 2013. Accessed January 22, 2017. http://www.wnyc.org/story/312823-black-leaders-once-championed-strict-drug-laws-they-now-seek-dismantle/.

9. Brian Mann. "Profile: Charles Rangel and the Drug Wars." WNYC. August 17, 2013. Accessed January 22, 2017. http://www.wnyc.org/story/313060-profile-charles-rangel-and-drug-wars/.

10. Yolanda Young. "Analysis: Black Leaders Supported Clinton's Crime Bill." NBCNews.com. April 8, 2016. Accessed January 24, 2017. http://www.nbcnews.com/news/nbcblk/analysis-black-leaders-supported-clinton-s-crime-bill-n552961.

11. Jessica Lussenhop. "Clinton Crime Bill: Why Is It so Controversial?" BBC News. April 18, 2016. Accessed January 24, 2017. http://www.bbc.com/news/world-us-canada-36020717.

12. E. Ann Carson and Elizabeth Anderson. *Prisoners in 2015.* NCJ 250229. Washington, D.C.: U.S. Department of Justice, 2016. Accessed February 26, 2017. https://www.bjs.gov/content/pub/pdf/p15.pdf.

13. Jacob Sullum. "The War on Drugs Now Features Roadside Sexual Assaults by Cops." Forbes. May 12, 2015. Accessed March 2, 2017. https://www.forbes.com/sites/jacobsullum/2015/05/07/will-texas-ban-roadside-sexual-assaults-by-drug-warriors/#48f361c7829e.

14. *Eckert v. Dougherty, et al.,* 15–2204, docket number 2:13-CV-00727-JB-WPL (D. N.M.). U.S. Court of Appeals for the Tenth Circuit. September 14, 2016.

15. *Young v. Hidalgo County,* 2:13-cv-01087-SMV-LAM, U.S. District Court for the District of New Mexico. November 8, 2013.

16. Ibid.

17. *United States v. Montoya de Hernandez,* 473 U.S. 531 (1985). July 1, 1985.

18. "The Constitution in the 100-Mile Border Zone." American Civil Liberties Union. Accessed March 3, 2017. https://www.aclu.org/other/constitution-100-mile-border-zone.

19. *United States v. Montoya de Hernandez,* 473 U.S. 531 (1985) (July 1, 1985).

20. Mark Thornton. "Alcohol Prohibition Was a Failure." Cato Institute. July 17, 1991. Accessed November 6, 2016. https://www.cato.org/publications/policy-analysis/alcohol-prohibition-was-failure.

21. Jeffrey A. Miron. *Drug War Crimes: The Consequences of Prohibition.* Oakland, CA: Independent Institute, 2004.

22. Charles Hanson Towne. *The Rise and Fall of Prohibition.* New York: Macmillan, 1923.

23. Jeffrey A. Miron. *Drug War Crimes: The Consequences of Prohibition.* Oakland, CA: Independent Institute, 2004.

24. Ibid.

25. Jeremy Kuzmarov. "What August Vollmer, the Father of American Law Enforcement, Has to Teach Us." *The Huffington Post*. October 4, 2016. Accessed February 26, 2017. http://www.huffingtonpost.com/jeremy-kuzmarov/what-august-vollmer-the-f_b_12333080.html.

26. Denise Schlegel. "Police Grants: What's Being Federally Funded in 2016?" PoliceGrantsHelp.com. February 1, 2016. Accessed November 12, 2016. http://www.policegrantshelp.com/Columnists/Denise-Schlegel/articles/71130006-Police-grants-Whats-being-federally-funded-in-2016/.

27. The National Highway Transportation Safety Administration alone has budgeted over $1 billion for traffic-ticket-based grants for 2017. *NHTSA/Budget Estimates Fiscal Year 2017*. Washington, DC: U.S. Department of Transportation. Accessed November 12, 2016. http://www.nhtsa.gov/staticfiles/administration/pdf/Budgets/FY2017-NHTSA_CBJ_FINAL_02_2016.pdf.

28. Sheriffs occupy a unique position, in that they are elected officials themselves and are not so easily controlled by their local governments.

29. Tim Reason. "Obama's Accounting Expert?" CFO. November 26, 2008. Accessed March 1, 2017. http://ww2.cfo.com/risk-compliance/2008/11/obamas-accounting-expert/.

30. Public Law 110–343; Div. A, Sec. 1, Title 1,§ 115(a)(3).

31. "Goldman Sachs' Revolving Door." CBS News. April 8, 2010. Accessed March 1, 2017. http://www.cbsnews.com/news/goldman-sachs-revolving-door/.

32. Caroline Wolf Harlow. *Defense Counsel in Criminal Cases*. Washington, D.C.: U.S. Department of Justice, Office of Justice Programs, Bureau of Justice Statistics, 2001. Accessed December 13, 2016. https://www.bjs.gov/content/pub/pdf/dccc.pdf.

33. "Jones v. U.S. Drug Enforcement Admin." 819 F. Supp. 698 (1993). Leagle .com. Leagle. April 21, 1993. Accessed December 13, 2016. http://www.leagle.com/decision/19931517819FSupp698_11453/JONES%20v.%20U.S.%20DRUG%20ENFORCEMENT%20ADMIN.

34. Ibid.

35. Emily Ekens. "84% of Americans Oppose Civil Asset Forfeiture." Cato at Liberty. December 13, 2016. Accessed December 13, 2016. https://www.cato.org/blog/84-americans-oppose-civil-asset-forfeiture?utm_content=bufferf7580&utm_medium=social&utm_source=facebook.com&utm_campaign=buffer.

36. William Blackstone. "Avalon Project—Blackstone's Commentaries on the Laws of England—Book the Fourth—Chapter the Twenty-Seventh: Of Trial, and Conviction." Avalon Project. Accessed December 13, 2016. http://avalon.law .yale.edu/18th_century/blackstone_bk4ch27.asp.

37. Whitley Kaufman. "Blackstone's Ratio." Accessed December 13, 2016. http://faculty.uml.edu/whitley_kaufman/law/BlackstonesRatio.htm.

38. Brad Tuttle. "Police All over the U.S. Are Issuing Fewer Traffic Tickets." *Time*. March 30, 2015. Accessed December 14, 2016. http://time.com/money/3762033/traffic-ticket-decrease-speed-limits-police/.

39. *Investigation of the Ferguson Police Department.* Washington, D.C.: U.S. Department of Justice, Civil Rights Division, 2015. Report.

40. James Baxter. "Traffic Tickets Are Big Business—National Motorists Association." October 13, 2016. Accessed December 14, 2016. https://www.motorists.org/blog/traffic-tickets-are-big-business/.

41. "Traffic Fines as Cash Cow." *Los Angeles Times.* February 6, 2010. Accessed December 14, 2016. http://articles.latimes.com/2010/feb/06/opinion/la-ed-fines6–2010feb06.

42. "Investigation of the Baltimore City Police Department." Justice.gov. August 10, 2016. Accessed December 14, 2016. https://www.justice.gov/opa/file/883366/download.

43. Since the lawsuit ended the stop-and-frisk policy in 2013, violent crime has declined from 77,563 incidents to 75,165 in 2015—a 3 percent drop: "New York Crime Rates 1960–2015." Disastercenter.com. Accessed February 17, 2017. http://www.disastercenter.com/crime/nycrime.htm.

44. "Stop-and-Frisk Data." Nyclu.org. Accessed February 17, 2017. http://www.nyclu.org/content/stop-and-frisk-data.

45. *David Floyd et al. v. City of New York.* U.S. District Court, Southern District of New York, August 12, 2013. https://www.justice.gov/sites/default/files/crt/legacy/2013/06/13/floyd_soi_6-12-13.pdf.

46. "Investigation of the Baltimore City Police Department." Justice.gov. August 10, 2016. Accessed December 14, 2016. https://www.justice.gov/opa/file/883366/download.

Chapter 7: Training the Police for Service Instead of Enforcement

1. A. J. Pinizzotto and E. F. Davis. *FBI Law Enforcement Bulletin* (United States, FBI). June 1999. Accessed June 11, 2017. https://leb.fbi.gov/1999-pdfs/leb-june-1999.

2. "IADLEST Model Minimum Standards." IADLEST.org. Accessed March 1, 2017. https://www.iadlest.org/Projects/ModelStandards.aspx.

3. "Census of Law Enforcement Training Academies, 2002 [United States] (ICPSR 4255)." June 9, 2005. Accessed November 13, 2016. http://www.icpsr.umich.edu/icpsrweb/NACJD/studies/4255.

4. Taken in part from *State and Local Law Enforcement Training Academies, 2013.* Vol. NCJ 249784. Washington, D.C.: U.S. Department of Justice, Bureau of Justice Statistics, 2016.

5. Ibid.

6. Brian A. Reaves. "Census of State and Local Law Enforcement Agencies, 2008." Bureau of Justice Statistics. July 2011. Accessed November 13, 2016. http://www.bjs.gov/content/pub/pdf/csllea08.pdf.

7. "Police Patrol Officer Salaries." Salary.com. November 2016. Accessed November 19, 2016. http://www1.salary.com/Police-Officer-Salary.html.

8. Ayn Rand and Leonard Peikoff. "Chapter 1." In *Philosophy: Who Needs It*. New York: Signet, 1984, 7.

9. "Code of Ethics." IACP.org. Accessed November 20, 2016. http://www .iacp.org/codeofethics.

10. Wesley G. Skogan and Kathleen Frydl. *Fairness and Effectiveness in Policing: The Evidence*. Washington, D.C.: National Academies Press, 2004.

11. Ibid.

12. Robert J. Kaminski and Jeffrey A. Martin. "An Analysis of Police Officer Satisfaction with Defense and Control Tactics." *Policing: An International Journal of Police Strategies & Management* 23, no. 2 (2000): 132–53. Emerald Group Publishing. Accessed January 15, 2017. http://www.emeraldinsight.com/doi/pdfplus/10 .1108/13639510010333697.

13. "The Problem-Solving Triangle." Center for Problem-Oriented Policing. Accessed January 15, 2017. http://www.popcenter.org/about/?p=triangle.

14. *State and Local Law Enforcement Training Academies, 2013*. Vol. NCJ 249784. Washington, D.C.: U.S. Department of Justice, Bureau of Justice Statistics, 2016.

15. Ibid.

16. "Cosmetology License Requirements by State." Beauty Schools Directory. Accessed January 16, 2017. http://www.beautyschoolsdirectory.com/faq/state_ req.php.

17. *State and Local Law Enforcement Training Academies, 2013*. Vol. NCJ 249784. Washington, D.C.: U.S. Department of Justice, Bureau of Justice Statistics, 2016.

Chapter 8: Police Legitimacy and Public Relations

1. See 18 U.S. Code § 1385.

2. Albert Meijer and Marcel Thaens. "Social Media Strategies: Understanding the Differences between North American Police Departments." *Government Information Quarterly* 30, no. 4 (2013): 343–50.

3. Michael J. Palmiotto and N. Prabha Unninthan. "The Impact of Citizen Police Academies on Participants: An Exploratory Study." *Journal of Criminal Justice* 30, no. 2 (2002): 101–106.

4. Ellen G. Cohn. "The Citizen Police Academy—A Recipe for Improving Public Relations." *Journal of Criminal Justice* 24, no. 3 (1996): 265–71.

5. See http://ncpaa.us.

6. Matthew T. Theriot. "School Resource Officers and the Criminalization of Student Behavior." *Journal of Criminal Justice* 37 (2009): 280–87.

7. Tom R. Tyler and Yuen J. Huo. "Chapter 1." In *Trust in the Law: Encouraging Public Cooperation with the Police and Courts*. New York, NY: Russell Sage Foundation, 2002, 7.

8. The Center for Court Innovation provides procedural-justice resources for prosecutors and judges; see www.courtinnovation.org.

Chapter 9: Handling Officers Who Abuse the Public Trust

1. "Raw Video: Chicago Police Dashcam Video of Laquan McDonald Shooting." YouTube. November 24, 2015. Accessed February 28, 2017. https://www.youtube.com/watch?v=1Zz03rvyhIk.

2. David March. CPD Case Supplementary Report—HX475653. Chicago: Chicago Police Department. December 4, 2015. Accessed May 6, 2016. http://www.documentcloud.org/documents/2642131-McD-6.html.

3. *People of the State of Illinois vs. Jason Van Dyke*. Circuit Court of Cook County. November 2015. Ordinal Document.

4. David March. CPD Case Supplementary Report—HX475653. Chicago: Chicago Police Department. December 4, 2015. Accessed May 6, 2016. http://www.documentcloud.org/documents/2642131-McD-6.html.

5. *Recommendations for Reform: Restoring Trust between the Chicago Police and the Communities They Serve*. Chicago: Police Accountability Task Force, 2016. Report.

6. Justin Glawe. "Exclusive: Lawyers Went to Rahm Emanuel, Then Quashed the Laquan McDonald Video." *Daily Beast*. January 6, 2016. Accessed May 6, 2016. http://www.thedailybeast.com/articles/2015/01/06/exclusive-lawyers-went-to-rahm-then-quashed-the-laquan-mcdonald-video.html.

7. Roger G. Dunham and Geoffrey P. Alpert. *Critical Issues in Policing: Contemporary Readings*. Long Grove, IL: Waveland Press, 2015.

8. "Introduction." In Michael K. Brown, *Working the Street: Police Discretion and the Dilemmas of Reform*. New York: Russel Sage Foundation, 1988, p. 9.

9. "Citizens Police Data Project." Accessed September 24, 2016. https://cpdb.co/officer/jason-van-dyke/7655.

10. *Recommendations for Reform: Restoring Trust between the Chicago Police and the Communities They Serve*. Chicago: Police Accountability Task Force, 2016. Report.

11. *Agreement between Fraternal Order of Police Chicago Lodge No. 7 and the City of Chicago*. Collective Bargaining Agreement, Chicago, IL. July 1, 2012.

12. Timothy Williams. "Cast-Out Police Officers Are Often Hired in Other Cities." *The New York Times*. September 11, 2016. Accessed January 5, 2017. http://www.nytimes.com/2016/09/11/us/whereabouts-of-cast-out-police-officers-other-cities-often-hire-them.html?_r=0.

13. Ibid.

14. Ibid.

15. Anthony L. Fisher. "Why It's So Hard to Stop Bad Cops from Getting New Police Jobs." Reason.com. September 30, 2016. Accessed February 3, 2017. http://reason.com/archives/2016/09/30/why-its-so-hard-to-stop-bad-cops-from-ge.

16. National Decertification Index. IADLEST.com. Accessed January 5, 2017. https://www.iadlest.org/projects/ndi20.aspx.

17. "Uniform Termination Notice for Securities Industry Registration." FINRA.org. Accessed January 5, 2017. http://www.finra.org/sites/default/files/form-u5.pdf.

18. National Practitioner Databank. Health Resources and Services Administration. Accessed January 5, 2017. https://www.npdb.hrsa.gov/.

19. Anthony L. Fisher. "Why It's So Hard to Stop Bad Cops from Getting New Police Jobs." Reason.com. September 30, 2016. Accessed February 3, 2017. http://reason.com/archives/2016/09/30/why-its-so-hard-to-stop-bad-cops-from-ge.

20. Roger L. Goldman. "State Revocation of Law Enforcement Officers' Licenses and Federal Criminal Prosecution: An Opportunity for Cooperative Federalism." 2003. Accessed February 3, 2017. https://www.nlg-npap.org/sites/default/files/RevocationGoldman.pdf.

21. Nomaan Merchant. "In the Wake of Michael Brown's Death, the Federal Government Wants to Require the Ferguson Police Department to Check All New Hires against a Database of Police Officers Stripped of Their Law Enforcement Licenses for Misconduct." *U.S. News & World Report.* March 9, 2016. Accessed February 3, 2017. http://www.usnews.com/news/us/articles/2016-03-09/database-of-problem-police-officers-may-get-test-in-ferguson.

22. Ibid.

23. Anthony L. Fisher. "Why It's So Hard to Stop Bad Cops from Getting New Police Jobs." Reason.com. September 30, 2016. Accessed February 3, 2017. http://reason.com/archives/2016/09/30/why-its-so-hard-to-stop-bad-cops-from-ge.

24. Emily Ekins. *Policing in America: Understanding Public Attitudes Toward the Police. Results from a National Survey.* Washington, D.C.: Cato Institute, 2016. Working paper.

25. "Legislation Opposed by the FOP in the 114th Congress." Fop.net. January 14, 2015. Accessed February 4, 2017. http://www.fop.net/SearchResult.aspx?Category=PAGES&index=0.

26. "Judge Dismisses Baltimore Police Union's Lawsuit Trying to Block Work of Civilian Review Board." ACLU.org. November 4, 2016. Accessed February 4, 2017. https://www.aclu.org/news/judges-dismisses-baltimore-police-unions-lawsuit-trying-block-work-civilian-review-board.

27. Martin Kaste. "Police Are Learning to Accept Civilian Oversight, but Distrust Lingers." NPR. February 21, 2015. Accessed February 4, 2017. http://www.npr.org/2015/02/21/387770044/police-are-learning-to-accept-civilian-oversight-but-distrust-lingers.

28. *Investigation of the Chicago Police Department.* Washington, D.C.: U.S. Department of Justice, 2017. Report.

29. Ibid.

30. William A. Geller, editor. *Police Leadership in America: Crisis and Opportunity.* Chicago: American Bar Foundation, 1985.

31. Ibid.

32. Ibid.

33. Douglas Werner Perez. *Common Sense about Police Review.* Philadelphia, PA.: Temple University Press, 1994.

34. Michael F. Armstrong. *They Wished They Were Honest: The Knapp Commission and New York City Police Corruption.* New York: Columbia University Press, 2012.

Chapter 10: The Police Force the Public Deserves

1. *Investigation of the Ferguson Police Department.* Washington, D.C.: U.S. Department of Justice, Civil Rights Division, 2015. Report.

2. Ibid.

3. Russ Zajtchuk and Christopher M. Grande. *War Psychiatry.* Falls Church, VA: Office of the Surgeon General, U.S. Army. 1995. Accessed November 25, 2016. http://fas.org/irp/doddir/milmed/warpsychiatry.pdf.

4. Sonny Provetto. "Stress . . . No Problem? Think Again." *Law Enforcement Today.* February 28, 2012. Accessed November 25, 2016. http://www.lawenforce menttoday.com/stress%E2%80%A6no-problem-think-again/.

5. "Alcohol Abuse among Law Enforcement Officers." Hazelden Betty Ford Foundation. November 2015. Accessed November 26, 2016. http://www.hazel denbettyford.org/articles/research/alcohol-abuse-and-law-enforcement.

6. "IADLEST Projects NDI 2.0." IADLEST.com. Accessed November 26, 2016. https://www.iadlest.org/projects/ndi20.aspx.

7. Jeanne Kuang. "Group Slams Police Union Hire of Officer Charged in Laquan McDonald Shooting." *Chicago Tribune.* May 5, 2016. Accessed February 15, 2017. http://www.chicagotribune.com/news/laquanmcdonald/ct-laquan-mcdonald-jason-van-dyke-court-met-20160323–20160331-story.html.

8. *Law Enforcement Use of Cell-Site Simulation Technologies: Privacy Concerns and Recommendations.* Washington, D.C.: Committee on Oversight and Government Reform. December 19, 2016. Accessed February 15, 2017. https://oversight .house.gov/wp-content/uploads/2016/12/THE-FINAL-bipartisan-cell-site-simu lator-report.pdf. Report.

9. Thomas Jefferson. *The Jeffersonian Cyclopedia: A Comprehensive Collection of the Views of Thomas Jefferson Classified and Arranged in Alphabetical Order under Nine Thousand Titles Relating to Government, Politics, Law, Education, Political Economy, Finance, Science, Art, Literature, Religious Freedom, Morals, Etc.,* edited by John P. Foley. New York: Funk & Wagnalls, 1900.

10. Frank Serpico. "Serpico: Police Corruption Is Here to Stay." *New York Post.* April 8, 2016. Accessed February 25, 2017.

Bibliography

Adekoya, Nelson, and Kurt B. Nolte. "Struck-by-Lightning Deaths in the United States." *Journal of Environmental Health* 67 (2005): 45–50. Accessed December 10, 2016. http://www.bls.gov/iif/oshwc/cfoi/jeh5_05_45–50.pdf.

Agreement between Fraternal Order of Police Chicago Lodge No. 7 and the City of Chicago. Collective Bargaining Agreement. Chicago, IL. July 1, 2012.

"Alcohol Abuse among Law Enforcement Officers." Hazelden Betty Ford Foundation. November 2015. Accessed November 26, 2016. http://www.hazeldenbettyford.org/articles/research/alcohol-abuse-and-law-enforcement.

Allen, Jonathan. "New York to Pay $15 Million in Wrongful Loitering Arrests." Reuters. February 8, 2012. Accessed February 1, 2017. http://www.reuters.com/article/us-newyork-unconstitutional-idUSTRE81804920120209.

Alvarado, Francisco. "1981: Miami's Deadliest Summer." *Miami New Times.* May 25, 2016. Accessed December 17, 2016. http://www.miaminewtimes.com/news/1981-miamis-deadliest-summer-6565290.

"The Annenberg Public Policy Center of the University of Pennsylvania—Americans Know Surprisingly Little about Their Government, Survey Finds." The Annenberg Public Policy Center of the University of Pennsylvania. September 17, 2014. Accessed January 2, 2016. http://www.annenbergpublicpolicycenter.org/americans-know-surprisingly-little-about-their-government-survey-finds/.

"Annual Estimates of the Resident Population by Sex, Age, Race, and Hispanic Origin for the United States and States: April 1, 2010 to July 1, 2015." U.S. Census Bureau. 2016. Accessed December 10, 2016. https://factfinder.census.gov/faces/tableservices/jsf/pages/productview.xhtml?src=bkmk.

Armstrong, Ken. "Dollree Mapp, 1923–2014: 'The Rosa Parks of the Fourth Amendment.'" The Marshall Project. December 8, 2014. Accessed November 2, 2016. https://www.themarshallproject.org/2014/12/08/

dollree-mapp-1923–2014-the-rosa-parks-of-the-fourth-amendment#
.7JfQUFKnR.

Armstrong, Michael F. *They Wished They Were Honest: The Knapp Commission and New York City Police Corruption.* New York: Columbia University Press, 2012.

Ashkenas, Jeremy, and Haeyoun Park. "The Race Gap in America's Police Departments." *The New York Times.* September 2, 2014. Accessed May 20, 2016. http://www.nytimes.com/interactive/2014/09/03/us/the-race-gap-in-americas-police-departments.html?_r=0.

Associated Press. "Ruby Ridge: 20 Years Later, Randy Weaver's Daughter Lives in Peace." PennLive.com. August 20, 2012. Accessed December 28, 2016. http://www.pennlive.com/midstate/index.ssf/2012/08/ruby_ridge_20_years_later.html.

Baker, Al, J. David Goodman, and Benjamin Mueller. "Beyond the Chokehold: The Path to Eric Garner's Death." *The New York Times.* June 13, 2015. Accessed December 11, 2016. http://www.nytimes.com/2015/06/14/nyregion/eric-garner-police-chokehold-staten-island.html?_r=0.

Balko, Radley. "A Decade after 9/11, Police Departments Are Increasingly Militarized." *The Huffington Post.* September 12, 2011. Accessed December 19, 2016. http://www.huffingtonpost.com/2011/09/12/police-militarization-9-11-september-11_n_955508.html.

Balko, Radley. *Overkill: The Rise of Paramilitary Police Raids in America.* Washington, D.C.: Cato Institute, 2006. Accessed December 27, 2016. https://object.cato.org/sites/cato.org/files/pubs/pdf/balko_whitepaper_2006.pdf.

Balko, Radley. "Rise of the Warrior Cop." *The Wall Street Journal.* August 7, 2013. Accessed December 27, 2016. http://www.wsj.com/articles/SB10001424127887323848804578608040780519904.

Balko, Radley. *Rise of the Warrior Cop: The Militarization of America's Police Forces.* New York: PublicAffairs, 2013.

Baum, Dan. "Legalize It All." *Harper's Magazine.* April 2016. Accessed November 7, 2016. http://harpers.org/archive/2016/04/legalize-it-all/.

Baxter, James. "Traffic Tickets Are Big Business—National Motorists Association." National Motorists Association. October 13, 2016. Accessed December 14, 2016. https://www.motorists.org/blog/traffic-tickets-are-big-business/.

Becker, Andrew, and G. W. Schulz. "Local Cops Ready for War with Homeland Security-Funded Military Weapons." *Daily Beast.* December 21, 2011. Accessed December 19, 2016. http://www.thedailybeast.com/articles/2011/12/20/local-cops-ready-for-war-with-homeland-security-funded-military-weapons.html.

Benjamin Burris v. Garnett Riley, et al., United States District Court for Western Virginia. November 18, 2015. Accessed June 11, 2017. http://rutherford.org/files_images/general/11-19-2015_Burruss-_complaint.pdf.

Big Tex. "The Face of Emmett Till (Updated)." *Daily Kos.* May 14, 2009. Accessed December 4, 2016. http://www.dailykos.com/story/2009/5/14/731205/-.

Blackstone, William. "Avalon Project—Blackstone's Commentaries on the Laws of England—Book the Fourth—Chapter the Twenty-Seventh: Of Trial, and Conviction." Avalon Project. Accessed December 13, 2016. http://avalon.law.yale.edu/18th_century/blackstone_bk4ch27.asp.

Boehm, Randolph. *Records of the Wickersham Commission on Law Observance and Enforcement.* Bethesda, MD: University Publications of America, 1996. Accessed December 2, 2016. http://www.lexisnexis.com/documents/academic/upa_cis/1965_WickershamCommPt1.pdf.

"Bossier Parish Crime Remains Low while Population Steadily Rises." Bossier Sheriff: Public—Crime Statistics. Accessed December 19, 2016. http://www.bossiersheriff.com/crime-statistics/.

Botelho, Greg. "Texas Shooting: Officer with Pistol Stops Rifle-Wielding Attackers." CNN. May 5, 2015. Accessed December 26, 2016. http://www.cnn.com/2015/05/05/us/texas-police-shooting-hero/.

Brinkley, Joel. "U.S. Panel Urges Testing Workers for Use of Drugs." *The New York Times.* March 3, 1986. Accessed December 18, 2016. http://www.nytimes.com/1986/03/04/us/us-panel-urges-testing-workers-for-use-of-drugs.html.

Brown, Jodi M., and Patrick A. Langan. "Policing and Homicide, 1976–98: Justifiable Homicide by Police, Police Officers Murdered by Felons." Bureau of Justice Statistics. March 2001. Accessed May 14, 2016. http://www.bjs.gov/content/pub/ascii/ph98.txt. Twelve percent of murdered officers were killed with their own weapon in the 22 years between 1976 and 1998.

Brown, Michael K. *Working the Street: Police Discretion and the Dilemmas of Reform.* New York: Russell Sage Foundation, 1981.

Brown, Robert W. "London in the 19th Century." April 16, 2004. Accessed January 08, 2016. http://www2.uncp.edu/home/rwb/london_19c.html.

Bump, Philip. "The Facts about Stop-and-Frisk in New York City." *Washington Post.* September 26, 2016. Accessed December 12, 2016. https://www.washingtonpost.com/news/the-fix/wp/2016/09/21/it-looks-like-rudy-giuliani-convinced-donald-trump-that-stop-and-frisk-actually-works/?utm_term=.9905b9c174bd.

Burch, Anrdea M. *Arrest-Related Deaths, 2003–2009—Statistical Tables.* NCJ 235385. November 2011. Accessed January 26, 2017. https://www.bjs.gov/content/pub/pdf/ard0309st.pdf.

Carson, E. Ann, and Elizabeth Anderson. *Prisoners in 2015.* NCJ 250229. Washington, D.C.: U.S. Department of Justice, 2016. Accessed February 26, 2017. https://www.bjs.gov/content/pub/pdf/p15.pdf.

Cato Institute. *The Cato Handbook for Policy Makers.* 8th ed. Washington, D.C.: Cato Institute, 2017.

Celona, Larry, Kirstan Conley, and Bruce Golding. "Police Fury at Mayor's Racial Smear." *New York Post.* December 4, 2014. Accessed December 11, 2016. http://nypost.com/2014/12/04/police-union-prez-rips-de-blasio-over-eric-garner/.

"Census of Law Enforcement Training Academies, 2002 [United States] (ICPSR 4255)." June 9, 2005. Accessed November 13, 2016. http://www.icpsr.umich.edu/icpsrweb/NACJD/studies/4255.

Chandler, George Fletcher, and Albert B. Moore. *The Policeman's Art: As Taught in the New York State School for Police.* New York: Funk & Wagnalls, 1923.

"Chicago Homicides." *Chicago Tribune.* Accessed February 18, 2017. http://crime.chicagotribune.com/chicago/homicides.

"Citizens Police Data Project." Accessed September 24, 2016. https://cpdb.co/officer/jason-van-dyke/7655.

Clark, Thomas C. "Mapp v. Ohio." Legal Information Institute. Accessed December 14, 2016. https://www.law.cornell.edu/supremecourt/text/367/643.

"Clerks of Court Generally Are Meeting the System's Collections Performance Standards." Office of Program Policy Analysis & Government Accountability. 2007. Accessed February 12, 2017. http://www.oppaga.state.fl.us/reports/pdf/0721rpt.pdf. Report.

"Code of Ethics." IACP.org. Accessed November 20, 2016. http://www.iacp.org/codeofethics.

Cohen, Stanley. *The Execution of Officer Becker: The Murder of a Gambler, the Trial of a Cop, and the Birth of Organized Crime.* New York: Carroll & Graf, 2007.

Cohn, Ellen G. "The Citizen Police Academy—A Recipe for Improving Public Relations." *Journal of Criminal Justice* 24, no. 3 (1996): 265–71.

Collins, Allyson, and Cynthia Brown. *Shielded from Justice: Police Brutality and Accountability in the United States.* New York: Human Rights Watch, 1998.

"The Constitution in the 100-Mile Border Zone." American Civil Liberties Union. Accessed March 3, 2017. https://www.aclu.org/other/constitution-100-mile-border-zone.

Cook, Rhonda. "Military Equipment Flowing to Local Law Enforcement Raises Questions." *Atlanta Journal Constitution.* January 27, 2013. Accessed December 19, 2016. http://www.ajc.com/news/military-equipment-flowing-local-law-enforcement-raises-questions/6KuK57UWg3mxGwqCh5Ab6O/.

Cooper, Alexia, and Erica L. Smith. *Homicide Trends in the United States, 1980–2008.* NCJ 236018. Washington, D.C.: U.S. Department of Justice, Office of Justice Programs, Bureau of Justice Statistics, 2011.

"Cops Called on 13-Year-Olds for Selling Cupcakes." NBCNews.com. November 15, 2010. Accessed March 1, 2017. http://www.nbcnews.com/id/40194328/ns/us_news-life/t/cops-called—year-olds-selling-cupcakes/#.WLcXOxiZPVo.

"Cosmetology License Requirements by State." Beauty Schools Directory. Accessed January 16, 2017. http://www.beautyschoolsdirectory.com/faq/state_req.php.

Costigan, Bryan. "Statement for the Record." Senate Committee on Homeland Security and Governmental Affairs, March 2015. Accessed December 26, 2016. https://www.google.com/url?sa=t&rct=j&q=&esrc=s&source=web &cd=10&ved=0ahUKEwjb39PXwpLRAhWBWCYKHbswDYcQFghVMA k&url=https%3A%2F%2Fwww.hsgac.senate.gov%2Fdownload%2F%3F id%3D05729f27-be22–48a1–95de-880e07cadc86&usg=AFQjCNEnYQt o7I7LQIq_1XL_WwhskM93sA&sig2=-k8pVT_7NP55X3Q4OGqNrw.

Cottrell, Catherine A., and Steven L. Neuberg. "Different Emotional Reactions to Different Groups: A Sociofunctional Threat-Based Approach to 'Prejudice.'" *Journal of Personality and Social Psychology* 88, no. 5 (2005): 770–789. Accessed October 22, 2016. http://psychology-dev.clas.asu.edu/sites/default/files/Different%20Emotional%20Reactions%20to%20Different% 20Groups-%20A%20Sociofunctional%20Threat-Based%20Approach%20 to%20_Prejudice_.pdf.

"Crime in the United States." Ucr.fbi.gov. May 18, 2014. Accessed February 19, 2017. https://ucr.fbi.gov/crime-in-the-u.s/2013/crime-in-the-u.s.-2013/cius-home.

Daly, Michael. "Baltimore Mayor Gave Permission to Riot." *Daily Beast.* April 28, 2015. Accessed January 25, 2017. http://www.thedailybeast.com/articles/2015/04/28/baltimore-mayor-s-tone-deaf-handling-of-city-s-riot-crisis.html.

David Floyd, et al. v. City of New York. U.S. District Court, Southern District of New York. June 12, 2013. *Justice.gov.* U.S. Department of Justice, June 12, 2013. Web. January 14, 2017.

Dawkins, Stephen. "Hoover Police to Purchase Armored Vehicle." *280 Reporter.* August 16, 2016. Accessed December 19, 2016. http://www.shelbycoun tyreporter.com/2016/08/16/hoover-police-to-purchase-armored-vehicle/.

DeGroat, Bernie. "Road Chat: Talking to Passengers Can Be as Dangerous as Using a Cell Phone." *Michigan News.* February 21, 2006. Accessed January 21, 2017. http://ns.umich.edu/new/releases/116-road-chat-talking-to-passengers-can-be-as-dangerous-as-using-a-cell-phone.

Department of Justice Report Regarding the Criminal Investigation into the Shooting Death of Michael Brown by Ferguson, Missouri Police Officer Darren Wilson. Washington, D.C.: U.S. Department of Justice, 2015. Report.

Do Not Resist. Dir. Craig Atkinson. Vanish Films, 2016. Documentary.

"The DOJ Report Doesn't Say How Freddie Gray Died, but It Does Explain Why." *Baltimore Sun.* August 11, 2016. Accessed January 25, 2017. http://www .baltimoresun.com/news/opinion/editorial/bs-ed-freddie-gray-doj-2016 0811-story.html.

Douglas, Todd. *A Republic, If You Can Keep It: A Chronicle of the American Counter-revolution.* Oklahoma City: Tate Pub & Enterprises Llc., 2015.

Dunham, Roger G., and Geoffrey P. Alpert. *Critical Issues in Policing: Contemporary Readings.* Long Grove, IL: Waveland Press, 2015.

Durose, Matthew R., et al. *Recidivism of Prisoners Released in 30 States in 2005: Patterns from 2005 to 2010.* NCJ 244205. April 2014. Accessed February 14, 2017. https://www.bjs.gov/content/pub/pdf/rprts05p0510.pdf.

Eckert v. Dougherty et al., 15–2204, docket number 2:13-CV-00727-JB-WPL (D. N.M.). U.S. Court of Appeals for the Tenth Circuit. September 14, 2016.

Eith, Christine, and Matthew R. Durose. *Contacts between Police and the Public, 2008.* Bureau of Justice Statistics. October 2011. Accessed December 5, 2016. https://www.bjs.gov/content/pub/pdf/cpp08.pdf. Report.

Ekens, Emily. "84% of Americans Oppose Civil Asset Forfeiture." Cato at Liberty. December 13, 2016. Accessed December 13, 2016. https://www.cato.org/blog/84-americans-oppose-civil-asset-forfeiture?utm_content=bufferf7580&utm_medium=social&utm_source=facebook.com&utm_campaign=buffer.

Ekins, Emily. "54% of Americans Say Police Using Military Weapons." Cato Institute. December 14, 2016. Accessed December 21, 2016. https://www.cato.org/blog/54-americans-say-police-using-military-weapons-goes-too-far.

Ekins, Emily. *Policing in America: Understanding Public Attitudes toward the Police. Results from a National Survey.* Washington, D.C.: Cato Institute, 2016. Working paper.

Ekins, Emily. "Poll: Americans Are Not as Divided on Policing as Headlines Suggest." *The Federalist.* January 30, 2017. Accessed February 28, 2017. http://thefederalist.com/2017/01/26/poll-finds-americans-not-divided-policing-headlines-suggest/.

Elbow, Steven. "Hooked on SWAT." Madison.com. August 18, 2001. Accessed February 25, 2017. http://host.madison.com/ct/news/local/writers/steven_elbow/hooked-on-swat/article_f1bc13e6-b29b-5ab0-a7cf-ba46b1b3860c.html.

Emsley, Clive. "A Typology of Nineteenth-Century Police." *Crime, Histoire & Sociétés* 3, no. 1 (1999): 29–44.

Engel, Robin Shepard, Jennifer M. Calnon, and Thomas J. Bernard. "Theory and Racial Profiling: Shortcomings and Future Directions in Research." *Justice Quarterly* 19, no. 2 (2002): 249–73.

Eric Garner Video—Unedited Version. YouTube. July 12, 2015. Accessed February 2, 2017. https://www.youtube.com/watch?v=JpGxagKOkv8.

"Ernesto Miranda." NNDB. 2016. Accessed September 19, 2016. http://www.nndb.com/people/596/000125221/.

"Estimated Violent Crime Rate." Uniform Crime Reporting Statistics. Accessed December 17, 2016. https://www.ucrdatatool.gov/Search/Crime/State/RunCrimeTrendsInOneVar.cfm.

Evans, G. W., C. Gonnella, L. A. Marcynyszyn, L. Gentile, and N. Salpekar. "The Role of Chaos in Poverty and Children's Socioemotional Adjustment." *Psychological Science* 16, no. 7 (2005): 560–65. Accessed December 8, 2016. https://pdfs.semanticscholar.org/1ed7/fe9d504d7100d787dd3b79baa464c83b02c9.pdf.

"The Excessive Militarization of American Policing." ACLU.org. April 17, 2015. Accessed December 18, 2016. https://www.aclu.org/files/field_document/ACLU%20-%20%20Militarization%20of%20Policing.pdf.

"Federal Bureau of Investigation—Shooting Incident 4/11/86 Miami, FL." Vault. FBI.gov. Accessed December 17, 2016. https://vault.fbi.gov/FBI%20Mi ami%20Shooting%204-11-86%20/Miami%20Shooting%204-11-86%20 Part%207%20of%2011%20.

Fingerhut, Hannah. "Beyond Distrust: How Americans View Their Government." Pew Research Center for the People and the Press. November 23, 2015. Accessed February 17, 2017. http://www.people-press.org/2015/ 11/23/beyond-distrust-how-americans-view-their-government/.

Fisher, Anthony L. "Why It's So Hard to Stop Bad Cops from Getting New Police Jobs." Reason.com. September 30, 2016. Accessed February 03, 2017. http://reason.com/archives/2016/09/30/why-its-so-hard-to-stop-bad-cops-from-ge.

"Freddie Gray's Death in Police Custody—What We Know." BBC News. May 23, 2016. Accessed January 25, 2017. http://www.bbc.com/news/world-us-canada-32400497.

Friedman, Robert R. "University Perspective: The Policing Profession in 2050." *American Police Chief Magazine.* August 2006. Accessed May 20, 2016. http://www.policechiefmagazine.org/magazine/index.cfm?fuseaction= display_arch&article_id=958&issue_id=82006.

Frost, Linda S. "Part 1." In *An Introduction to Policing,* edited by John S. Dempsey. 8th ed. Sydney, Australia: Cengage Learning, 2015, 7.

Fryer, Roland G., Jr. "An Empirical Analysis of Racial Differences in Police Use of Force." National Bureau of Economic Research. July 2016. Accessed January 25, 2017. http://www.nber.org/papers/w22399.pdf.

"Fusion Center Encourages Improper Investigations of Lobbying Groups and Anti-War Activists." ACLU.org. February 25, 2009. Accessed January 2, 2017. https://www.aclu.org/news/fusion-center-encourages-improper-investiga tions-lobbying-groups-and-anti-war-activists?redirect=cpredirect% 2F38835.

Gallagher, J. J. "Aug. 2016: Chicago's Bloodiest Month in Two Decades." ABC News. September 1, 2016. Accessed December 26, 2016. http://abcnews .go.com/US/aug-2016-chicagos-bloodiest-month-decades/story?id= 41792681.

Geller, William A., editor. *Police Leadership in America: Crisis and Opportunity.* Chicago: American Bar Foundation, 1985.

"Gideon v. Wainwright." Legal Information Institute, Cornell University. Accessed March 1, 2017. https://www.law.cornell.edu/supremecourt/text/372/ 335.

Glass, Andrew. "Reagan Declares 'War on Drugs,' October 14, 1982." *Politico.* October 14, 2010. Accessed December 18, 2016. http://www.politico.com/ story/2010/10/reagan-declares-war-on-drugs-october-14-1982-043552.

Glawe, Justin. "Exclusive: Lawyers Went to Rahm Emanuel, Then Quashed the Laquan McDonald Video." *Daily Beast.* January 6, 2016. Accessed May 6, 2016.http://www.thedailybeast.com/articles/2015/01/06/exclusive-lawyers-went-to-rahm-then-quashed-the-laquan-mcdonald-video.html.

Goldman, Roger L. "State Revocation of Law Enforcement Officers' Licenses and Federal Criminal Prosecution: An Opportunity for Cooperative Federalism." 2003, 121–50. Accessed February 3, 2017. https://www.nlg-npap .org/sites/default/files/RevocationGoldman.pdf.

"Goldman Sachs' Revolving Door." CBS News. April 8, 2010. Accessed March 1, 2017. http://www.cbsnews.com/news/goldman-sachs-revolving-door/.

Gonnerman, Jennifer. "Before the Law." *The New Yorker.* June 8, 2015. Accessed February 14, 2017. http://www.newyorker.com/magazine/2014/10/06/ before-the-law.

"The Government War on Kid-Run Concession Stands." Freedom Center of Missouri. Accessed January 21, 2017. http://www.mofreedom.org/2011/07/ the-government-war-on-kid-run-concession-stands/.

Green, Jonah. "NYPD Could Take Down Plane in an 'Extreme Situation': Ray Kelly." *The Huffington Post.* November 26, 2011. Accessed December26,2016.http://www.huffingtonpost.com/2011/09/26/nypd-could-take-down-plan_n_980883.html. Video.

Harlow, Caroline Wolf. *Defense Counsel in Criminal Cases.* Washington, D.C.: U.S. Department of Justice, Office of Justice Programs, Bureau of Justice Statistics, 2001. Accessed December 13, 2016. https://www.bjs.gov/content/ pub/pdf/dccc.pdf.

Harrell, Erika. *Black Victims of Violent Crime.* NCJ 214258. Washington, D.C.: U.S. Department of Justice Office of Justice Programs, 2007. Accessed February 18, 2017. https://www.bjs.gov/content/pub/pdf/bvvc.pdf.

"Head of the Civil Rights Division Vanita Gupta Delivers Remarks at University of North Carolina Center for Civil Rights Conference." Justice.gov. December 2, 2016. Accessed December 5, 2016. https://www.justice.gov/ opa/speech/head-civil-rights-division-vanita-gupta-delivers-remarks-university-north-carolina-center.

Healy, Gene. *Deployed in the U.S.A.: The Creeping Militarization of the Home Front.* Washington, D.C.: Cato Institute, 2003.

"History." Federal Law Enforcement Training Accreditation. Accessed September 20, 2016. https://www.fleta.gov/history.

"History of the DEA." DEA.gov. Accessed February 25, 2017. https://www.dea .gov/about/history.shtml.

Hjelmgaard, Kim. "Ambush-Style Killings of Police up 167% This Year." *USA Today.* November 3, 2016. Accessed December 5, 2016. http://www .usatoday.com/story/news/nation/2016/11/02/ambush-style-killings-police-up-300/93155124/.

Hollywood Florida Police Attack Man for Refusing to Give His Name. YouTube. December 27, 2016. Accessed January 4, 2017. https://www.youtube.com/ watch?v=XUsuTsdSxL4.

Horowitz, Craig. "The NYPD's War on Terror." NYMag.com. 2011. Accessed December 26, 2016. http://nymag.com/nymetro/news/features/n_8286/.

"H.R. 2461 (101st): National Defense Authorization Act for Fiscal Years 1990 and 1991." GovTrack.us. Accessed December 18, 2016. https://www.govtrack .us/congress/bills/101/hr2461/text.

"'I Have My Own Army in the NYPD—The Seventh Largest Army in the World': Bloomberg's Bizarre Boast about City's Police Force." *Daily Mail Online*. December 1, 2011. Accessed December 28, 2016. http://www.dailymail .co.uk/news/article-2068428/Bloomberg-I-army-NYPD-State-Depart ment-New-York-City.html.

"IADLEST Model Minimum Standards." IADLEST.org. Accessed March 1, 2017. https://www.iadlest.org/Projects/ModelStandards.aspx.

"IADLEST Projects NDI 2.0." IADLEST.com. Accessed November 26, 2016. https://www.iadlest.org/projects/ndi20.aspx.

"Idaho Criminal Intelligence Center." Idaho Criminal Intelligence Center. Accessed December 26, 2016. https://www.isp.idaho.gov/icic/.

"Investigation of the Baltimore City Police Department." Justice.gov. August 10, 2016. Accessed December 14, 2016. https://www.justice.gov/opa/file/ 883366/download.

Investigation of the Chicago Police Department. Washington, D.C.: U.S. Department of Justice, 2017. Report.

Investigation of the Ferguson Police Department. Washington, D.C.: U.S. Department of Justice, Civil Rights Division, 2015. Report.

Jefferson, Thomas. *The Jeffersonian Cyclopedia: A Comprehensive Collection of the Views of Thomas Jefferson Classified and Arranged in Alphabetical Order under Nine Thousand Titles Relating to Government, Politics, Law, Education, Political Economy, Finance, Science, Art, Literature, Religious Freedom, Morals, Etc.* Edited by John P. Foley. New York: Funk & Wagnalls, 1900.

Jones, Susan. "After Two Raids, DOJ Decides No Criminal Charges against Gibson Guitar Company." CNS News. August 7, 2012. Accessed December 27, 2016. http://www.cnsnews.com/news/article/after-two-raids-doj- decides-no-criminal-charges-against-gibson-guitar-company.

"Jones v. U.S. Drug Enforcement Admin." 801 F. Supp. 15 (M.D. Tenn., 1992). Justia US Law. Accessed December 13, 2016. http://law.justia.com/cases/ federal/district-courts/FSupp/801/15/1945074/.

"Jones v. U.S. Drug Enforcement Admin." 819 F. Supp. 698 (1993). Leagle.com. Leagle. April 21, 1993. Accessed December 13, 2016. http://www.leagle .com/decision/19931517819FSupp698_11453/JONES%20v.%20U.S.%20 DRUG%20ENFORCEMENT%20ADMIN.

"Judge Dismisses Baltimore Police Union's Lawsuit Trying to Block Work of Civilian Review Board." ACLU.org. November 4, 2016. Accessed February 4, 2017. https://www.aclu.org/news/judges-dismisses-baltimore- police-unions-lawsuit-trying-block-work-civilian-review-board.

Kaminski, Robert J., and Jeffrey A. Martin. "An Analysis of Police Officer Satisfaction with Defense and Control Tactics." *Policing: An International*

Journal of Police Strategies & Management 23, no. 2 (2000). Emerald Group Publishing. Accessed January 15, 2017. http://www.emeraldinsight.com/doi/pdfplus/10.1108/13639510010333697.

Kaste, Martin. "Police Are Learning to Accept Civilian Oversight, but Distrust Lingers." NPR. February 21, 2015. Accessed February 4, 2017. http://www.npr.org/2015/02/21/387770044/police-are-learning-to-accept-civilian-oversight-but-distrust-lingers.

Katzenbach, Nicholas DeB. *The Challenge of Crime in a Free Society: A Report by the President's Commission on Law Enforcement and Administration of Justice.* Washington, D.C.: U.S. Government Printing Office, 1967.

Kaufman, Whitley. "Blackstone's Ratio." Accessed December 13, 2016. http://faculty.uml.edu/whitley_kaufman/law/BlackstonesRatio.htm.

"Keene, New Hampshire." Keene, New Hampshire. NH 03431. Accessed December 19, 2016. http://www.city-data.com/city/Keene-New-Hampshire.html. Profile.

Kelling, George L., and Mark H. Moore. *Perspectives on Policing.* Washington, D.C.: Office of Justice Programs, U.S. Department of Justice. National Criminal Justice Reference Service. Accessed November 27, 2016. https://www.ncjrs.gov/pdffiles1/nij/114213.pdf.

Kennedy, Robert C. "The Big Chief's Fairy Godmother." *The New York Times.* 2001. Accessed February 20, 2017. http://www.nytimes.com/learning/general/onthisday/harp/0906.html.

Kerstetter, Wayne A. "Who Disciplines the Police? Who Should?" In *Police Leadership in America: Crisis and Opportunity*, edited by William A. Geller. Chicago: American Bar Foundation, 1985, 149–82.

Khoo, Isabelle. "Morgan Freeman Calls Black History Month 'Ridiculous.'" *The Huffington Post.* February 10, 2017. Accessed February 26, 2017. http://www.huffingtonpost.ca/2017/02/10/morgan-freeman-black-history-month_n_14642958.html.

Kindig, Jesse. "Selma, Alabama, (Bloody Sunday, March 7, 1965) | The Black Past: Remembered and Reclaimed." Black Past.org. March 7, 1965. Accessed December 5, 2016. http://www.blackpast.org/aah/bloody-sunday-selma-alabama-march-7-1965.

Kindy, Kimberly, Marc Fisher, Julia Tate, and Jennifer Jenkins. "A Year of Reckoning: Police Fatally Shoot Nearly 1,000." *The Washington Post.* December 24, 2015. Accessed December 10, 2016. http://www.washingtonpost.com/sf/investigative/2015/12/26/a-year-of-reckoning-police-fatally-shoot-nearly-1000/.

Kuang, Jeanne. "Group Slams Police Union Hire of Officer Charged in Laquan McDonald Shooting." *Chicago Tribune.* May 5, 2016. Accessed February 15, 2017. http://www.chicagotribune.com/news/laquanmcdonald/ct-laquan-mcdonald-jason-van-dyke-court-met-20160323–20160331-story.html.

Kuzmarov, Jeremy. "What August Vollmer, the Father of American Law Enforcement, Has to Teach Us." *The Huffington Post*. October 4, 2016. Accessed February 26, 2017. http://www.huffingtonpost.com/jeremy-kuzmarov/ what-august-vollmer-the-f_b_12333080.html.

Law Enforcement Equipment Working Group. "Recommendations Pursuant to Executive Order 13688." WhiteHouse.gov. May 2015. Accessed December 18, 2016. https://www.whitehouse.gov/sites/default/files/docs/le_ equipment_wg_final_report_final.pdf.

"Law Enforcement Officers Killed United States, 1961–2012." Accessed December 5, 2016. http://www.albany.edu/sourcebook/pdf/t31542012.pdf.

"Law Enforcement Officers Killed United States, 1961–2012." *Sourcebook of Criminal Justice Statistics*. 2013. Accessed March 1, 2017. http://www.albany .edu/sourcebook/.

Law Enforcement Use of Cell-Site Simulation Technologies: Privacy Concerns and Recommendations. Washington, D.C.: Committee on Oversight and Government Reform, 2016. December 19, 2016. Accessed February 15, 2017. https://oversight.house.gov/wp-content/uploads/2016/12/THE-FINAL-bipartisan-cell-site-simulator-report.pdf. Report.

Lee, Jaeah. "Here's the Data That Shows Cops Kill Black People at a Higher Rate than White People." Mother Jones. September 10, 2014. Accessed January 26, 2017. http://www.motherjones.com/politics/2014/08/police-sho otings-ferguson-race-data.

"Legislation Opposed by the FOP in the 114th Congress." Fop.net. January 14, 2015. Accessed February 4, 2017. http://www.fop.net/SearchResult .aspx?Category=PAGES&index=0.

Lentz, Susan A. "The Invention of Peel's Principles: A Study of Policing 'textbook' History." *Journal of Criminal Justice* 35, no. 1 (2007): 69–79. Accessed December 5, 2016. http://ac.els-cdn.com.webster.sunybroome. edu:2048/S0047235206001449/1-s2.0-S0047235206001449-main. pdf?_tid=f13db7a4-bb08-11e6-aeb6-00000aab0f26&acdnat=1480 955956_b1f26ebe0f88cb4105869abbb3cfd6ff.

Linder, Douglas O. "Emmett Till Murder Trial: Selected Testimony." UMKC.edu. 2014. Accessed December 4, 2016. http://law2.umkc.edu/faculty/proj ects/ftrials/till/tillaccount.html.

Lott, John R., Jr. "A Transaction-Costs Explanation for Why the Poor Are More Likely to Commit Crime." *The Journal of Legal Studies* 19, no. 1 (1990): 243–45. Accessed December 8, 2016. http://www.jstor.org.webster.suny broome.edu:2048/stable/pdf/724420.pdf.

Lussenhop, Jessica. "Clinton Crime Bill: Why Is It so Controversial?" BBC News. April 18, 2016. Accessed January 24, 2017. http://www.bbc.com/news/ world-us-canada-36020717.

"Lyndon B. Johnson: Special Message to the Congress on Crime and Law Enforcement, March 9, 1966." The American Presidency Project.

Accessed December 2, 2016. http://www.presidency.ucsb.edu/ws/?pid= 27478.

Macartney, Suzanne. *Poverty Rates for Selected Detailed Race and Hispanic Groups by State and Place: 2007–2011.* ACSBR/11–17. Washington, D.C.: U.S. Census Bureau, 2013. February 2013. Accessed February 18, 2017. https://www.census.gov/prod/2013pubs/acsbr11–17.pdf.

"Major Current Responsibilities of Police." Aba.com. 1980. Accessed February 27, 2017. http://www.americanbar.org/publications/criminal_justice_sec tion_archive/crimjust_standards_urbanpolice.html#1-1.1.

Mann, Brian. "Profile: Charles Rangel and the Drug Wars." WNYC. August 17, 2013. Accessed January 22, 2017. http://www.wnyc.org/story/313060 -profile-charles-rangel-and-drug-wars/.

March, David. CPD Case Supplementary Report—HX475653. Chicago: Chicago Police Department. December 4, 2015. Accessed May 6, 2016. http:// www.documentcloud.org/documents/2642131-McD-6.html.

Margolick, David. "Beating Case Unfolds, as Does Debate on Lawyer." *The New York Times.* March 16, 1991. Accessed December 14, 2016. http://www .nytimes.com/1991/03/17/us/beating-case-unfolds-as-does-debate-on- lawyer.html.

Marzulli, John, and Alison Gendar. "20 Yrs. Ago: Cop Shooting Led to War Gangs." *New York Daily News.* February 24, 2008. Accessed December 17, 2016. http://www.nydailynews.com/news/crime/20-yrs-shot-nypd-began- crushing-drug-gangs-article-1.307155.

McBride, Alex. "Supreme Court History." PBS. Accessed September 19, 2016. http://www.pbs.org/wnet/supremecourt/rights/landmark_miranda.html.

McDermott, Ryan M. "Marilyn Mosby Never Should Have Charged Officers in Freddie Gray Death, Lawyers Say." *The Washington Times.* July 27, 2016. Accessed January 25, 2017. http://www.washingtontimes.com/news/ 2016/jul/27/marilyn-mosby-never-should-have-charged-officers-i/.

McMains, Vanessa. "Johns Hopkins Study Suggests Medical Errors Are Third- Leading Cause of Death in U.S." *The Hub.* May 3, 2016. Accessed Febru- ary 15, 2017. https://hub.jhu.edu/2016/05/03/medical-errors-third-leading- cause-of-death/.

Meijer, Albert, and Marcel Thaens. "Social Media Strategies: Understanding the Differences between North American Police Departments." *Government Information Quarterly* 30, no. 4 (2013): 343–50.

Merchant, Nomaan. "In the Wake of Michael Brown's Death, the Federal Gov- ernment Wants to Require the Ferguson Police Department to Check All New Hires against a Database of Police Officers Stripped of Their Law Enforcement Licenses for Misconduct." *U.S. News & World Report.* March 9, 2016. Accessed February 3, 2017. http://www.usnews.com/news/us/ articles/2016–03–09/database-of-problem-police-officers-may-get-test- in-ferguson.

Meyer, Ali. "Unemployment among Black Youth 393% Higher Than National Rate." CNS News. November 9, 2013. Accessed February 4, 2017. http://

www.cnsnews.com/news/article/ali-meyer/unemployment-among-black-youth-393-higher-national-rate.

Miller, Joel. *Profiling Populations Available for Stops and Searches.* London: Home Office, Policing and Reducing Crime Unit, Research, Development and Statistics Directorate, 2000.

Miron, Jeffrey A. *Drug War Crimes: The Consequences of Prohibition.* Oakland, CA: Independent Institute, 2004.

The Modern Militia Movement. Jefferson City: Missouri Information Analysis Center, 2009. February 20, 2009. Accessed January 2, 2017. http://constitution.org/abus/le/miac-strategic-report.pdf. Report.

Morgan, Jan. *Rampant Injustice.* YouTube. October 31, 2012. Accessed December 28, 2016. https://youtu.be/bFALonjLay0.

Moskos, Peter. *Cop in the Hood: My Year Policing Baltimore's Eastern District.* Princeton, NJ: Princeton University Press, 2009.

National Decertification Index. IADLEST.com. Accessed January 5, 2017. https://www.iadlest.org/projects/ndi20.aspx.

National Practitioner Databank. Health Resources and Services Administration. Accessed January 5, 2017. https://www.npdb.hrsa.gov/.

"New York Crime Rates 1960–2015." Disastercenter.com. Accessed February 17, 2017. http://www.disastercenter.com/crime/nycrime.htm.

1961 Commission on Civil Rights Report. Washington, D.C.: U.S. Government Printing Office, 1961.

"Obama's Father's Day Remarks." *The New York Times.* June 15, 2008. Accessed January 30, 2017. http://www.nytimes.com/2008/06/15/us/politics/15text-obama.html.

"Officer Deaths by Year." National Law Enforcement Officers Memorial Fund. Accessed December 17, 2016. http://www.nleomf.org/facts/officer-fatalities-data/year.html.

"The Oklahoma Question." Oklahoma Information Fusion Center. Accessed December 26, 2016. https://www.ok.gov/okfusion/About_The_OIFC/The_Oklahoma_Question/index.html.

Ortega, Tony. "What Frank Serpico Started: The Knapp Commission Report." *Village Voice.* April 18, 2011. Accessed December 7, 2016. http://www.villagevoice.com/news/what-frank-serpico-started-the-knapp-commission-report-6663567.

Paddock, Barry, Rocco Parascandola, and Corky Siemaszko. "Eric Garner's Death Ruled a Homicide: NYC Medical Examiner." *NY Daily News.* August 1, 2014. Accessed December 11, 2016. http://www.nydailynews.com/new-york/nyc-crime/eric-garner-death-ruled-homicide-medical-examiner-article-1.1888808.

Palmiotto, Michael J., and N. Prabha Unninthan. "The Impact of Citizen Police Academies on Participants: An Exploratory Study." *Journal of Criminal Justice* 30, no. 2 (2002): 101–106.

Pamer, Melissa. "Los Angeles 1992 Riots: By the Numbers." NBC Southern California. April 20, 2012. Accessed December 14, 2016. http://www

.nbclosangeles.com/news/local/Los-Angeles-1992-Riots-By-the-Num
    bers-148340405.html.

People of the State of Illinois vs. Jason Van Dyke. Circuit Court of Cook County.
    November 2015. Ordinal Document.

"People v Debour." New York State Unified Court System. 2016. Accessed
    December 14, 2016. http://www.courts.state.ny.us/reporter/archives/p_
    debour.htm.

Perez, Douglas Werner. *Common Sense about Police Review.* Philadelphia, PA:
    Temple University Press, 1994.

Pine, Joslyn T. *Wit and Wisdom of the American Presidents: A Book of Quotations.*
    Mineola, NY: Dover Publications, 2001.

Pinker, Steven. *The Better Angels of Our Nature: Why Violence Has Declined.* New
    York: Penguin Books, 2012.

Pinto, Nick. "The Bail Trap." *The New York Times.* August 13, 2015. Accessed
    February 14, 2017. https://www.nytimes.com/2015/08/16/magazine/the-
    bail-trap.html?_r=0.

"Platform—The Movement for Black Lives." The Movement for Black Lives. August 1,
    2016. Accessed November 30, 2016. https://policy.m4bl.org/platform/.

"Police Patrol Officer Salaries." Salary.com. November 2016. Accessed November
    19, 2016. http://www1.salary.com/Police-Officer-Salary.html.

Prestigiacomo, Amanda. "5 Things You Need to Know about Black Lives Matter."
    Daily Wire. July 11, 2016. Accessed November 29, 2016. http://www
    .dailywire.com/news/7353/5-things-you-need-know-about-black-
    lives-matter-amanda-prestigiacomo.

"The Problem-Solving Triangle." Center for Problem-Oriented Policing. Accessed
    January 15, 2017. http://www.popcenter.org/about/?p=triangle.

"Profiles of Those Forced to 'Pay or Stay.'" NPR. May 19, 2014. Accessed Febru-
    ary 13, 2017. http://www.npr.org/2014/05/19/310710716/profiles-of-those-
    forced-to-pay-or-stay.

Provetto, Sonny. "Stress . . . No Problem? Think Again." *Law Enforcement Today.*
    February 28, 2012. Accessed November 25, 2016. http://www.lawen
    forcementtoday.com/stress%E2%80%A6no-problem-think-again/.

"Public Trust in Government: 1958–2014." Pew Research Center for the People
    and the Press. November 13, 2014. Accessed January 2, 2016. http://
    www.people-press.org/2014/11/13/public-trust-in-government/.

Rand, Ayn, and Leonard Peikoff. "Chapter 1." In *Philosophy: Who Needs It.* New
    York, NY: Signet, 1984, 7.

Raw Video: Chicago Police Dashcam Video of Laquan McDonald Shooting. YouTube.
    November 24, 2015. Accessed February 28, 2017. https://www.youtube
    .com/watch?v=1Zz03rvyhIk.

Rayfield, Jillian. "The Right to BearCats: Local Police Gun for Armored Tanks."
    TPM. March 7, 2012. Accessed December 19, 2016. http://talkingpoints
    memo.com/muckraker/the-right-to-bearcats-local-police-gun-for-
    armored-tanks.

Reason, Tim. "Obama's Accounting Expert?" CFO. November 26, 2008. Accessed March 1, 2017. http://ww2.cfo.com/risk-compliance/2008/11/obamas-accounting-expert/.

Reaves, Brian A. "Census of State and Local Law Enforcement Agencies, 2008." Bureau of Justice Statistics. July 2011. Accessed November 13, 2016. http://www.bjs.gov/content/pub/pdf/csllea08.pdf.

Recommendations for Reform: Restoring Trust between the Chicago Police and the Communities They Serve. Chicago: Police Accountability Task Force, 2016. Report.

Report of the Independent Commission on the Los Angeles Police Department. Los Angeles, National Criminal Justice Reference Service, 1991. Report.

"Report of the National Advisory Committee on Civil Disorders." Ncjrs.gov. Accessed December 6, 2016. https://www.ncjrs.gov/pdffiles1/Digitization/8073NCJRS.pdf.

Report of the National Advisory Committee on Civil Disorders—Summary of Report. New York: Bantam Books, 1968.

Report of the National Commission on Law Observance and Enforcement. Vol. 14. Washington, D.C.: U.S. Government Printing Office, 1931. Report.

Reynolds, Elaine A. *Before the Bobbies: The Night Watch and Police Reform in Metropolitan London, 1720–1830.* Stanford, CA: Stanford University Press, 1998.

"Richard Nixon: Remarks about an Intensified Program for Drug Abuse Prevention and Control." The American Presidency Project. Accessed November 6, 2016. http://www.presidency.ucsb.edu/ws/?pid=3047.

Richards, Jennifer Smith, Angela Caputo, Todd Lighty, and Jason Meisner. "92 Deaths, 2,623 Bullets: Tracking Every Chicago Police Shooting over 6 Years." *Chicago Tribune.* September 17, 2016. Accessed February 18, 2017. http://www.chicagotribune.com/news/watchdog/ct-chicago-police-shooting-database-met-20160826-story.html.

Richardson, Valerie. "Police More Reluctant to Shoot Blacks Than Whites, Study Finds." *The Washington Times.* May 2, 2016. Accessed January 25, 2017. http://m.washingtontimes.com/news/2016/may/2/police-more-reluctant-shoot-blacks-whites-study-fi/.

"Rudy Giuliani." History.com. 2014. Accessed December 17, 2016. http://www.history.com/topics/rudy-giuliani.

Rutz, David. "Black Lives Matter Leader Stands by Controversial Tweets." *Washington Free Beacon.* July 11, 2016. Accessed December 10, 2016. http://freebeacon.com/issues/black-lives-matter-leader-stands-controversial-tweets/.

Schlegel, Denise. "Police Grants: What's Being Federally Funded in 2016?" PoliceGrantsHelp.com. February 1, 2016. Accessed November 12, 2016. http://www.policegrantshelp.com/Columnists/Denise-Schlegel/articles/71130006-Police-grants-Whats-being-federally-funded-in-2016/.

"Scottsboro Timeline." PBS—American Experience. Accessed December 4, 2016. http://www.pbs.org/wgbh/amex/scottsboro/timeline/index.html.

Seper, Jerry. "Brutal DEA Agent Murder Reminder of Agency Priority." *The Washington Times*. March 5, 2010. Accessed December 18, 2016. http://www.washingtontimes.com/news/2010/mar/05/dea-has-25-year-burning-reminder/.

Serpico. Dir. Sidney Lumet. Perf. Al Pacino, John Randolph. Paramount Pictures Release, 1973. Film.

Serpico, Frank. "Serpico: Police Corruption Is Here to Stay." *New York Post*. April 8, 2016. Accessed February 25, 2017. http://nypost.com/2016/04/08/serpico-police-corruption-is-here-to-stay/.

Shapiro, Joseph. "As Court Fees Rise, the Poor Are Paying the Price." NPR. May 19, 2014. Accessed February 13, 2017. http://www.npr.org/2014/05/19/312158516/increasing-court-fees-punish-the-poor.

Shapiro, Joseph. "Measures Aimed at Keeping People Out of Jail Punish the Poor." NPR. May 24, 2014. Accessed February 13, 2017. http://www.npr.org/2014/05/24/314866421/measures-aimed-at-keeping-people-out-of-jail-punish-the-poor.

Siegel, Jacob. "The Monsters Who Screamed for Dead Cops." *Daily Beast*. December 23, 2014. Accessed November 29, 2016. http://www.thedailybeast.com/articles/2014/12/23/who-started-new-york-s-dead-cops-chant.html.

Silverglate, Harvey A. *Three Felonies a Day: How the Feds Target the Innocent*. New York: Encounter Books, 2011.

Skogan, Wesley G., and Kathleen Frydl. *Fairness and Effectiveness in Policing: The Evidence*. Washington, D.C.: National Academies Press, 2004.

Smedley, Audrey. "Race—The Power of an Illusion." *Anthropology Newsletter*. 1997. Accessed December 10, 2016. http://www.pbs.org/race/000_About/002_04-background-02–09.htm.

Soergel, Andrew. "War on Terror Could Be Costliest Yet." *U.S. News & World Report*. September 9, 2016. Accessed February 25, 2017. https://www.usnews.com/news/articles/2016–09–09/war-on-terror-could-be-costliest-yet.

Somashekhar, Sandhya, Wesley Lowery, Keith L. Alexander, Kimberly Kindy, and Julie Tate. "Unarmed and Black." *The Washington Post*. August 8, 2015. Accessed December 11, 2016. http://www.washingtonpost.com/sf/national/2015/08/08/black-and-unarmed/.

"State and Major Urban Area Fusion Centers." Department of Homeland Security. Accessed December 26, 2016. https://www.dhs.gov/state-and-major-urban-area-fusion-centers.

"Statute of Westminster 1275." Project Gutenberg, World Library Foundation. Accessed February 14, 2017. http://www.gutenberg.us/articles/eng/statute_of_westminster_1275.

"Stop-and-Frisk Data." Nyclu.org. Accessed February 17, 2017. http://www.nyclu.org/content/stop-and-frisk-data.

"Substance Abuse and Mental Health Services Administration Survey on Drug Use and Health." NIDA.gov. June 2015. Accessed February 26, 2017. https://www.drugabuse.gov/publications/drugfacts/nationwide-trends.

Sullivan, Laura. "Inmates Who Can't Make Bail Face Stark Options." NPR. January 22, 2010. Accessed February 14, 2017. http://www.npr.org/templates/story/story.php?storyId=122725819.

Sullum, Jacob. "The War on Drugs Now Features Roadside Sexual Assaults by Cops." *Forbes*. May 12, 2015. Accessed March 2, 2017. https://www.forbes.com/sites/jacobsullum/2015/05/07/will-texas-ban-roadside-sexual-assaults-by-drug-warriors/#48f361c7829e.

Summary of Law Enforcement Officers Killed and Assaulted—2015. Washington, D.C.: FBI, 2016. Accessed February 23, 2017. https://ucr.fbi.gov/leoka/2015/officers-feloniously-killed/leoka-felonious-summaries-2015.pdf. Report.

Sweeney, Annie, and Hal Dardick. "Chicago: Front Line in War on Terror." *Tribune Digital*. November 11, 2010. Accessed December 26, 2016. http://articles.chicagotribune.com/2010–11–11/news/ct-met-terrorism-chicago-police-1114–20101111_1_david-coleman-headley-chicago-cops-mumbai.

Table 43—Arrests, "Crime in the United States—2014." FBI. September 19, 2015. Accessed December 10, 2016. https://ucr.fbi.gov/crime-in-the-u.s/2014/crime-in-the-u.s.-2014/tables/table-43.

Taibbi, Matt. *The Divide: American Injustice in the Age of the Wealth Gap*. New York: Spiegel & Grau Trade Paperbacks, 2014.

"10 U.S. Code Chapter 18—Military Support for Civilian Law Enforcement Agencies." LII/Legal Information Institute. Accessed December 18, 2016. https://www.law.cornell.edu/uscode/text/10/subtitle-A/part-I/chapter-18.

"The Terrorism Statistics Every American Needs to Hear." Global Research. May 19, 2014. Accessed December 26, 2016. http://www.globalresearch.ca/the-terrorism-statistics-every-american-needs-to-hear/5382818.

"Terry v. Ohio." Legal Information Institute, Cornell University. Accessed March 1, 2017. https://www.law.cornell.edu/supremecourt/text/392/1.

Theriot, Matthew T. "School Resource Officers and the Criminalization of Student Behavior." *Journal of Criminal Justice* 37 (2009): 280–87.

"Thirty Years of America's Drug War: A Chronology." PBS—Frontline. Accessed December 18, 2016. http://www.pbs.org/wgbh/pages/frontline/shows/drugs/cron/.

Thornton, Mark. "Alcohol Prohibition Was a Failure." Cato Institute. July 17, 1991. Accessed November 6, 2016. https://www.cato.org/publications/policy-analysis/alcohol-prohibition-was-failure.

Towne, Charles Hanson. *The Rise and Fall of Prohibition*. New York: Macmillan, 1923.

"Traffic Fines as Cash Cow." *Los Angeles Times*. February 6, 2010. Accessed December 14, 2016. http://articles.latimes.com/2010/feb/06/opinion/la-ed-fines6–2010feb06.

Tuttle, Brad. "Police All Over the U.S. Are Issuing Fewer Traffic Tickets." *Time*. March 30, 2015. Accessed December 14, 2016. http://time.com/money/3762033/traffic-ticket-decrease-speed-limits-police/.

"2015 Washington Post Database of Police Shootings." *The Washington Post*. Accessed December 10, 2016. https://www.washingtonpost.com/graphics/national/police-shootings/.

"2016 Chicago Murders—Explore Data." DNAinfo Chicago. December 2016. Accessed December 26, 2016. https://www.dnainfo.com/chicago/2016-chicago-murders/explore-data.

"2010 Census Summary File 1, Ferguson, Missouri." American Factfinder. 2010. Accessed November 29, 2016. http://factfinder.census.gov/faces/tableservices/jsf/pages/productview.xhtml?src=bkmk.

Tyler, Tom R., and Yuen J. Huo. "Chapter 1." In *Trust in the Law: Encouraging Public Cooperation with the Police and Courts*. New York, NY: Russell Sage Foundation, 2002, 7.

"Uniform Termination Notice for Securities Industry Registration." FINRA.org. Accessed January 5, 2017. http://www.finra.org/sites/default/files/form-u5.pdf.

United States v. Montoya de Hernandez, 473 U.S. 531 (July 1, 1985).

United States v. Salerno, 481 U.S. 739 (May 26, 1987).

U.S. Department of Justice. "The War on Crime: The End of the Beginning." Justice.gov. Accessed December 2, 2016. https://www.justice.gov/sites/default/files/ag/legacy/2011/08/23/09–09–1971.pdf. News release.

U.S. Department of Justice, Bureau of Justice Statistics. *State and Local Law Enforcement Training Academies, 2013*. NCJ 249784. Washington, D.C.: U.S. Department of Justice, 2016.

U.S. Department of Transportation. *NHTSA/Budget Estimates Fiscal Year 2017*. Accessed November 12, 2016. http://www.nhtsa.gov/staticfiles/administration/pdf/Budgets/FY2017-NHTSA_CBJ_FINAL_02_2016.pdf.

Venugopal, Arun. "Black Leaders Once Championed the Strict Drug Laws They Now Seek to Dismantle." WNYC. August 15, 2013. Accessed January 22, 2017. http://www.wnyc.org/story/312823-black-leaders-once-championed-strict-drug-laws-they-now-seek-dismantle/.

"Views of Race Relations Are More Negative Now Than They Have Been for Much of the 2000s." Pew Research Center's Social & Demographic Trends Project. June 21, 2016. Accessed November 30, 2016. http://www.pewsocialtrends.org/2016/06/27/2-views-of-race-relations/st_2016-06-27_race-inequality-ch2–03/.

Warren, Earl. "Miranda v. Arizona." Legal Information Institute, Cornell University School of Law. 2010. Accessed December 14, 2016. https://www.law.cornell.edu/supremecourt/text/384/436.

Whitehead, Don. *Attack on Terror: The FBI against the Ku Klux Klan in Mississippi*. New York: Funk & Wagnalls, 1970.

"Wickersham Report on Police." *American Journal of Police Science* 2, no. 4 (1931): 337–48. Accessed December 1, 2016. http://ljournal.ru/wp-content/uploads/2016/08/d-2016–154.pdf.

Williams, Timothy. "Cast-Out Police Officers Are Often Hired in Other Cities." *The New York Times.* September 11, 2016. Accessed January 5, 2017. http://www.nytimes.com/2016/09/11/us/whereabouts-of-cast-out-police-officers-other-cities-often-hire-them.html?_r=0.

Williams, Walter E. "The True Black Tragedy: Illegitimacy Rate of Nearly 75%." CNS News. May 19, 2015. Accessed January 30, 2017. http://www.cnsnews.com/commentary/walter-e-williams/true-black-tragedy-illegitimacy-rate-nearly-75.

Wilson, Christopher P. *Cop Knowledge: Police Power and Cultural Narrative in Twentieth-Century America.* Chicago: University of Chicago Press, 2000.

Wiseman, Samuel. "Discrimination, Coercion, and the Bail Reform Act of 1984: The Loss of the Core Constitutional Protections of the Excessive Bail Clause." *Fordham Urban Law Journal* (2009): 122–56. Accessed February 14, 2017. http://ir.lawnet.fordham.edu/cgi/viewcontent.cgi?article=2298&context=ulj.

Wootson, Cleve R., Jr. "Yesterday's Ku Klux Klan Members Are Today's Police Officers, Councilwoman Says." *The Washington Post.* October 11, 2016. Accessed November 29, 2016. https://www.washingtonpost.com/news/local/wp/2016/10/11/yesterdays-ku-klux-klan-members-are-todays-police-officers-councilwoman-says/.

Young v. Hidalgo County, 2:13-cv-01087-SMV-LAM, U.S. District Court for the District of New Mexico, November 8, 2013.

Young, Yolanda. "Analysis: Black Leaders Supported Clinton's Crime Bill." NBCNews.com. April 8, 2016. Accessed January 24, 2017. http://www.nbcnews.com/news/nbcblk/analysis-black-leaders-supported-clinton-s-crime-bill-n552961.

Zajtchuk, Russ, and Christopher M. Grande. *War Psychiatry.* Falls Church, VA: Office of the Surgeon General, U.S. Army, 1995. Accessed November 25, 2016. http://fas.org/irp/doddir/milmed/warpsychiatry.pdf.

Index

Montana Analysis and Technical
  Information Center, 61
Moore, Mark, 32
Mosby, Marilyn, 111–12
Mother Jones report on arrest-related
  deaths, 117–19
Movies, heroic cops in, 204–6
Murrah Federal Building, 61

Narcotics investigations, 52. *See also*
  Drug war
National Advisory Commission on
  Civil Disorders, 36, 48
National Center for State Courts, 94
National Citizens Police Academy
  Association, 191
National Commission on Law
  Observance and Enforcement
  report, 33–35
National Decertification Index, 213
National Defense Authorization Act
  (NDAA), 55
National Guard units, 184
Nation-states, 27, 28
Neighborhood watch programs, 134
Net Capital Rule, 147
New Castle, New York, 80
New Haven, Connecticut, 67
New Jersey, 96
New York City Police: criminality in,
  37; Fort Apache, the Bronx, 50;
  militarization of, 59; origins of,
  31–32; stop and frisk policy,
  135–36
Nietzche, Friedrich, 199
1984 (Orwell), 232
Nixon, Richard, 45, 52, 137–44
Nonviolent protests, 36
North Charleston, South Carolina, 116
No-win situations, 11–12, 16–17

Obama, Barack, 118–19
Office of National Drug Control Policy
  (ONDCP), 53

Officer evaluation, 71
Officer Friendly myth, 116
Officer-involved shooting, personal
  account of, 175–79
Oklahoma fusion center, 61
Ombudsman's office, 219
Omnibus Crime Control and Safe
  Streets Act (1968), 38
Online newsrooms, 186
Operation Exodus, 58
Operations standards, 161–62
Order maintenance function, 19–20,
  21, 25–26, 157
Organizational integrity, 83
Organized crime, 143
Orwell, George, 3
Overlapping jurisdictions, 31

Paradox of policing, 1–3
Paramilitary training, 164
Paramilitary units, 63–70
Parking violations, 91–93
Parole and probation supervision
  fees, 94
Pastore, Nick, 67
Paul, Ron, 60
Paulson, Henry, 146–47
Peaceful protest marches, 48
Peace officers, 19–20, 56–57, 151–52,
  157–58, 168–70, 189
Peel, Robert, 6, 19, 27, 29–30, 230
People v. Debour (1976), 41
Perception of fairness, 77
Perceptiveness, 159
Persecution, perception of, 8
Phone data, police capturing, 232
Physical and/or psychological cruelty,
  34
Physical defense and control tactics
  training, 173
Physical fitness, 160
PIO (public information officer),
  186
Plea bargain, 90